MW01234192

Essential GIMP for Web Professionals

ISBN 0-13-019114-0

9 780130 191144

90000

The Prentice Hall Essential Web Professionals Series

- *Essential GIMP for Web Professionals*
  Michael J. Hammel

- *Essential ColdFusion 4.5 for Web Professionals*
  Micah Brown and Mike Fredrick

- *Essential Design for Web Professionals*
  Charles Lyons

- *Essential Flash™ 5 for Web Professionals*
  Lynn Kyle

- *Essential Flash™ 4 for Web Professionals*
  Lynn Kyle

- *Essential ASP for Web Professionals*
  Elijah Lovejoy

- *Essential PHP for Web Professionals*
  Christopher Cosentino

- *Essential CSS & DHTML for Web Professionals*
  Dan Livingston and Micah Brown

- *Essential JavaScript™ for Web Professionals*
  Dan Barrett, Dan Livingston, and Micah Brown

- *Essential Perl 5 for Web Professionals*
  Micah Brown, Chris Bellow, and Dan Livingston

- *Essential Photoshop® 5 for Web Professionals*
  Brad Eigen, Dan Livingston, and Micah Brown

Essential GIMP for Web Professionals

Michael J. Hammel

Prentice Hall PTR
Upper Saddle River, NJ 07458
www.phptr.com

Library of Congress Cataloging-in-Publication Data

Hammel, Michael.
    Essential GIMP for web professionals / Michael Hammel.
        p. cm.
    Includes index.
    ISBN 0-13-019114-0
    1. Internet programming. 2. World Wide Web. I. Title.

QA76.625.L68 2000
005.2'76--dc21   00-063702

Editorial/Production Supervision: Nicholas Radhuber
Acquisitions Editor: Miles Williams
Marketing Manager: Kate Hargett
Manufacturing Manager: Alexis R. Heydt
Cover Design Director: Jerry Votta
Cover Design: Anthony Gemmellaro
Interior Design Director: Gail Cocker-Bogusz
Series Design: Patti Guerrieri

Prentice Hall books are widely used by corporations and government agencies for training, marketing, and resale.

The publisher offers discounts on this book when ordered in bulk quantities. For more information, contact: Corporate Sales Department, Phone: 800-382-3419; Fax: 201-236-7141; E-mail: corpsales@prenhall.com; or write: Prentice Hall PTR, Corp. Sales Dept., One Lake Street, Upper Saddle River, NJ 07458.

Printed in the United States of America

10 9 8 7 6 5 4 3 2 1

ISBN 0-13-019114-0

Prentice-Hall International (UK) Limited, *London*
Prentice-Hall of Australia Pty. Limited, *Sydney*
Prentice-Hall Canada Inc., *Toronto*
Prentice-Hall Hispanoamericana, S.A., *Mexico*
Prentice-Hall of India Private Limited, *New Delhi*
Prentice-Hall of Japan, Inc., *Tokyo*
Pearson Education Asia Ltd., *Singapore*
Editora Prentice-Hall do Brasil, Ltda., *Rio de Janeiro*

Contents

v

Preface

In the past few years the World Wide Web has become a medium where writers, editors, and software developers have migrated, either by choice or by request, to the world of publishing. Beyond the need to develop content—the articles and other information we find online—these new publishers are finding it necessary to learn about the world of graphic arts. The Web, unlike print publishing, is actually an easy medium upon which to learn about color, texture, form, and function. That's because the medium used for display is the same medium used for creation: the computer. Tools are available for many platforms to create the simple logos and the many navigation aides we find on the Web today. The GIMP is one such tool.

Developed originally for the Linux platform, the GIMP now runs on most major flavors of UNIX and on both OS/2 and Microsoft Windows-based platforms. A port is also underway for the BeOS platform. Despite the underlying differences in these computer systems, the GIMP itself is the same on all of them. GIF images are the same no matter what platform you work on, so using the GIMP to create a GIF image is the same on all of those platforms.

The user interface for the GIMP is similar to Adobe's Photoshop, a tool popular with computer-based artists but which is inordinately expensive. In fact, much of what the GIMP does is modeled after Photoshop and tools like it. There are many advantages to using the GIMP instead of Photoshop:

1. The GIMP has an open architecture making it easy to extend its feature set.

2. The GIMP on UNIX, BeOS, and OS/2 won't crash your OS if something goes wrong.

3. The GIMP supports scripting using multiple languages (Perl, Scheme, and Python in the 1.2 release)

4. The GIMP fixes various architectural problems found in Photoshop which amounts to better performance in various areas (layer composition, for example).

But for many new graphic artists the best reason to work with the GIMP is price—the GIMP is free. It is included with all Linux distributions and can also be downloaded from the gimp.org Web site or one of its mirror locations. Photoshop does deal with printing issues much better than the current version of the GIMP (Pantone colors, for example, are not supported in the GIMP) so if you need to worry about getting your images onto the printed page, Photoshop is currently a better solution (at least for high end publishing; it can still be used for prints where color matching does not have to be quite so accurate). But for new artists and those who don't make a living creating the artwork, the cost of Photoshop is prohibitive. The GIMP fills the gap by providing a quality alternative at a reasonable (nonexistent) price.

◆ How This Book Is Laid Out

What we want to do with a book like this is to address the needs of those people who are new to graphic design and who need to generate graphics for Web pages. To accomplish this we break the book into five parts:

• Part 1: *GIMP Basics for Web Image Production* introduces the basics of the GIMP that relate heavily to Web image production.
• Part 2: *Drawing, Painting, and Color Management* moves into color, drawing, and painting issues.
• Part 3: *Formatting Images in Web Pages and Animation Issues* looks at generating Web images versus gallery images.

- Part 4: *Capturing Images, Applying Special Effects, and Scripting* looks at advanced features like effects and rendering filters.
- The last part consists of a set of appendixes that can be used for quick reference.

Each of the four parts contains two or more chapters and ends with a project showing how to use what was learned in that section. The appendices contain handy references for color management features, filters, and the Perl scripting interface. Although you can skip forward through the book, you may want to read it front to back if you're new to both the GIMP and graphic design.

This book is not a comprehensive reference for the GIMP. Such a text would easily take up 1,000 or more pages and is far more detailed for someone who just wants to jump in and quickly get started. You won't be an expert after reading this text—but you will be able to get some work done. And you'll have the base upon which to start a more detailed study of the GIMP.

◆ The Projects

Each of the four parts concludes with an example that demonstrates the features covered in the preceding chapters. These examples are referred to as Site Design chapters and show how you might approach designing the front page of a new Web site. Although these examples show basic layout and design for a fictional Web site, this book doesn't actually cover how to decide where buttons go, how to decide upon a site color scheme, or how to fit it all into the HTML. That would take another text on its own. The focus here is to show how to use the GIMP to generate the various images you'll be needing. With the exception of the chapter on making Image Maps, how you create your HTML will be up to you.

◆ Writing About Open Source Tools

The GIMP is part of a moderately new design philosophy with software—that is, the software is freely available to developers to maintain and distribute. This philosophy has been termed Open Source or Free Software, depending on whom you talk to. At the time that this book was started, the GIMP's 1.2 release was in early beta testing. If you're not familiar with beta testing, it means that the software developers have agreed that no new features are to be added and a period of time is to be spent making sure the existing features work properly. The initial beta test date might be more familiar to you the way Microsoft refers to it, which is "Launch Date."

The hard part about writing a book on a beta-level product, including one from an Open Source project, is that the product tends to change often and sometimes without notice. Fortunately, the maintainers of the GIMP project are actually well organized. Keeping up with the latest developers' releases helps in knowing what has been changed or added. Plus they're really friendly people who have never refused to answer any of my questions, no matter how silly they might have seemed. Hopefully, I've managed to catch all the updates to the 1.2 release of the GIMP before this book went to print. Since the book was timed to be delivered at about the same time GIMP 1.2 was to be released, it should match closely with the final 1.2 version. Even better, the book should be hitting the shelves at about the same time the 1.2 release is starting to be widely distributed with the popular Linux distributions. In that case, you might actually get a copy with the right information at the time you actually need it.

Isn't Open Source fun?

Acknowledgments

Since many of the developers of the GIMP don't often get the public glory that we writers get, I thought it important to at least name a few of the people who've helped me over the past few years: John Beale, Zach Beane, Tom Bech, Marc Bless, Simon Budig, Seth Burgess, Jay Cox, Andreas Dilger, Austin Donnelly, Larry Ewing, Scott Goehring, Tuomas Kuosmanen, Peter Kirchgessner, Karin Kylander, Olof S. Kylander, Nick Lamb, Elliot Lee, Marc Lehmann, Ralph Levien, Adrian Likins, Tor Lillqvist, Ingo Luetkebohle, Josh MacDonald, Vidar Madsen, Torsten Martinsen, Federico Mena Quintero, Adam D. Moss, Shuji Narazaki, Michael Natterer, Sven Neumann, Miles O'Neal, Jay Painter, Manish Singh, Mike Sweet, and Owen Taylor. This is in no way the complete list of developers for the GIMP, but each of these people has, in one way or another, helped me out with some GIMP issue over the past four or five years. And for this I am eternally grateful. If I left anyone out of this list, my sincerest apologies.

1 GIMP and the Web

◆ What We Do On the Web

The Web is a tool for distribution. Anything that can be digitized can be made available to the public: music, software, news, books, images, recorded speeches, recipes, grandma's last will and testament. Anything. The only difference between these items is how they are presented to an audience. Music comes in MP3 formats. Video news feeds are often in G2 format from Real, Inc. But the majority of information is presented in some form of markup language. The most common of these languages is HTML. And it is from HTML that most Web site designers derive their need for artwork.

HTML-based pages are often static, meaning they are created once and sit as a file on a Web server waiting for users to request them. Some pages are dynamic. These are pages that are gener-

1

ated right as the user requests them. Dynamic pages put a heavy load on a server with many visitors, so small companies and small Web sites often try to generate static pages on a scheduled basis instead of loading the server with dynamic requests. In either case, HTML pages are usually chock full of graphic images: logos, background images, navigation buttons, animations, and thumbnails. Each of these serve a different purpose and have different requirements for the designer. Fortunately, none of them is very difficult to produce with the GIMP.

Logos are used to identify a site, product, trademark, corporation, or individual. They are generally images which show up on just about every page of a site. Background images are placed behind text or other images. They provide a style or theme for a Web page. Although they provide no real functionality for a site (the site can usually exist without the background image), they are a key component for presenting a site's identity. Because they are so key to an identity, logos are often used as background images.

Animations are most useful in advertisements, however, I can't in good conscience encourage their use. Web-based inline animations are only available using the GIF file format, which supports animation in about the same way a "page flip" book supports it. Both work and both are extremely inefficient (would you rather watch page flip books or a movie?). Still, you can't avoid their use on the Web. Animations are a moderately complex topic and will be discussed briefly here in Part 3.

Navigation buttons include rectangular, oval, and randomly shaped images used to move around a Web site. An alternative to buttons are image maps, which are ordinary images with various regions linked to other areas at the site. You'll often see navigation buttons used when you move a mouse over some text and it changes color or shape—these are known as JavaScript rollovers. Each of these buttons is actually two different images: the one displayed when the mouse is over it and the one displayed when the mouse is somewhere else. Image maps do not change when you move the mouse over them, although the status bar at the bottom of the browser window may show the destination link depending on where the mouse is over the image. Most of these images are created before the Web page itself is created. The images are static. But for some situations a dynamically created image is more desirable. Stock price charts are an example of dynamically created images. The GIMP's scripting interface allows you the option of using it in *batch* mode, which means the user interface is not started. This allows programs to run unattended to generate images. We'll look at scripting with the GIMP in Part 4.

◆ What GIMP Does for the Web

The GIMP provides a means of creating images for use on the Web (it can also be used for print, but that topic is beyond the scope of this text). Images can be created from scratch, like logos or backgrounds, or manipulated from scanned or other digital images. You can create image maps, buttons, galleries of photos, or even cut up an image to fit into an HTML table.

What you can't do with the GIMP is generate programmatic interfaces to your pages. This is known as CGI (for server-side programs) or JavaScript and Java (for client-side programs). Such programs, even though they may generate images or automate the display of images, are usually created manually using a programming language like Perl. Perl can also be used with the GIMP, but the GIMP does not generate Perl code.

◆ The User Interface

If you've ever worked with Adobe Photoshop then the GIMP's user interface should be familiar to you. The initial window consists of a number of rows and columns of buttons with a menu bar at the top—this is the *Toolbox*. Each button enables a different tool for use in the *Canvas*. Figure 1-1 shows the Toolbox. Note that single-clicking on a button sets the tool mode to that tool. Double-clicking on the button sets the tool mode and also opens the Tool Options dialog. Most tools have configurable options. This dialog remains open when you change tools, and will display the options (if any) for the currently selected tool.

Canvases are where you do your drawing, painting, and so forth. Figure 1-4 shows a blank Canvas and some of its features. You can open a new, blank window using either the *File->New* menu option from the Toolbox, the *File->New* menu option in the Canvas menu, or by typing *Ctrl-N* in either the Toolbox or a Canvas window(*Ctrl-O* will open an existing image). You will be given an option as to what the window will display—either a transparent (i.e., empty) background, a white background, or the current foreground or background colors.

Each Canvas is made up of *rulers* along the left and top sides, scrollbars on the bottom and right sides, the display area (usually white in a new window), a *status bar* below the bottom scrollbar, a pop-up menu, *quick mask* buttons, and the *Navigation Preview* button. All of these are initially visible (the menu opens when you

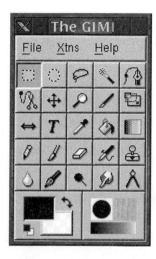

FIGURE 1-1 The GIMP Toolbox

FIGURE 1-2 Foreground/background colors

FIGURE 1-3 Brush, pattern, and gradient quick tools

click on its arrow or when you press the right mouse button inside the display area) and most can be toggled off (invisible) using the *File->Preferences* option in the Toolbox. There are other features which are not visible: multiple layers (only the background layer is created initially, you'll create others later) and *guides*. Guides are created by clicking in one of the rulers and dragging it into the display area. A guide is just a straight line to which selection outlines and layer edges can be attached, making alignment much simpler. We'll see these in action in later chapters.

Closing the Canvas window is done by typing *Ctrl-W* in the display area. If changes have been made to the window you will be asked if you want to save them. Closing the Canvas window does not exit the GIMP. To exit, you select *File->Quit* from the Toolbox or Canvas window menus or just type *Ctrl-Q* in any window.

The GIMP understands most common image file formats, ranging from JPEG and GIF to TGA, TIFF, XPM, PCX, Postscript,

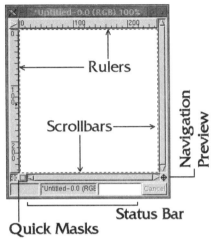

FIGURE 1-4 The Canvas window and its features

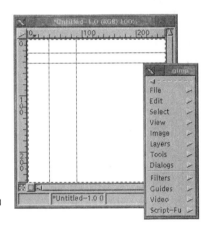

FIGURE 1-5 A Canvas window with guides and the Canvas window Menu displayed

PNG, and WMF. If you open an image and it's too large for the display, or if you resize the Canvas window, you can move around the image within the display area in three ways. First, moving the scrollbars will get you around. Second, the middle mouse button when clicked (or, if you only have two buttons, then both pressed at the same time) and dragged will do the same thing. Finally, a new feature to 1.2, the Navigation Preview, allows you to see a thumbnail version of the image with an outlined region showing the display area of the Canvas window. You can drag the outline around the thumbnail and the Canvas window's display area is updated accordingly.

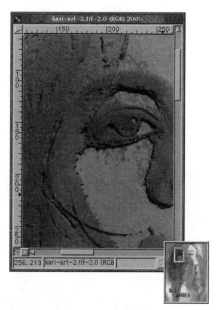

FIGURE 1-6 The Navigation Preview

Although you can change the resolution (number of dots per inch, for example) for the image, you won't need to do so for Web images. The default is 72DPI, and the rulers along the sides of the Canvas window will show units in pixels. You can change from pixels to inches for the units used in the rulers, although this probably won't be all that helpful. Such features are more important to artists working on images destined for print.

The Canvas window menu is an important part of the GIMP. If you're used to the Microsoft and Mac world of applications, you're probably expecting a menu bar to access features. The GIMP is designed for artists, who value screen space on their monitors like movie producers value summer blockbusters. Because of this, you'll find a number of features designed to save screen space. The Canvas window menu is one such feature. The menu can be accessed by clicking on the menu arrow in the upper left corner of any Canvas window or by pressing and holding the right mouse button in the display area of the window. The GIMP uses the notion of an *active window*, which means that the menu item you select is applicable to the window which is active. Which window is active depends on which window was last clicked in. Want to make a Canvas window active and not take the chance of accidentally making changes to it? Click in the status bar over the name of the window.

The *Canvas menu* gives you access to nearly all the features of the GIMP, including those found in the Toolbox (only a few options under the *Xtns* menu in the Toolbox are also not available here). This menu contains a number of submenus, including options for editing (cut and paste), selecting (feathering, growing, shrinking, and so forth), and the vast set of color and effects filters. If you want quick access to it, you can *tear off* the menu and it will then get its own window. This can be confusing if you have multiple Canvas windows open since the menu is Canvas-specific. Fortunately, the GIMP knows which window the menu belongs to. However, if you use tear-off menus you'll need to keep track of which ones they belong to on your own since visually it will not be obvious. The key: don't use tear-off menus.

◆ Saving Your Work

We've already talked about opening existing image files and starting with a blank Canvas window. Once you've completed your work (and if you're smart, periodically while you're working), you'll want to save the image. The GIMP has its own file format called XCF (an acronym for the Experimental Computing Facility at Berkeley where the GIMP was born). If your image has more than one layer and you specify to use filename extensions to identify the file and also specify ".xcf" as the suffix to the filename, then your image will be saved in an XCF formatted file. This is good—all the information that the GIMP knows about while running will be saved here. If you choose another suffix, say .jpg or .gif, then GIMP will try to save the image using these formats. This can be troublesome if you have more than one layer since JPEG images, for example, don't understand layers or multiframed images. The key here is to use the right format for the job. Save your work in a XCF format at all times until you're ready to flatten the layers (which means to combine them into a final, single layer). At that time, with a single layer, you can save it to some other file format. We'll talk more about the differences between GIF and JPEG in Part 3, where we get into the meat of imaging for the Web.

FIGURE 1-7 The Save As dialog

◆ Terminology—You Say Potato, I Say Option Menu

One of the problems with working on multiple computer platforms is terminology. There are standards for terms, and the geeks among us are used to them, but the average person needs a little primer every now and then. Well, here's yet another primer.

The GIMP uses terminology which is similar to, but slightly different than, PC and Mac systems. Mac users may be familiar with the term "palette" when describing a window that pops open in response to selecting a menu item, for example. In the GIMP (and on LINUX and UNIX systems in general), these are referred to as "dialog boxes." We'll refer to just about every window that opens in the GIMP that isn't either the Toolbox or a Canvas as a dialog box of some sort.

Dialog boxes contain buttons, scrolled lists, and other things. One of the less familiar items can be found in the Layers and Channels dialog (type *Ctrl-L* in a Canvas window to open this dialog). Here you'll find a *notebook* with three tabs labeled "Layers," "Channels," and "Paths." Clicking on the Layers tab puts you on the Layers *page* of the notebook. Clicking on the Paths tab puts you on the Paths page. Easy enough once you know the terms we'll be using.

Menus are also a little confusing since they come in various forms. The traditional menu is called a *pull-down menu,* like the

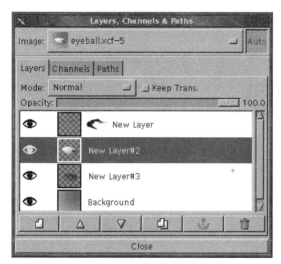

FIGURE 1-8 Layers and Channels dialog

menu you get when you click on *File* in the Toolbox's menu bar. This is also known as a *pop-up menu*. Some menus are presented like a button, so that when you click on it the menu opens with the currently selected menu item displayed over the button. Change the selected item and the button's text changes when the menu closes. These are called *option menus*. Usually, option menus are used in places where only a few options are available. Pop-up menus are used in most other places. *Tear-off* menus are versions of pop-up menus; you can identify these by the dashed line across the top of the menu. Click on the dashed line to tear off the menu. Click on it again to close the window the menu is placed in after being torn off.

The last bit of terminology has to do with buttons. You're familiar with simple push buttons—click on them and something happens. Alternatives to this are *radio* buttons, which are a series of diamond (usually) shaped options. You can click on only one of these—they are mutually exclusive. The other possibility is an ordinary *toggle* button. Click it once to turn it on and it appears depressed into the screen. Click it again and it is disabled, making it appear like it is sticking out from the screen. Radio buttons are just a series of interrelated toggle buttons.

It's an easy bit of terminology but important to understand as we go through this text. But don't let yourself get swallowed up by the terms—the GIMP is a tool for getting work done. When in doubt, forget the terms and just experiment for a while. You can always come back and put names to features later.

◆ Features You'll Learn to Love

There are many features in the GIMP with which you will become very familiar over time. A few of these are important to point out right from the start. Without an understanding of these, you may find your work a bit more tedious.

The Layers and Channels features, the dialog of which you've seen previously when we talked about terminology, are indispensible to the GIMP artist. Layers in particular will be used often, even for the most minor of artwork. These can be thought of like a series of clear acetate sheets laid one atop the other. The final image is viewed through these sheets; this is known as the *composite* image (compositing means to combine the layers). An example of the use of layers is in the creation of shadows. The top layer may contain some text, below which is a blurred and offset copy of the text. The composite of these two layers gives the appearance of the text lying above the background a sort of 3D appearance.

The Layers and Channels dialog has many options for adding, deleting, moving, and managing layers in general. You'll be creating *masks* for layers—regions which are blocked from use in the composite image—as well as applying different methods of composition for each layer. Finally, the Layers and Channels dialog also contains the new *Paths* option, which allows you to create and edit lines and curves in your image. We'll discuss layers in more detail in Chapter 2, "Layers."

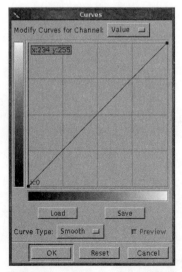 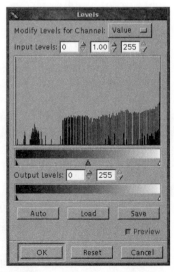

FIGURE 1-9 The Curves and Levels dialogs

Color management is another area you'll be dealing with on a daily basis. Most of the color tools are found in the Canvas menu, under the *Image->Colors* option. Tools like Curves, Levels, Hue/Saturation, and Desaturate are all used to manage colors globally within a layer or within a selection (selections are a discussion on their own, and we'll deal with them in Chapter 3, "Selections and Masks").

Finally, effects filters are where you are most likely to want to jump to right now. The heck with all this basics stuff—show me the fractals! Well, if you're into experimenting, open a new Canvas window and try out the *Filters->Render* options from the Canvas menu. The menu options here all lead to effects filters which render (i.e., draw) images without or with little regard to the image's current contents. In other words, they are cool to play with and you don't need any existing image to do something fun with them. But once you're done there, come back here. There are a lot of other effects filters, and they all have important purposes for the Web.

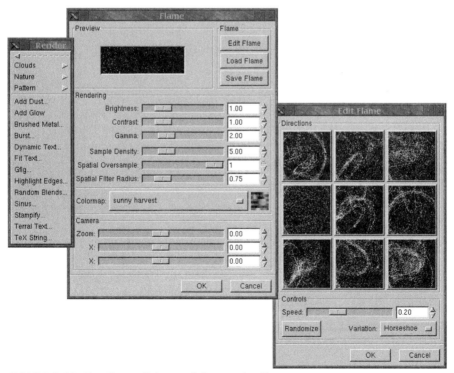

FIGURE 1-10 The Flame dialog and the Render filters menu

RECAP

We've covered some basics here, an introduction for those who are brand new to the GIMP and the Web. Getting started with a new tool often requires a little help with understanding what it is you're looking at, and that's what we've done in this chapter. But we're just getting started. In the next chapter we're going to look at layers, one of the most useful core features of the GIMP. Understanding layers is key to understanding how both static and animated images are made. Without layers, there would be no 3D effects, no drop shadows, no beveled edges. We'll look at what layers are and how to do something useful with them.

2 Layers

IN THIS CHAPTER

- Layer Features
- Moving and Transforming Layers
- Blending Layers
- Opacity and Transparency
- Compositing
- Recap
- Advanced Projects

Layers are so key to the creation of any artwork, no matter how simple, that it doesn't make much sense to discuss anything else until you've gotten a grasp of them. Layers give you the ability to make changes that can be backed out or reproduced easily, and allows you to make changes at a later date without affecting other aspects of the image.

In this chapter we start building the basic knowledge you need to do real work. The chapter is short and introductory in nature (we won't be creating any images just yet, but we're heading that way). We will, however, do a few simple experiments to illustrate what layers are and how they can be used.

◆ Layer Features

Layers are like sheets of clear acetate on an overhead projector—you lay them one on top of another with the light shining through to create the final image on the overhead screen. But you can do a lot more with layers than with the acetate sheets. Layers don't have to be the same size and can even be bigger than the actual image (such layers get cropped later or the image size is increased to enclose them, depending on your needs). You can align layers by their edges manually or automatically, move the layers around the image area individually or in groups, add masks to them, change their position in the stack, their method of composition, and even their opacity. You can, in fact, do just about anything with layers—except drop them on the floor and forget the order they were in.

The Layers and Channels dialog is where layers are managed for all Canvas windows. This dialog can be opened using the *File->Dialogs->Layers and Channels* menu option from the Toolbox or by typing *Ctrl-L* in the Toolbox or any Canvas window. It can also be opened from the *Layers->Layers and Channels* Canvas menu option.

The dialog consists of three main parts:

1. The image selection options

2. The notebook pages

3. The page specific buttons

Notebook Pages

Image Selection Options

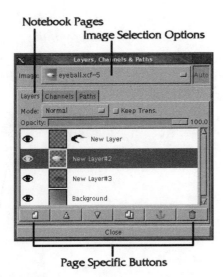

Page Specific Buttons

FIGURE 2-1 The Layers and Channels dialog, with major features indicated

Across the top of the dialog you will find the image selection options. An option menu takes up most of this region and allows you to manually select which Canvas layers to view. Next to this is a button labeled "Auto." By default, this button is depressed and causes the dialog to display the layers for the active window automatically, even when the active window changes.

Below these two items lives the notebook in which you can choose to work with either layers, channels, or paths. We'll only be looking at layers for now, and since that is the default page you won't need to change anything.

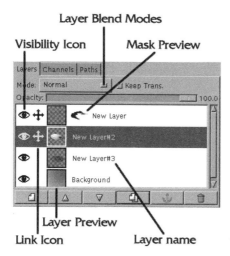

FIGURE 2-2 The Layers page, with features indicated

The layers page consists of the blend modes option menu, an opacity slider, a toggle for using or ignoring transparency within the layer, and a scrolled region in which each layer for the active Canvas will be displayed. Below this scrolled region are the layer buttons. These are, from left to right:

1. The new layer button—adds a new, blank layer above the currently selected layer.

2. The raise layer button—switches the position of the current layer with the layer above it, if there is one.

3. The lower layer button—switches the position of the current layer with the one below it, if there is one.

4. The duplicate layer button—duplicates the current layer, adding the duplicate layer above the current one.

5. The anchor layer button—composites a floating layer with the current layer or mask.

6. The delete layer button—deletes the current layer.

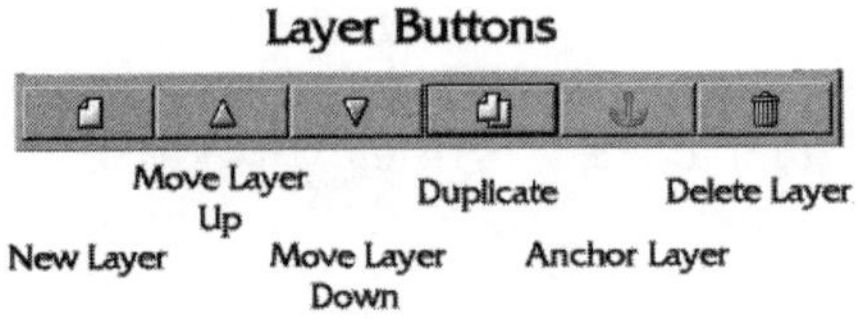

Layer Buttons

Move Layer
Up
New Layer   Duplicate   Delete Layer
Move Layer   Anchor Layer
Down

FIGURE 2-3 The layer buttons

Each layer has several parts to it. The layer name is displayed on the right of each layer entry in the scrolled region. Double-click on this and a dialog opens allowing you to change the name. Two previews are also available for each layer: the layer preview (also referred to as a thumbnail) and its mask. A mask is a grayscale image where black regions mask out the same pixels from that layer, white regions let the pixels be used as they are, and gray pixels allow the pixels to be used with varying levels of transparency applied to them. Not all layers will have masks (you have to add them manually), but when one is available for a layer its preview is displayed to the right of the layer image preview. We'll get to masks a little later in this chapter.

The other two parts to a layers entry in the scrolled region of the layers page are the visibility and link icons. The former looks like an eye and, when visible, means the layer is used in the composite image you see in the Canvas display. If you click on this it turns the eye icon off, so the layer is not used in the composite image. The link icon allows you to join multiple layers together so that movement of one layer affects all of the linked layers.

The scrolled region will initially have only one layer, the background layer. You can add a new layer quickly by clicking on the New Layer button at the bottom of the dialog. Additionally, you can duplicate the current layer by clicking on the Duplicate Layer button. Oh, and the current layer? That's selected by clicking anywhere on a layer entry. The easiest way, which avoids accidentally opening the Layer Name dialog or toggling the visibility or link icons, is to click on the layer preview.

Like the Canvas menu, the Layers menu location is not obvious to the new user. Right-mouse clicking on a layer entry in the scrolled region will open the menu. The options in the menu are applicable to the currently selected layer which will be whatever layer you clicked on to open the menu (the layer will be highlighted). This menu contains options that perform the same functions as the Layer buttons as well as options for dealing with layer masks, generating selections from transparent regions, and combining layers. We'll look at some of these in a little more detail as we go through this chapter.

◆ Moving and Transforming Layers

Like their acetate cousins, layers can be moved around within the stack. What you see in the Canvas display area is what you get on the overhead projector—similar to only the region over the lit area of the projector shows up on the screen, even if some parts of the sheet hang over the edge. Layers are like that too. You can move the layers off the edge of the display area without losing any data. You can also resize (or scale—there is difference between these two) a layer to make it larger than the viewable area. Later, when you combine layers (i.e., composite them) you can decide if you want to chop off those overhanging areas. The process of moving, resizing, or scaling layers is known as a transformation.

You can move layers around the image area or up and down the layer stack. Moving layers is simple. First, lets make a Canvas with a couple of layers. Type *Ctrl-N* to open a new window. Use the default size (256x256). When the window is open, open the Layers and Channels dialog and duplicate the existing layer by clicking on the Duplicate Layer button. Now add a new layer by clicking on the New Layer button. When prompted, make the new layer 50x50 pixels in size. We want it smaller than the original image so we can see what moving a layer looks like. Finally, double-click on the three layer names and name them "Small" (top layer), "Duplicate" (middle layer), and "Original" (the background layer).

To move a layer around the image, and keep it in place in the layer stack, use the Move tool. This is the button in the Toolbox which looks like two double-ended arrows crossing each other (to be specific, the icon is called a *fleur*). Click on this button, then click on the top layer (the "Small" layer) in the Layers dialog. Now, while holding down the shift key, left click in the Canvas and drag the mouse around. Notice the outline of the layer moves. If you don't hold down the shift key, the GIMP will determine which layers pixel the mouse is over, switches the active layer to that layer, and applies the move operation to that layer.

FIGURE 2-4 The layers as you should see them

This behavior can be confusing for new users, so just be certain to hold down the Shift key during layer moves until you've had some time to get used to it.

Move Tool **FIGURE 2-5** The Move tool

Moving up and down the layer stack is even easier. The simplest method is to use the Layer Up and Layer Down buttons at the bottom of the Layers page. These do just what you expect—move the layer up or down one spot in the stack. If the current layer cannot be moved in one or the other direction, the appropriate button will be "grayed out," which means you can't use it. You can also use options within the Layers menu to move a layer up or down, but the fastest way to move a layer more than one spot in the stack is to just drag, drop it. Left click on the preview, hold the mouse button down and drag it over where you want the layer to go, then let go of the button. The stack is updated immediately.

In our simple example you have three layers. Try moving the top or middle layer to the bottom of the stack—it doesn't work! Why? The bottom layer does not have an *alpha channel,* which means it can't have any transparency. If it moved up the stack, anything below it would never be visible. But you can get past this—just add an alpha channel to the bottom layer. In the Layers menu, select "Add Alpha Channel." If this option is not available, then the layer already had an alpha channel. All background layers in new Canvases are created *without* an alpha channel. If you create GIF images with a transparency (which we'll talk about in Chapter 9, "Web Imaging"), you'll want to make sure you add the alpha channel to that background layer.

Now put the layers back in order—"Small" on top, "Duplicate" in the middle." Click on the Small layer in the dialog to make it active. Click on the left side ruler and drag out a guide to the middle of the window. Do the same from the top ruler so the two guides intersect near the middle somewhere. Verify that the Move tool is still selected (it should be) and move the Small layer so its top edge aligns with the horizontal guide and its right edge aligns with the vertical guide. Notice how the edges of the layer want to attach themselves to the guides? With the edges aligned, try moving the guides again (just place the cursor over a guide, then click and drag). They, too, want to align with the edges of the layer. This makes alignment using guides rather easy. You can also turn off this gravitational effect by selecting the *View->Snap to Guides* option in the Canvas menu. Note that changing this only affects the current Canvas, it is not a global change.

FIGURE 2-6 Layer alignment with guides

There is one special type of layer—the floating layer. These layers are temporary—they are created when a selection within a layer is transformed (moved, rotated, etc.) or when something is pasted into the image. There is only one of these at any given time and you must specify what to do with it before you can continue work on other layers. A floating layer can either be turned into a new layer at the top of the stack or anchored into the current layer. If it is anchored, its pixels will replace the pixels at the same locations within the image of the current layer, or if the layers mask is active, the pixels within the mask.

We can create a floating layer pretty easily, and this little experiment will let you use some of the other tools in the GIMP we haven't talked about yet. First, make the middle layer active by clicking on its preview. Then click on the Bucket Fill tool in the Toolbox (it looks like a paint bucket). Now click in the Canvas window. The middle layer turns black (as long as you haven't changed any colors—you shouldn't have since we haven't talked about doing so yet!). Now click on the Rectangular selection in the Toolbox (upper left corner—the button with the box outline). In the Canvas window click in the upper left quadrant of the window and drag diagonally to the lower right a ways. A selection will appear bounded by the *marching ants*. Click inside the selection (notice how the cursor looks like the fleur again?) and drag it to the upper right and release the mouse button. Look in the Layers and Channels dialog—a floating selection is shown at the top of the stack. Right mouse click on it in the dialog and select *New Layer*.

FIGURE 2-7 A floating layer

What this shows is how you can make selections of one layer into new layers. This is an important step to remember since you'll often want to cut out parts of one image and place it over another background. Using these floating layers is the first step in managing such processes.

One last step that has to do with transforming layers involves changing the size of a layer. There are two ways to do this, and both are accessed via the Layers menu. The first option is to *resize* a layer. This will change the dimensions of the layer without changing the dimensions of the image it contains—in effect, it adds transparent padding around the image. Selecting *Resize Layer* from the Layers menu will allow you to set the new size and position the existing contents within the new layer dimensions. An alternative to this is to *scale* the layer. This option also changes the size of the layer, but it forces the layer's contents to be scaled to fit the new dimensions.

 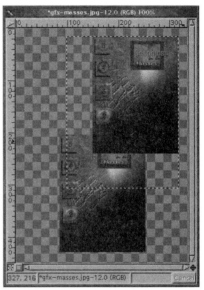

FIGURE 2-8 An original layer with (a) resized and (b) scaled versions

◆ Blending Layers

Transformations are only a small part of what layers provide. *Blend modes* are another. A blend mode allows you to specify how the current layer will be visually combined with the layers below it. The composite image displayed in the Canvas is generated by starting with the bottom layer and combining each successive layer higher in the stack. Each higher layer's blend mode is used to determine how the pixels in that layer and the current composite (the image as it's made up from all previous layers) are combined.

Setting the blend mode is simple—just select the mode desired from the Blend Mode option menu in the Layers page. There are 15 methods to blend a layer. Table 2-1 summarizes these modes. The default mode is Normal, which means that any pixels in the current layer that are not transparent replace the respective pixels in the composite image. A pixel can have different amounts of transparency. In any mode, the amount of transparency in a pixel determines how much of the current layers pixel is combined with the composite images pixel.

Table 2-1 Layer blend modes

Blend mode	What it does
Normal	Current layer pixel replaces composite pixel
Dissolve	Lower opacity setting adds random holes to current layer
Multiple (Burn)	Current layer darkens composite; lighter pixels in current layer have less effect (white is neutral—no effect)
Divide (Dodge)	Current layer lightens composite
Screen	Current layer lightens composite; darker pixels in current layer have less effect (black is neutral—no effect)
Overlay	50% gray is neutral; white pixels lighten composite, black pixels darken it
Difference	Absolute value of composite pixel—current layer pixel
Addition	Composite pixel + current layer pixel; maximum value of 255 (white)
Subtract	Composite pixel—current layer pixel, but with a minimum value of 0 (black)
Darken	Pixels in current layer that are darker than composite replace those pixels
Lighten	Pixels in current layer that are lighter than composite replace those pixels
Hue	Replaces composite pixels hue with the current layers hue, which effectively shifts the visible color of the pixel
Saturation	Same as hue, but affects the saturation of the pixel. The result sets the purity of the color—from pure to completely washed out (i.e., white or gray).
Color	Actually a mix of saturation and hue, with the effect being that the current layers color is mixed with the lightness of the lower layers composite
Value	Like hue and saturation, with the result being the visible color strength of the composite pixel being used with the color of the current layers pixel.

Blending layers is done for a number of reasons. First, it's an inexpensive way to generate effects. Blend modes take up no extra memory nor do they use any of your Undo levels. Ctrl-Z will undo the last operation, with a maximum number of levels of undo specified in the Preferences dialog (which you can find in the File menu of the Toolbox). Undo levels can take up a lot of memory, so using blend modes to make changes to the composite image can be a big help on memory limited systems.

Many 3D effects are generated using blend modes. Using similar colors for slightly blurred text in two successive layers, with one layer slightly offset from the other, and setting the appropriate blend mode (often overlay, multiply, or screen) can produce text that appears to be rounded across its surface. You can also use the Screen blend mode on a desaturated layer of an image to bring out underexposed regions of a scanned photo. Blend modes serve many purposes, not all of which are initially obvious.

◆ Opacity and Transparency

We've talked about transparency already but haven't really defined it. In the Layers page of the Layers and Channels dialog you see an Opacity slider which, by default, is set all the way to the right. This means the current layer's pixels are fully opaque—you can't see through them. By moving the slider to the left, you allow more and more of the lower layers to show through. The slider affects the current layer as a whole. In other words, the setting for opacity is applied equally to all pixels in the layer. And each layer can have a different setting (the slider only shows the setting for the currently active layer, but it changes as you select different layers).

Opacity (which is the opposite of transparency) for pixels goes beyond what the opacity slider shows. Each pixel in a layer also has an alpha channel along with its three color channels (the Red, Green, and Blue channels). The value for a pixel's alpha channel can be anywhere from 0 (completely opaque) to 255 (completely transparent). So, even with the opacity slider set to fully opaque for the layer, individual pixel may still be partially or completely transparent.

Pixels may also be fully or partially transparent based on the *layers mask*. White pixels in the mask cause the respective pixels in the layer to be transparent. Black pixels let those pixels in the layer show as they are (with whatever level of transparency they might already have). Gray pixels in the mask apply varying levels of transparency to their respective layer pixels.

When you're working on an image, try to apply transparency with masks first. You want to use the masks because you can change the mask (or remove it) without affecting the actual pix-

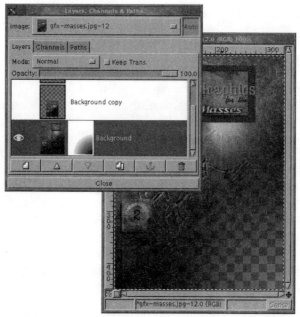

FIGURE 2-9 The layer mask preview is displayed to the right of the layer preview

els in your image. That's a key point—avoid actually changing pixels unless you absolutely have to! At times you'll need to apply the mask (an option in the Layers menu) to the layer, which will remove the mask but update the layer pixels. This usually becomes necessary because some filters won't work on layers that have masks. Layer masks on their own don't actually change layer pixels, only the way those pixels are composited. *Applying* the mask to the layer *does* change the layer pixels (and the mask goes away because it's no longer needed for computing the composite image). Applying the mask means to apply to mask values into the alpha channel of the pixels in the layer. The layer pixels are modified by this process. Like the blend modes, the opacity slider only affects how the layer is composited with other layers in the Canvas's display. It doesn't actually change the pixels in the layer. Unlike layer masks, however, the opacity slider can *never* actually change the layer pixels (i.e., you cannot physically apply the opacity slider setting to the layer).

Sound confusing? It can be when you look at it like this, but don't try to think so technical. Just keep in mind this simple rule: If you need to remove pixels from a layer, do it with masks. The Eraser tool (in the Toolbox) should only be used when you're cleaning up edges of transparent regions in a final image, but even then it's probably better to work with masks first, then merge the layers. Use the opacity slider only when you want to "ghost" a layer, making the whole layer seem partially transparent. Keep in mind that masks use up memory and changes to masks use up undo levels; the opacity slider affects neither.

All of this has to do with generating transparency for pixels. Another option in the Layers page, the *Keep Transparency* toggle determines if the transparency for pixels in a layer should be honored while you work on the layer. With the toggle set (pressed in) the level of transparency for a pixel as determined by its alpha channel (but *not* by the mask or Opacity slider!) is considered when painting or drawing into that layer. For example, if a pixel is fully transparent and you try to paint on it, nothing happens. If the pixel is 50% transparent, then you'll get 50% of the paint you applied and the pixel will remain 50% transparent. This becomes useful when you want to change the color of text. Text is applied to transparent layers, which means all the pixels, except where the text is, are transparent. With Keep Transparency turned on, you can just do a Bucket Fill on the text layer to change the color of the text—the rest of the pixels in that layer will remain unaffected.

This last example brings us to something you should be aware of regarding layer transparency: selections. In the Layers menu, the option Alpha To Selection will allow you to generate a selection around the nontransparent regions of a layer. We'll talk in more detail about selections in the next chapter, but for now you should keep in mind that this option only works on pixels that have greater than 50% opacity (i.e., their alpha channel value is set to 128 or less).

◆ Compositing

Remember how we talked about the image that is displayed in the Canvas being made by combining all the layers together? Well, that's called the *composite* image, and combining layers is known as *compositing*. Images used on the Web come in three basic formats: GIF, JPEG, and PNG. JPEG and PNG allow only a single image (not one with multiple layers). GIF files can have multiple frames, which are essentially multiple layers. In any case, you need to know how to turn that multilayered image into the right format. We'll discuss file formats in more detail in Chapter 9. For now, keep in mind that there are two ways to composite an image from a set of layers: *merging* and *flattening*.

Merging and flattening essentially do the same thing: combine visible layers (i.e., layers which have the eye icon visible in the Layers and Channels dialog). However, they each do this a little differently. First, there are two ways to merge: merge down and merge visible layers. The former will merge the current layer with the next visible layer down in the stack, if any. The latter will merge all the visible layers into a single layer located in the stack at the same point as the lowest visible layer. All layers which are not visible are left untouched and in place in the stack.

Flattening does the same thing except that it discards layers which are not visible. It will also fill in any transparent regions (areas which had no opaque pixels in any of the visible layers) with the current background color. It's important to remember this difference between flattening and merging. If you're trying to create a round button then you'll have transparent regions in the image. You have to use the GIF format, but more important you can't flatten the layers—you have to merge them! If you have leftover layers that are not visible after merging, delete them, and save the image to a GIF file. Don't forget to save the XCF version (the one with all the layers) before doing this! You may want to come back later and make changes.

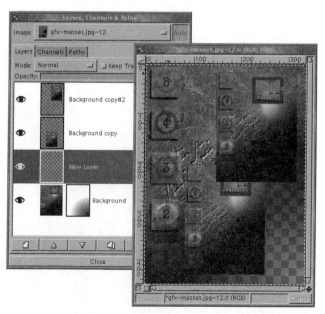

FIGURE 2-10a Original image with multiple layers

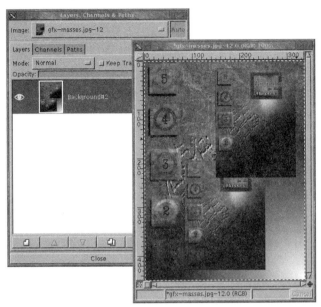

FIGURE 2-10b Flattened image with current background applied to transparent pixels

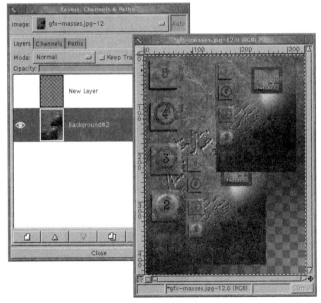

FIGURE 2-10c Merged image with leftover invisible layers

Merging and flattening can be undone. Just type *Ctrl-Z* to get back all the layers you had originally. This is handy, for example, in creating buttons with the same form but with different text. You can create a single XCF file with multiple layers. One layer is the button, the other layers contain the various text you'll use. Then you set the visibility for a given button/text combination, merge or flatten, save, then undo to get all the layers back. Reset the visibility for the next button and repeat. You can keep all the button images in a single, layered XCF file this way.

RECAP

Layers are an important part of any GIMP project. The biggest question people ask is how to get a single framed GIF image out of a layered XCF file. We've answered that in this chapter—merge the layers, deleting invisible layers if necessary. With practice you'll learn to love layers. In fact, you'll wonder how you ever lived without them!

The next chapter introduces you to the other major aspect of the GIMP you can't live without—selections. Like this chapter, the next will be moderately short and contain a few simple selection exercises. After that, we'll work on a real world project. Honest!

ADVANCED PROJECTS

These are pretty basic projects, but we're just trying to get used to the layers dialog and dealing with layers in general.

1. Open a new Canvas and duplicate the original layer four times. Change the name of each layer. Add a white layer mask to two of the duplicates. Now bucket-fill those two layers. Did the layer get filled, or did the mask? Why? How can you fix this? Hint: clicking on previews never causes serious finger cramps. Make sure the layers are white and the layer masks are black for those two layers.

2. Turn off the visibility in all the layers except one with a mask. The Canvas should show the gray checkerboard pattern that represents transparency. Why? Click on the one visible layer to make it active. Click on the layer mask preview to make it active. Make a rectangular selection and fill the selection with white. (The default foreground color is black; look at the Toolbox, do you see a way to swap the foreground color with the background color? It's

fairly obvious.) What do you see? Now, hold down the Alt key and click on the layer mask. Now what do you see? Do it again. Now hold down the Ctrl key and click on the layer mask? What do you see now? Repeat the Ctrl-click process on the layer mask one more time. You should see a white box, right?

3. Make this visible layer the last layer in the stack. Just click on the preview and drag it down to the bottom layer's preview. What happens? Why? How can you make this visible layer the new bottom layer? Hint: Look at the layer's menu for the bottom layer.

4. Extra credit: Scale the layers so they're all different sizes, filling them with different colors (try clicking on the foreground color box in the Toolbox to change its color—how do you think you can reset the colors to black and white?), then moving them so they're all visible. Remember: Moving a layer is easier if you hold down the shift key!

3 Selections and Masks

IN THIS CHAPTER

- Layer Transparency Revisited
- Faster Is Better—Quick Masks
- Shaped and Freehand Selections
- Selecting by Color
- Outlining Selections with the Bezier and Intelligent Scissors Tools
- Guides, Joins, and Cuts
- Preparing for a Selection
- Saving Your Selections
- Tilted Ovals
- Recap
- Projects

Selections, like layers, play an important role in image development with the GIMP. A selection is simply an outline around a region which you want to work on. The outline is enclosed by an animated dashed line, referred to as the "marching ants." You can make multiple selections (not physically touching) within a single layer, feather them to make soft edges for bucket fills, stroke them to draw lines, and most importantly, selectively apply effects. Combined with your experience with layers, using selections will complete your GIMP basics and allow you to do some real work.

◆ Layer Transparency Revisited

In the last chapter we said that layers were so key to working with the GIMP that it didn't make much sense to talk about anything else until you understood them. Transparency in layers can be set in a number of ways, but when it comes to using transparency to make selections we're only concerned about the alpha channel for layer pixels. The alpha channel determines how opaque the pixel will appear, just as the red, green, and blue channels determine how much of each of those colors the pixel contains.

In the layers menu there is an option for using the alpha channel to create a selection. The option is labeled *Alpha To Selection*. It works by checking the level of transparency for each pixel. Any pixel that is more than 50% opaque (i.e., less than 50% transparent) will be included in the selection. This option does not take into consideration the layers mask. A separate option, *Mask To Selection*, can be used to generate a selection from the mask. Here, the selection is generated from any pixels in the mask that are 50% gray or lighter. Any pixels that are darker are left out of the selection.

The important distinction here is that generating a selection from the alpha channel of a layer (or its mask) is quick and quite easy, but is not necessarily as accurate as you might like. Still, for hard edges surrounded by fully transparent pixels, it's the best method for generating a selection.

◆ Faster Is Better—Quick Masks

A new feature of the 1.2 release of the GIMP is the Quick Mask. On the lower left corner of the Canvas window you'll find two small buttons. The one on the left is pressed in under normal use—this is the *Normal Mode* button. The button to its right is the *Quick Mask* button. When you click it, the Canvas window takes on a reddish shade. A new channel will be added (look at the Channels page of the Layers and Channels dialog). You can draw or paint into the Canvas window anywhere you like—this doesn't change the image even if the region you're drawing over gets occluded. When you click back onto the *Normal Mode* button the region you painted in becomes a selection. This is like creating a layer mask and then using the Mask to Selection menu option to create a selection outline. However, instead of generating a mask, the Quick Mask just generates a selection—it doesn't actually mask out anything.

The purpose of the Quick Mask is to allow you to manually paint over the region around which you want a selection. This is far easier to do than using some of the other outline tools (which we'll talk about later in this chapter), much faster to perform, and often more accurate. You can zoom in on a region (use the equal (=) key to zoom in, the minus (–) key to zoom out, or use the the *View->Zoom* options from the Canvas menu). Zooming lets you paint more accurately.

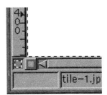

FIGURE 3-1 The Quick Mask tool

◆ Shaped and Freehand Selections

There are many other methods of generating selections. The most simple of these are the shaped selections: rectangular and elliptical. The former are created using the Rectangular Selection tool from the Toolbox (upper left corner; we used it in Chapter 2, "Layers," to demonstrate floating selections). Rectangular selections can be altered in various ways by holding down the Shift, Alt, and Ctrl keys. Table 3-1 summarizes these variations. Elliptical selections, which are created using the Elliptical Selection tool to the right of the Rectangular tool, are modified in similar ways.

Table 3-1 Changing the behavior of the Rectangular Selection tool

Selection Tool	CTRL key	SHIFT	CTRL-SHIFT
Rectangular and Elliptical	Click point becomes center of selection	Forces selection to be square or elliptical	Does both

Normally, selections anchor a corner point to where you click and the selection expands out in the direction you drag the cursor. The Ctrl key will cause the selections center to be anchored on the click point.

The Alt key, when pressed, can be used to reposition a selection after it has been drawn. If you try to move the selection without pressing the Alt key, then the contents of the layer bounded by the selection will be moved and a floating layer will be created to hold it.

The Freehand Selection tool (top right in the first row of the Toolbox) allows you to create selections just by drawing an outline. The outline follows the path of the cursor as you move around the Canvas window. When you let go of the left mouse button (which you hold down as you drag around the window), the end point is connected to the starting point to create a closed selection. The outline you create can cross back on itself; the GIMP will simply determine which parts are inside the selection. Think of the shapes you could make by twisting a necklace a few times and try to figure out which parts would be inside. Keep in mind that "inside" is determined by starting on the left side of the Canvas and traveling to the right, counting the odd number times you cross the selection boundary. Even numbered crossings put you outside the boundary.

Okay, so this in/out scenario is a bit confusing. But the good news is you don't usually use the Freehand tool for this type of selection (unless you're trying to do something fairly artsy). Instead, the Freehand tool is often used to generate an initial boundary inside where more sophisticated selections will be used. For example, you can draw around a person's head in a scanned photograph and then use the Select By Color (the discussion of which is coming in just a moment) option to isolate the dark or light regions around the eyes.

◆ Selecting by Color

A more sophisticated selection can be created by making use of the colors within an image. There are two ways to do this: the Fuzzy Select tool and the Select By Color menu option (in the Canvas menu, under the *Select* option). Both tools require you to click on a pixel in a layer. With the Fuzzy Select tool (which should be the first button in the second row) you'll get any pixels that are within the threshold specified and are continuous from the initial click point. In other words, you get a single closed selection which encompasses the pixel at the click point and any pixels whose color is near that pixel (with *near* being defined by the threshold setting). The Select By Color option works similarly, but will include any pixel within the bounds of the threshold level even if it is not in a continuous region containing the initial click point. With this method you can get many small closed selections peppered around the image display.

FIGURE 3-2 The Fuzzy Select tool

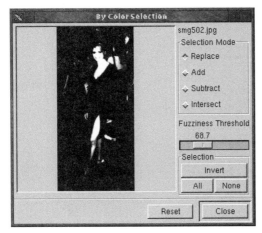

FIGURE 3-3 Selecting by Color will include any pixels within the specified threshold, even if the regions are not continuous

With both tools you can limit the area in which the selection is to be created by creating an initial bounding selection. Create a rectangular selection, for example, around some houses in a picture of a city block. Then use the Select By Color dialog's Intersect option and click inside the bounding box in the image. The result is a selection that is bounded by the original rectangular selection and whose pixels meet the threshold criteria for the click point.

The Fuzzy Select can work similarly except that this tool has no dialog option for setting the intersect mode. Instead, you need to hold down the Ctrl and Shift keys at the same time. Fuzzy Select also allows you to drag while you hold the mouse button down to increase the threshold range.

Selections, no matter how they are created, have hard edges by default. That means the boundary of the selection runs directly over a single pixel. However, selections can be feathered, which means their edges drift out to include pixels beyond the edge. These extra pixels are only partially used with the selection. For example, applying a bucket fill inside a feathered selection will make the selection appear to have smooth, fading edges.

Feathering has another effect on the multiple enclosed regions of a Select By Color selection: It can join some of those regions. Why this happens is not important. What it means to the Web developer is that Select By Color can be used to select spots you definitely want to work on, and feathering will make changes to those regions blend much more seamlessly.

◆ Outlining Selections with the Bezier and Intelligent Scissors Tools

Fuzzy Select and Select By Color allow you to choose regions based on color, not shape (unless the colors provide distinct boundaries, such as a cloudless blue sky over a city landscape). To make a selection around a person, for example, you need more control of the selection outline. The Freehand selection offers one possibility, but it requires a steady hand and tremendous patience to get it just right. If you're in a hurry, you need the Bezier and Intelligent Scissors tools.

Both the Bezier and Intelligent Scissors tools allow you to drop *anchor points* (also referred to as *control points*) around some shape in the image. Initially, with the Bezier tool, straight lines are drawn between these points. You can change them to curves to match the outline of the shape you're trying to select by adjusting the *handles* on the control points. The handles are small blocks that sit on straight lines extending from either side of an anchor point.

Anchor points are created when the Bezier tool is selected and you click in the Canvas. (Each point will have two handles: one for managing the shape of the curve on either side of the anchor point.) When you click to drop an anchor point on the image, it will make life easier if you drag the cursor a little to stretch the handles out. When you are ready to close the outline you can click on the original anchor once again. Now, click on any control point to make it active. Then click and drag the handles to adjust the curve of both sides of the anchor. To adjust the curve on only one side, hold down the Shift key before you click and drag a handle. Be careful: You need to click in the box shape at the end of the handle! If you accidentally click outside that region, but the click is inside the bounded region of the Bezier curves, then the selection becomes active and the marching ants start their dance. If this isn't what you wanted, type Ctrl-Z to undo the selection and get back the Bezier anchors and their handles.

Anchor points can be moved after they've been created. First, click on the anchor to make it active, then hold down the Ctrl key while you click in and drag the anchor point around. If you don't hold down the Ctrl key, you'll cause the handles to revert back to their original state of being 180 degrees apart.

Intelligent Scissors work in much the same way as the Bezier selection tool. You click around some shape to drop anchor points. To close the selection before activating it, you click on the original control point. As you drop a new control point onto the canvas it is connected with a jagged line. The intelligence is in the GIMP's attempt to find edges between the two points, edges where colors or contrast vary significantly.

After you've dropped a number of points you can Ctrl-Click on them to move them around. This changes the jagged line between adjacent points. You can click on the jagged line between points to add new ones. To get more accurate selections with Intelligent Scissors, zoom in on the image and add more control points. Clicking inside the solid edged border connecting the control points will activate the selection.

◆ Guides, Joins, and Cuts

Remember how you could align layers using guides? Well, you can do the same thing with selections. Under the *View* option of the Canvas menu you'll find a toggle for *Snap To Guides*. This option allows you to set whether selection boundaries for Rectangular, Elliptical, Freehand, and Bezier selections gravitate towards the horizontal and vertical guides. When enabled, it causes the first three types of selections boundaries to snap towards the guides. In the case of Bezier selections, the anchor points are pulled towards the guides. This happens only if you're relatively close to the guides, however.

Snapping to the guides makes it easy to select perfect circles. You can use two horizontal and two vertical guides to mark the radius of the circle, then drag from the upper left intersection of the guides to the lower right intersection. Similarly, you can use guides to mark the horizontal and vertical outlines of a ship or building, then with joined rectangular selections to outline the object.

Joined selections are simple. You use a key to modify the behavior of a selection. For both rectangular and elliptical selections, the Shift key causes a new selection to be added to any existing selection. This allows you to have, for example, two elliptical selections active at the same time even though they aren't physically touching in the Canvas. An unfortunate feature of selection modifiers is that they are context sensitive—that means a modifier, like the Shift modifier or the Ctrl modifier, can perform two functions. For rectangular and elliptical selections, the Shift key also causes the click point to become the center of the selection. What happens if you want to add a selection to an existing one, but don't want the new selection to be perfectly square or circular? Hold the shift key down, start dragging, then—without letting go of the mouse button—release the shift key. The selection reverts to using the click point as an anchor for a corner. What if a selection already exists and you want a new selection that is perfectly square? Just get rid of the original selection first using Shift-Ctrl-A or just click once (but don't drag the mouse) outside the existing selection. Then create your new one.

Where the Shift key can join two selections, the Control key can be used to make a cutout of an existing selection. Try this:

1. Make a rectangular selection in a new, blank Canvas window.

2. Hold down the Control key and make another selection inside the first one.

You've made a cutout of the first selection. A cutout will be created (when the Control key is pressed before you start the second selection) anywhere the two selections overlap. You can make intersecting selections as well by holding down the Shift and Ctrl keys at the same time. An intersection of two selections means the resulting selection will only include those areas which overlap.

Because these modifiers are overloaded (meaning they perform two functions: determining shape and joining selections), you need a way to determine just what is happening and when. The key: pressing the keys *before* you press the mouse button determines the method of joining or cutting selections. Once you start dragging the mouse, the join/cut mode is set and the keys now determine the shape and/or anchor point for the selection. If you press the keys *after* you start dragging then you only modify the shape and/or anchor point.

◆ Preparing for a Selection

As you see, there are many tools to make a selection, but a good selection can go beyond using just these tools. Recognizing color and brightness aspects of the desired region can help in determining which tool to use and for preparing that region for the selection.

For example, if you have a region you want as a selection where the colors in that region closely match their surroundings but whose brightness is considerably different, you can use a contrast-enhanced, desaturated version of the layer to generate the selection. This new layer is only temporary and is used just to create the selection, which is then used on the original layer.

To use this particular technique you start by duplicating the layer. Make sure the duplicate layer is active and choose *Image->Colors->Desaturate* from the Canvas menu. This will make the duplicate layer a grayscale version of the original. Next, choose *Image->Colors->Brightness-Contrast* (or Levels or even Curves). Now use the dialog to increase the contrast between the two regions—the area you want to select and the area you don't. Once this contrast has created a definitive line between the two areas you can use Fuzzy Select to make your selection. Click back on the original layer to use the selection on the original, and delete the temporary layer if you have no further use for it.

◆ Saving Your Selections

You'll find there are times you use the same selection over and over again. It would be nice to be able to save the selection, especially complex ones, so you don't have to recreate it each time. Fear not—selections can be saved! Once the selection has been made, choose the *Select->Save To Channel* option in the Canvas menu. This will create a new channel (in the Channels page of the Layers and Channels dialog) which is a black and white representation of the selection.

In order to use a saved selection, click on the channel to make it active. Note that this will deactivate the layer on which you were just working. Now choose the *Channel to Selection* option (right mouse click on the channel name to open the Channels menu). A selection is created in the Canvas. Now you need to return to the Layers page of that dialog and click on the layer again to reactivate it. You're now ready to use the saved selection once again.

◆ Tilted Ovals

Accurate selections can be difficult but are required for serious artwork. Most Web sites won't have much need for making a cutout
of someone's flowing hair for seamless display over random colored backgrounds, but you never know. Stranger things have
been seen.

Getting an accurate selection is a learned skill. Imagine, for
example, if you have a photograph of a circular sign taken from
an angle. The sign in the photo will appear to be a tilted oval.
How can you make a selection of this quickly? The elliptical selection would be optimal, but it doesn't tilt—the selections are
always up and down or left and right. How do you create an elliptical selection that is tilted? It turns out to be rather easy and
requires little more than what you've learned already.

The first thing to do is set some guides to the outside edges—
left, right, top, and bottom—of the ellipse you want to select. Then
drag an elliptical selection from the upper left to the lower right
intersections of these guides. Create a new, blank layer. Bucket fill
the elliptical selection with white. Now get rid of the guides; you
won't need them anymore.

Set the opacity of the new layer to about 50%. We want the
original image to show through. Now we come to the new piece
of information—using the *Transform* tool. Double-click on its
Toolbox button, which should be just to the left of the *Flip* tool
button (which itself looks like a double-ended arrow). This will
open the Tool Options dialog. Choose the *Shearing* option. By
default, shearing occurs to the left and right (not up and down).
Choose *Alpha To Selection* from the Layers menu for the new layer,
then click on the selection. A bounding box is drawn around the
selection. Clicking in the Canvas and dragging left or right will
shear the bounding box. Do this until the vertical lines in the
bounding box appear to match the direction of tilt for the object
you're trying to select. Clicking the *Shear* button in the Shear
Information dialog box will perform the shearing and create a
floating layer. If the partially transparent white oval appears to
match the shape of the object you want to select, then choose *New
Layer* from the Layers menu (to convert the floating layer into a
real one) followed by *Alpha To Selection*. At this point you have a
selection that should match your object. You can later delete the
two temporary layers that were created during this process. If the
tilted transparent oval didn't quite match, you can use Ctrl-Z to
undo the operation and try again.

RECAP

Like layers, selections are an integral part of the GIMP with which Web designers need to become both familiar and comfortable. There are many tools for selections in the GIMP, such as the Rectangular, Elliptical, Freehand, Fuzzy, and Bezier tools, as well as the Select By Color dialog. And there are many methods for using features within the GIMP to generate selections, such as using a contrast-enhanced desaturated layer and the Fuzzy Select tool.

PROJECTS

Draw an oval selection using the Freehand Selection tool and then cross it repeatedly in circular swirls. After you let go of the mouse button and the marching ants start their dance, try to figure out which parts are internal to the selection. Then select the Bucket Fill tool and click inside the Canvas. See if your guesses were right about what parts were included and which weren't. Do the same thing again, but try more convoluted crossing patterns.

On a new, blank (white) layer, add a layer mask. Click on the mask to make it active. Now use the Freehand tool to draw a crazy outline. Fill the selection with black. Apply the layer mask. What happens? Choose *Alpha To Selection* from the layer menu. Now save this new selection to a channel. How would you retrieve that selection from the channel?

Do the same thing again, but this time, right after you draw the crazy outline, choose *Select->Feather* from the Canvas menu. Set the number of pixels to feather to 10 or even 20. Then repeat the rest of the project. What happens when you do the *Alpha To Selection*? What does the saved selection look like compared to the original layer?

Start with a scanned photo (or digital image from a stock photo collection). Duplicate the layer, then desaturate the duplicate. Choose *Image->Colors->Levels*. There are two color bars in this dialog; the upper one has three triangles (black, gray, and white, respectively, left to right). Drag the gray (middle) triangle to the left. What happens? Drag it to the right. What happens? What happens if you move the black or white triangle? How can this be used to isolate regions for selections?

Repeat the last project, but choose *Image->Colors->Curves*. Play with this to change the white and black levels in the image. Learning how the *Image->Colors* menu options can be used in this way is important in understanding how good selections can be made. This technique is basically how you would select things (like hair) from their backgrounds.

4 Font Techniques

chapter

IN THIS CHAPTER

- The Standard Text Tool
- GIMP Dynamic Text—GDynText
- Working with Text Layers
- Text Effects
- Recap
- Projects

Now that you've learned the two most basic pieces to the GIMP puzzle, layers and selections, we're going to dive into some real world issues. The first of these are logos. I find it hard to imagine any Web artist who hasn't had some need to create a custom logo, or at least edit or work on an existing one. Logos are basically ordinary text, using various fonts, and run through a bundle of effects filters. They're not usually difficult to create, but can become complex depending on their intended use. Fortunately, once you get the steps down for a specific logo, you can automate it using scripting, making it easy to recreate the exact same design each time.

In this chapter we'll look at what text tools exist and how they can be used for some simple effects. In the next chapter we'll perform our first Site Design project: a corporate logo for a fictional company.

◆ The Standard Text Tool

One area of big improvement in the 1.2 release of the GIMP is in text handling. There are now two ways to work with text, the standard Text Tool and the newer Dynamic Text tool, also known as GDynText. Each has pluses and minuses, so chances are good you'll end up using one or the other at different times.

The standard Text Tool dialog is shown in Figure 4-1. The major advantage of the standard tool over GDynText is in choosing a particular font. Using the Filter page of the Text Tool dialog, font searches can be limited by foundary name and by weight and slant, among others. Selecting the Adobe foundary, for example, would limit the fonts displayed in the Font page to only those fonts which come from Adobe. The usefulness of this feature becomes obvious when you already have 2,000 fonts installed and then add five more from a particular foundary. You want to try them out right away, but don't know their font names. Finding them using the standard Text Tool is quick and simple.

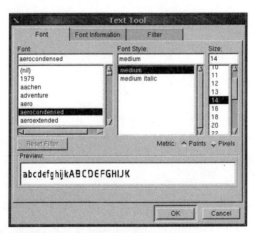

FIGURE 4-1 The standard Text Tool

To use the Text Tool simply click on its icon in the Toolbox. Then, in any Canvas, click once with the left mouse button. The Text Tool dialog opens. You can filter the set of available fonts first, then select the font you want to use from the Font page of the dialog. Set the size and style (if more than one style is available). Type in the text you want to create in the Preview window. By default, the GIMP will display a set of letters (lower- and upper-case versions of A through K) using the specified font characteristics. When you're ready, click on the OK button and the text is rendered in the current layer of the Canvas from which the dialog was opened. If you want to use a different color for the text, be sure to set the foreground color in the Toolbox prior to clicking the OK button in the Text Tool dialog.

◆ GIMP Dynamic Text—GDynText

The Dynamic Text Tool is a little more sophisticated than the standard tool. It allows you to create multiline text, set the justification for the lines, specify the font color, rotate the text, and even get the source text from a file. Although finding the font of choice is a bit harder, GDynText is generally a much better tool for working with text in the GIMP.

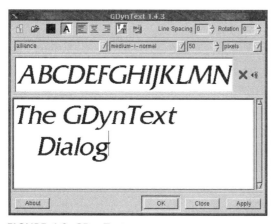

FIGURE 4-2 GDynText

Since the default Text Tool is the standard tool, you need to manually request to use GDynText. Double-click on the Text Tool icon in the toolbox to open the Tool Options dialog for that tool. There is a toggle button here for using Dynamic Text. Click this and then click on the Canvas to open the GDynText dialog. If you close the Tool Options dialog after you've selected to use Dynamic Text, then that setting will remain in effect from then on. You'll need to reset that toggle in the Tool Options to get back to the standard Text Tool dialog.

◆ Working with Text Layers

No matter which tool you use, text is converted from its font specifications into a rendered image in a layer. This means that although you can read the text, to the GIMP that layer is just another set of pixels. If you use the standard Text Tool, once you've rendered the text you can never go back to edit it. Any changes you want will require you to reopen the Text Tool dialog, select your font characteristics, retype your text and so forth, to recreate the rendering.

With GDynText, however, you can save the information used to render the text. You'll notice that when you click on the Canvas with the Dynamic Text option selected you get both the GDynText dialog and a message window stating that the layer you're working on is not a GDynText layer. So GDynText will create a new layer for you when you click the OK button, a layer which contains the font characteristics and original text saved internally to the GIMP. If you click on that new layer again with GDynText active, the dialog will be filled with the original text settings, allowing you to edit the text quite easily.

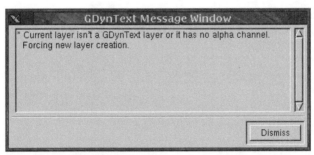

FIGURE 4-3 GDynText and message window

Although GDynText keeps track of the original settings, those settings are not obvious just by looking at the Canvas or the Layers dialog. You can have GDynText set the layer name to the settings by holding down the Shift key when you click on the OK button for the GDynText dialog. This will place the font name, size, and other characteristics, along with the actual text used, in the layer name. Be warned, however: This will create a really long layer name, even for short amounts of rendered text. This doesn't cause a problem, but the only way to see all of the information is to scroll horizontally in the Layers dialog.

FIGURE 4-4 GDynText OK button tool tip

Although GDynText allows you to save the text characteristics, it doesn't keep track of any effects you might apply to the rendered layer. This means that if you change the color of the text with a bucket fill and then blur it, for example, and then edit the text, you'll lose the bucket fill and blur effects. For this reason it's often preferable to apply effects to duplicate text layers, setting the layer name to the effect used and any relevant settings. Later, you can edit the original text layer and recreate each of the duplicate layers effects step by step.

◆ Text Effects

Okay, enough of this introductory stuff—let's do something interesting! The number of effects you can create starting with text is limitless. We're going to look at four quick and easy effects, just to show you the power behind the program.

3D Text Effect 1 - Levels

The first example we'll look at will create 3D text. This turns out to be a really simple process even though the GIMP is not a 3D tool. We're simply going to add depth to the text by fooling the eye with shadows and blurs. The easiest way to handle this is to simply run through the steps and then explain what happened.

1. Open a new Canvas with a white background.

2. Select the Dynamic Text Tool and click in the Canvas.

3. Click on the color box in the dialog and set the color to red.

4. Select a font with fat, smooth letters. Most systems will have helvetica or lucida, but use these only if the lettering in the Preview window is smooth along the edges. In our example we're using Alliance.

5. Type in some text, then click the OK button. A new layer is produced with your text.

6. The layer is positioned in the upper left of the Canvas. Move it to the center of the window.

7. Duplicate the layer, then click on the original layers name to make it active again. Turn off the visibility of the duplicate layer.

8. Type Ctrl-A to select the entire layer. Make sure the Keep Transparency toggle in the Layers dialog is set. Then fill the layer with black.

9. Resize the original layer—you want to add some space to the top and right of the text. Don't scale it! Resize it! You'll want a lot of extra space, but be certain the text remains at or near the lower left corner. Note: the original position of the rendered text shouldn't change, only the size of the layer should change.

10. Turn off the Keep Transparency toggle for this layer.

11. Type Ctrl-A to select the entire layer again.

12. Choose *Filters->Blur->Motion Blur* from the Canvas menu. Set the length to 10 or 15 and the angle to 135. The blur type should be the default—linear. Click OK to apply the effect to the black layer.

13. Choose *Merge Visible Layers* from the Layers menu. This will combine the black layer with the white background.

14. Choose *Image->Colors->Levels* from the Canvas menu.

15. In the Levels dialog there are a set of three triangles (black, gray, and white, respectively, left to right) just below the histogram display. Click the left mouse button on the black triangle and drag about halfway to the right. Then drag the gray slider nearly all the way to the right. You now have the extruded part of the text.

16. Turn on the visibility of the duplicate layer. That puts the red face back on your 3D text!

FIGURE 4-5 3D text example

Although this is a wordy example, it's not really hard. In fact, if we assumed your experience was anything more than beginner we could have left out much of this description. But this is the first real project we've done so we might as well be thorough.

So why does this work? We're just fooling the eye with shadows. Shadows are the key to showing depth in two dimensions. The motion blur generated the depth, but it wasn't a solid depth (it looked like a blur, of course). When we merged this with the white background and applied the Levels changes, the dark pixels got darker, filling in the blurred regions and making them appear solid.

Note that if you moved the black and gray triangles too far to the right in the Levels dialog you would end up with rough edges around the extruded part of the text. You have to play with this a bit depending on the shape defined by the font you choose in order to keep the edges smooth. But no matter what font you choose, the effect is not much more than a blur, merge, and contrast adjustment (the latter applied using the Levels dialog).

This particular effect works best with fat letters that render smoothly along their edges. The effect won't work well, for example, on text that looks like handwritten script or old english fonts. After a while you'll recognize this, but initially you just have to use trial and error to see what works and what doesn't.

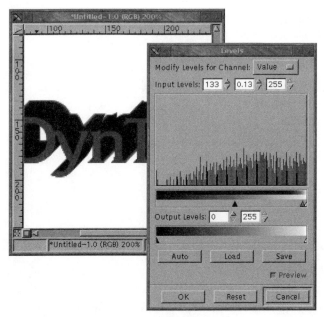

FIGURE 4-6 Level settings used in example

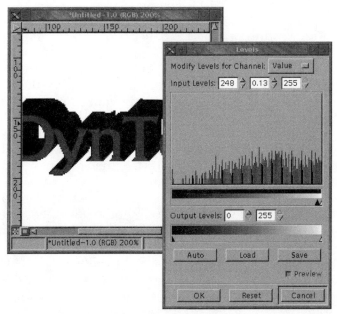

FIGURE 4-7 Levels adjusted too far—blockiness shows through

3D Text Effect 2—Blend Modes

Another method for generating 3D text is to use multiple layers and layer blend modes. The types of effects you can generate with blend modes goes far beyond what you did with the last, simple example. With blend modes, you can apply highlights and shadows that follow the natural contours of the text, just as if it were really in three dimensions.

As with the last example, we'll give the step-by-step instructions first and then explain what we did and why it works.

1. Start with a new Canvas. Be sure the foreground and background colors are set to their defaults. Add a text layer with a 15 pixel border. Use a font where the letters are thick to allow this effect to show more clearly.

2. Duplicate the layer twice, turning Keep Transparency off in the top and bottom text layers. The bottom layer would be the original text layer.

3. Apply a 5 pixel (vertical and horizontal) Gaussian Blur to the top text layer. The blur filters are available from the Canvas menu under the *Filters->Blur* option. There are two types of Gaussian Blur. Use the IIR version for this example, although there really isn't a huge difference between the two.

4. Gaussian Blur the bottom text layer 8 pixels both horizontally and vertically.

5. Offset the top layer by –2 pixels in x and y. This is done by opening the Offset dialog from the *Image->Transforms->Offset* Canvas menu option. You can use negative values in the fields for X and Y.

6. Offset the bottom layer 3 pixels in x and y.

7. Open the Curves dialog (*Image->Colors->Curves*) and adjust the Value curve as shown in Figure 4-11 to lighten the top layer. Be sure to click OK to apply the change and close the dialog.

8. Set the layer mode for the top layer to Screen.

That should be it.

Like in the last example, we're playing tricks again with shadows. When you blurred the top and bottom layers you applied the softness necessary for the rounded sides to the lettering. By offset-

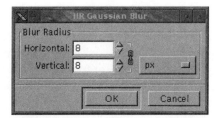

FIGURE 4-8 Gaussian Blur IIR dialog

FIGURE 4-9 The three layers before offsetting the top and bottom layers

FIGURE 4-10 The image after offsetting the layers

ting the top and bottom, you changed where the dark and light regions of the blur overlapped. Setting the top layer to Screen added that layer to whatever was showing below it. In places where the two blurred regions overlapped this created the appearance of depth. The process works with any shape—it doesn't have

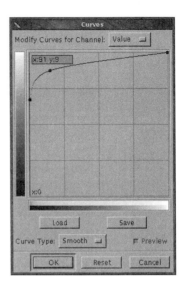

FIGURE 4-11 Curves setting for top layer

FIGURE 4-12 The final 3D effect

FIGURE 4-13 A variation on this technique can produce a cutout effect

to be text, although depth is easier to show if it's less regularly shaped. With a rectangle, for example, you might have to change the layer mode for the middle layer to Overlay.

In effect, what you're trying to do is add highlights and shadows with the top and bottom layers. The highlights and shadows are what give the text a 3D look. Again, we're just using tricks with light and color to make the eye think it sees depth.

The hard-edged text can be blurred 1 or 2 pixels and used as a mask on the final image. A soft blur might extend around the text giving the appearance of a haze or glow. In some cases this might look like a shadow, but in other cases you just want the 3D text without the soft edge. A proper mask can provide this, as long as it's applied to a merged version of the three layers.

There are many variations on this method. If you had applied the Curves adjustment to the bottom layer and set that layers mode to the difference, you'd get something that looked like it was pressed into the paper instead of standing out from it (you might have to change the order of the layers, or change more than one layers blend mode). The Addition, Lighten, Screen, and Overlay modes can all give rounded edges with a lighter layer over a darker one. It just depends on the colors in each layer and the shape of the object being worked on. Note that you'll get more dramatic effects by using variations of color rather than ordinary black text as we used in Figures 4-8 through 4-13.

Shadowed Text

Drop shadows are the kinds of shadows you see on the wall of a building when you're out in the sunlight. The shadow doesn't necessarily touch you. Imagine a ball floating over a table. The drop shadow is on the table. These types of shadows show 3D by adding depth to a scene. Perspective shadows are similar to drop shadows but they tend to flow out to a point on the horizon. They show 3D in perspective, expressing longer distances, and often start from the base of your object (whatever you're adding a shadow to).

Both types of shadows are easy to create in the GIMP, thanks to a couple of standard *Script-Fu* scripts. Script-Fu is the name of one of the scripting interfaces available for the GIMP. In this case, the scripts are written in the Scheme language, not that it matters that much. You use the scripts pretty much the way you use any other effects filter—by choosing it from a menu.

Start with a new window and add a text layer. In this example it doesn't matter as much which font you use. The scripts for generating drop shadows work well no matter what. Be certain the text is in a layer on its own—don't anchor it to the background layer. Then click on the text layer to make sure it's the active layer.

In the Canvas menu, under *Script-Fu->Shadows*, select the *Drop Shadow* option. The dialog that appears looks like Figure 4-14. Positive X and Y values will offset the shadow to the lower right, negative values to the upper left. The blur radius should be kept moderately small for Web images. If you're working on images destined for print, then you'll want a much larger blur radius than the default setting of 15 pixels. Additionally, the default setting for the Allow Resizing toggle is on. This will allow the Drop Shadow script to resize your Canvas if necessary to accommodate the shadow layer. This probably isn't what you want. Turn it off. The opacity setting can be left at 80 in most cases, although I find I set it to 100 for many of my shadows.

FIGURE 4-14 Drop Shadow dialog

The Color bar allows you to specify the color for the shadow. Most shadows are going to be shades of gray and the default black color will work well using variations of the blur radius. However, you can add a little color to the shadow to account for reflected light by changing this setting.

Once you've made your changes, click on the OK button. The script will generate the offset shadow in a new layer and place that layer below the currently active text layer.

Shadows show up well when the background has a high contrast—black shadow on white background, for example. Shadows usually have soft edges too, which means they fade into the background. If you try to generate a shadow for text which will have transparent regions, you'll end up having to dither that shadow down to fit into the 256 colors of a GIF image. The shadow may not look right in this case. Soft-edged shadows and GIFs don't work well together.

FIGURE 4-15 Drop Shadow for text

FIGURE 4-16 Dithered shadow for indexed GIF doesn't look good

Rotated and Arc'd Text

Rotating text is easy, and there are a number of ways to do it. First, you can use GDynText to rotate the text before you've created it. The rotation field in the upper right corner of the dialog allows you to specify the angle of rotation in degrees, from +360 to –360. The text will be rendered at this angle when you click on the OK button.

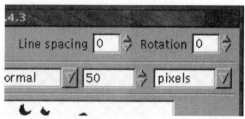

FIGURE 4-17 GDynText's rotation option

You can also rotate text after it's been rendered. The Transform tool in the Toolbox offers an interactive method of rotating a layer or selection. Double-click on its icon in the Toolbox to open its Tool Options dialog. Make sure the Rotation Transform option is selected in this dialog. Click in the text layer. The Rotation Information dialog will open. You can drag the slider under the Rotation Angle field to interactively select a rotation angle. When you do this, a set of grid lines will rotate in the Canvas showing the angle of rotation. Once you click on the Rotate button in this dialog the layer will be rotated. This method can also be applied to a selection. The rotation will create a floating layer and leave a cutout in the shape of the selection in the original layer.

Placing text around a curve is possible in the GIMP, but it's not easy. You can use the Text Circle script under **Xtns->Script-Fu->Logos** to place text around an arc, but you can't have the text follow any random curve. If you want text to follow a wavy path you'll need to create the letters or phrases separately, then rotate each one to fit the path.[1] With GIMP 1.2 you have a little help with alignment; you can draw a path using the Path Tool and then use it as a path along which you can align your text. We'll be taking a closer look at paths in Chapter 7, "Drawing and Painting."

FIGURE 4-18 Text along a curve, created manually by rotating individual letters

---

1. There is a tool for Linux called Sketch which can handle text along random curves. This is, at the time of this writing, the closest thing Linux has to Adobe Illustrator. Although it's currently the best vector drawing tool for Linux, and certainly quite good for things like text along curves, it still has a ways to go before it could reasonably be compared to the caliber of Illustrator.

RECAP

In this chapter we looked at using fonts and GIMP's text tools for creating text effects. You saw how layer blend modes can be used to simulate contoured text, and how simple extrusion of text requires nothing more than a motion blur and contrast enhancement. Text effects for logos require an understanding of how to generate text and how to manipulate it within layers.

Text is an important part of image design for a Web site. With the GIMP, managing text is simple using the text tools. In the next chapter we're going to look at a real world example. We'll generate the Wilbur Widgets Design Studio front page, and talk about the wide set of predefined logos on which we can base our own.

PROJECTS

In the layer blend mode example, what happens if you change the background from the white default to, say, red? Reset the background to white.

Try applying (and then undoing with Ctrl-Z) a red bucket fill to each of the text layers, one at a time. What happens? What if you apply a bucket fill to the top layer *after* you turn Keep Transparency back on? You'll get a Neon sign effect if you apply the bucket fills to both the top and bottom layers with Keep Transparency turned on, but not if you also apply it to the middle layer. Why not?

How can you get a copy of this text and place it in another image? Hint: It's harder to do if you have to use multiple layers.

3D is easy when you think about how shadows work. The simplest 3D example is a sphere. Just make a circular selection. Then switch the default foreground and background colors. Next, double-click on the Gradient Tool (the one next to the Bucket Fill), and select a Radial blend (from the middle options menu). Now drag from one point to another in the selection. Changing the starting point of your drag will change the apparent direction of lighting on the sphere. If it doesn't look quite right, make sure the foreground is set to white and the background is set to black.

5 Site Design 1: Logos

In This Chapter

- Goals for This Site Design Project
- Basics of Logo Design for the Web
- The Quick and Dirty Logo
- Creating the Wilbur Widgets Logo
- Scaling Issues
- Recap

Most Web designs focus around a core identity, a logo that presents the basic image of the site. Designing logos is a full-time job for some people, but most users of the GIMP won't have to work quite that hard. Besides the wide array of predefined logos available, the GIMP provides a set of common features which make logo design simple and painless.

In this chapter we'll generate the Wilbur Widgets Design Studio front page, and talk about the wide set of predefined logos on which we can base our own. Over the course of the book we'll expand upon this project with other Site Design chapters.

◆ Goals for This Site Design Project

Every project should have a goal and this one is no exception. The Wilbur Widgets Design Studio is in need of a logo for their Web site. The logo will not be used in print, so we're free to focus on Web issues alone for this project.

The studio isn't sure what they want for a logo, so we're going to offer a series of text logos on which to base their idea. The first thing we need from them is what text should be displayed in the logo. They want the studio name, Wilbur Widgets, and a company tag line, "Purveyors of fine art everywhere." We won't judge the merits of the tag line, just do as the client asks.

We recommend that a JPEG image be used for the logo on a white background. This makes it easier to generate anti-aliased text. A logo created with a transparent background can be cute but can also make a smooth edge look jagged because of limitations in using GIF images (which is currently the only way to use transparency with respect to existing and older browsers). We're also skipping transparency because, well, we haven't talked about it yet in this book. We'll get to it in a later chapter.

◆ Basics of Logo Design for the Web

Before we get started, let's take a look at what makes a good logo design for a Web site. The first thing is position on the page. A logo needs to be highly visible on the front page and noticeable, but out of the way, on any other page. The logo is an identifying mark for your site. People should become familiar with it.

The front page logo will be larger than on other pages. It will also occupy a position on the page around which the rest of the pages' contents must flow. This doesn't necessarily mean right smack in the middle. It just means the layout must be consistent.

The next key element in the logo design, and page layout in general, is the color scheme. It's less important how many colors you have (though this is a consideration for some of your visitors) than which colors you mix together. Purples and greens make lousy counterparts; bronze and yellow fit more comfortably.

Once color and position are defined, your next step is to choose the way you'll develop your artwork. The GIMP is a raster tool, which means it works on a pixel-by-pixel basis. The drawback to this is that there are practical limits to how far you can scale the image up. Vector art allows for scaling an image up fairly easily.

Since logos are often used both online and in print, you often want to work with vector art for the logos. However, in this design, Wilbur Widgets has told us they don't care about print versions of the logo. So we can work happily with the GIMP for now.

Online logos are usually fairly simple—they tend to have few colors and little or no transparency. Since even small scaling changes can reduce the clarity of the logo, special effects are usually not applied to any great length. Logos are often just simple patterns with the occasional drop shadow. Creating logos in this manner will allow you to size the logo down to be less obtrusive, but still visible, on other pages within the site.

◆ The Quick and Dirty Logo

With the basics and our clients needs in mind, we jump straight to the simplest method of logo generation: GIMP Script-Fu logos. These are a set of predefined logo generators that come with the standard distribution. Most will work as is, though a few may require that you choose a different font other than the default setting.

There are 28 predefined logo generators. Figure 5-1 shows the tear-off menu you'll see when you select *Xtns->Script-Fu->Logos* from the Toolbox menus. Each of these options will open a dialog window that allows you to specify a font, color, size, and various other features for the logo. Figures 5-2 and 5-3 show examples of two of these, the Basic I and the Cool Metal logos.

The stock set of logos can produce a wide range of standard styles. What changes, normally, is the font you use, the colors you choose and, in some cases, the textures you apply to the text and/or background. Since all of the logos are Script-Fu scripts, you can even copy them to your .GIMP/script-fu directory and modify them for your own projects.

Since we don't know what the client is really looking for, we'll choose these two options as a starting point.

FIGURE 5-1 The Script-Fu logo menu

FIGURE 5-2 The Basic 1 logo dialog

FIGURE 5-3 The Cool Metal logo dialog

FIGURE 5-4 Basic 1 Wilbur Widgets logo

FIGURE 5-5 Cool Metal Wilbur Widgets logo

Notice that we made the Cool Metal logo all uppercase. The reason is that this logo-generating script attempts to apply a drop shadow and reflective lettering at the base of the text. If we used mixed case then any descenders in the text (parts of the letters that drop below the baseline of the text) would cause the effect to become distorted.

FIGURE 5-6 Cool Metal Wilbur Widgets logo using mixed case

In case you're wondering, the Cool Metal logo gets its name from the reflective nature and coloring of the logo. In black and white, this may not be so obvious.

Another thing to note is that fonts on Linux come in two basic forms: scalable and nonscalable bitmapped. The latter are usually those found in the directory /usr/X11R6/lib/X11/fonts/75dpi and are designed specifically for use on computer displays. Scalable fonts are designed so that they scale much better. Using a 75dpi Times font yields the result seen in Figure 5-7. Figure 5-8 shows the same logo using a scalable Times font. Make sure you use the right font if you expect to scale the font to something higher than around 36 points, depending on the font.

FIGURE 5-7 Wilbur Widgets logo using 75dpi Times font

FIGURE 5-8 Wilbur Widgets logo using the scalable version of Times font

◆ Creating the Wilbur Widgets Logo

Now that we have some samples, we need to add the tag lines requested by the client. This is simple enough to do. We'll use a different font for the tag line (Alliance), and make it black. The next issue is position. For the Basic I logo we can place the tag line below the text to the right of the letter g's descender. This makes for a nice block alignment of the entire logo.

To make this change to the Basic I logo we want to first use a Guide to locate the top of our new text tag line. Then we want to add a text layer and align it with the Guide.

1. Click on the top ruler and drag down, placing the guide just below (but not touching) the existing text.

2. Open the Text Tool dialog and select a font. We're using Alliance here, but you'll need to pick from whatever is available on your system.

3. Type the tag line in the Text Tool dialog, set the appropriate font size (you may want it larger than the default setting), and click on OK.

4. You'll have a floating selection for the text. Click on its layer name and select "New Layer" to make it a new layer.

5. Select the Move tool. Holding the Shift key down, move the text layer so its top edge aligns with the Guide. This should happen automatically if you left the default settings turned on. Layer edges automatically align with Guides unless you turn that feature off (see *View->Snap To Guides*).

FIGURE 5-9 Updated Wilbur Widgets logo, with guide displayed

If for some reason the new text layer is not visible, check the Layers and Channels dialog. The new text layer should be at the top of the stack of layers. If not, click on the layer name and move it up using the up arrow button in that dialog. That's all there is to updating this logo. It's not fancy, but it's clean and useful.

The Cool Metal offers a more difficult problem. The 3D effect leaves no space to place the tag line near the bottom of the text. Doing so would block out the reflection and/or drop shadow and reduce the visual effect. The only places left are behind the text or above it. Behind won't work—the tag line is too long and will be hard to read if placed behind the company name. So the tag line has to go on top. There are actually a few other options to this, such as text along an arc, but we're not far enough along to deal with that yet, so we'll just stick to straight text.

Since there really isn't any existing space to place the tag line, we'll have to add some to this canvas window. Then we'll need to scale the background to fit that new canvas size, move the existing layers down a bit, and insert the new text.

1. Resize the canvas using the *Image->Canvas Size* option of the Canvas menu. Click on the chain link next to the ratio fields to allow you to change the Y ratio without changing the X ratio. Set the Y ratio to 1.2, which will increase the height of the Canvas window. At the bottom of this dialog is a small box showing the current size of the Canvas window inside a region that will be the new size. If the change isn't obvious when you change the Y ratio, move the mouse out of the dialog and back in—these two boxes should be updated. Drag the inside box down. This will force the additional space in the Canvas to be added along the top edges of the existing layers.

2. Now, scale the background to fit. Click on the background layer's name in the Layers and Channels dialog. Open the Layers menu and select *Layer to Image Size*. The layer should scale itself to fill the new space you just added.

3. Add a guide along the top of the text. Drag a guide down from the top ruler and place it just above the company name.

4. Add the tag text layer.

5. Align the new text layer with the guide. You may want to center the tag line, or maybe offset it to the right or left a little. Hey, you're the Web designer, be creative!

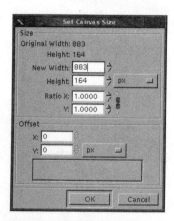

FIGURE 5-10 The Canvas Size dialog. Note the boxes at the bottom, for adjusting the position of the existing layers after the canvas has been resized

FIGURE 5-11 Cool Metal logo after the tag line has been added

After looking at our examples, Wilbur Widgets Design Studio has decided that they like the Basic I logo, but want a minor change. They want a horizontal stripe through the company name with the color fading opposite of the way it does in the logo. This is a simple addition, and we can even jazz it up a little.

1. Click on the top layer of the Basic I logo.

2. Click on the New Layer button of the Layers and Channels dialog. Just use the default values provided for the layer size.

3. Click on the Rectangular Selection tool in the Toolbox. Make a thin horizontal selection through the company name.

4. Click on the Gradient Tool and drag it from right to left in the selection you just made. This will create a smooth gradient that flows from white on the right to black on the left.

FIGURE 5-12 The final Wilbur Widgets logo

Now, to add a little pizazz, change the layer mode for this new layer to Difference. This should enhance the 3D effect on some of the lettering. Even in black and white it looks pretty good! If you don't like the color version, you can try adjusting the curves for the individual color channels of the stripe layer.

One more note on these logos. Notice that we used a white background. Our image will be saved as a JPEG, so there is no transparency. To eliminate what are known as the "jaggies," we've anti-aliased the text with the surrounding white backgrounds. This means that the white background of the logo needs to match the white background of the page it will be used on. So your site should have a white background—at least in the places where the logo is to be used. If you change the background of the page, you'll probably want to change the background of the logo.

This is the drawback to the Web right now. The only format that allows for transparency and high quality images is PNG, but few browsers support this format completely yet. Perhaps in a few years...

◆ Scaling Issues

The image we've created is simple enough to repeat if necessary, and in fact most of the settings will be saved by the Basic I Logo script. What you really can't do, at least not without distorting the image, is to scale the logo to be larger after you've finished it. You need to know ahead of time how large you want it. The default setting of 100 pixels for the font size in both the Basic I and Cool Metal logos generates an image that is about 750 pixels wide, far too large for a Web page. You'll want to redo this with a setting of about 12–24 pixels for a reasonable Web page logo.

RECAP

In this chapter we used all of the skills you've learned so far in this book, and even added a few extras like using the Gradient tool. The logo is just the first step in designing a useful Web page. However, we still have a few more basics to learn before we can get into HTML design. The next few chapters will look at dealing with color in your images, and how to use the GIMP's core set of drawing tools.

6 Color Management

IN THIS CHAPTER

- Gamma, and Why You Can't Do Much About It
- Curves and Levels
- Brightness / Contrast
- Hue / Saturation
- Softening Images and Bringing Out Hidden Detail
- Low Resolution Images with Posterize, Normalize, and Indexing
- When Do You Adjust Color?
- Recap
- Projects

One thing the GIMP doesn't do well is match the exact color necessary for prepress (i.e., print) operations. Support for Pantone colors, for example, is not available. However, the limitations here are only with prepress. The GIMP still offers a wealth of color management tools for the Web designer. In this chapter, we'll look at some of the more useful color management features, what you can do with them, and why you'd want to use them.

◆ Gamma, and Why You Can't Do Much About It

When designing for the Web you have to take into consideration a number of cross-platform issues. The most common problems deal with how various features of HTML and DHTML are supported by various Web browsers. Support for JavaScript, for example, is not always complete on every platform, especially not in older browsers.

For graphics work, a more serious problem is the differences you'll find in monitors, especially monitors designed for PCs and those designed for the Mac. Engineers and serious design artists often refer to the term *gamma* to describe how bright or dark monitors appear when displaying images. What the technical explanation is for this term doesn't really matter for this text. All you need to remember is that it refers to the apparent brightness of the display, and that Macs tend to display brighter than PCs.

The unfortunate part of this difference is that there really isn't much you can do as a designer to get around the problem. Plans are being worked out for browsers to support PNG, a relatively new file format like GIF or JPEG which supports setting gamma values directly in the image file. The browsers will check this setting and then display the image appropriately, no matter what the gamma settings of the monitor might be. But this is all work in progress and not expected to be available for a year or even longer, so for now there isn't much you can do. Take heart, though. At least for the foreseeable future the majority of visitors to any Web site are on PCs. Keeping your images the right brightness on a PC, then, will help ensure that a majority of visitors get the right view of your image.

◆ Curves and Levels

You can't control gamma correctness, but you can do quite a bit to clean up the color quality of your images. GIMP has many tools for this sort of work. Much of the time you'll find you use these features to clean up scanned images more than you will to work on drawings you created directly in the GIMP, but they do work well on images you create for use as tiled backgrounds also.

In Chapter 4, "Font Techniques," we took our first look at the Curves dialog (*Image->Colors->Curves*). Initially, it doesn't look like a curve—it's a diagonal line in a graph with two colored axis. You manipulate the line by clicking on it and dragging. The direction of the drag determines how the pixels in the current layer are to be updated. Dragging down and/or to the left tends to darken the image. Dragging up and/or to the right tends to lighten the image.

Changes to the curve are global unless you have an existing selection. The changes also affect only the current layer. You can make updates to any of the color channels (red, green, or blue) or to the overall lightness and darkness of the image.

FIGURE 6-1 Curves dialog

Curves adjustments can be used on all channels equally (using the default Value channel) or on each channel independently. This allows you to change the contrast between similarly colored pixels. This often helps to increase the color quality in an image, bringing out shadows or adding emphasis to existing highlights.

While curves adjust how light or dark existing pixels are, levels adjusts the range of colors in a layer. The levels diagram displays a histogram showing the range of colors (depending on which channel is being examined). If the histogram does not stretch all the way to the left and right sides of the window, then the tonal range is not stretched as far as it can go. In other words, the black pixels are not as black as they could be and/or the white pixels are not as white as they could be. If you were working with the red channel then the darkest red pixels are not as dark as they could be. By moving the triangular sliders beneath the histogram left or right you change the range of color tone in the image.

Levels adjustments differ from curves adjustments in that the latter can change the brightness of any set of pixels within the existing range while the former changes only the existing range. You can think of levels as a rough adjustment tool and curves as a fine adjustment tool.

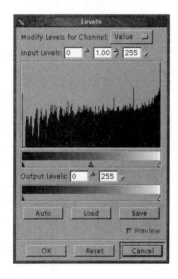

FIGURE 6-2 Levels dialog

Levels adjustment, particularly the Auto-Levels features in the Levels dialog, are often used to color-adjust a newly scanned photo. Curves adjustments are used to extend or reduce the effects of highlights or shadows. Both curves and levels adjust the color of an image but not its brightness (also known as "lightness").

Let's look at two quick examples of the Curves and Levels dialogs in action. In the first example, we'll see how the Curves dialog can be used to change a simple gradient into a three dimensional wave.

1. Start with gray gradient and open the Curves dialog.

2. Click on some point in the gradient; note the vertical marker in dialog. This marker designates the location on the diagonal line (known as the curve) that matches the pixel you clicked on.

3. Click in the Curves dialog on the intersection point where the curve and the vertical marker meet to set an anchor point.

4. To the right of the marker, click on the curve and drag it down. This will make the gradient darker near the point you clicked on in the Canvas.

5. Click and drag the curve down to the left of the marker. Again, this makes the gradient darker near your original click point.

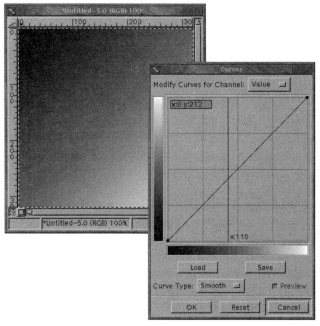

FIGURE 6-3 Simple diagonal gradient and the Curves dialog. Clicking on any pixel brings up the curves marker

What you've done is to cause the rate of change in the gradient to increase within certain parts of the image, specifically those pixels with a value (brightness) near the value of the pixel you clicked on initially. This is just one example of what you can do with curves. This example shows how the curve can be adjusted to generate a special effect (simulating undulating waves). Curves can also be used to increase the contrast between specific colors by using the Channel menu at the top of the dialog.

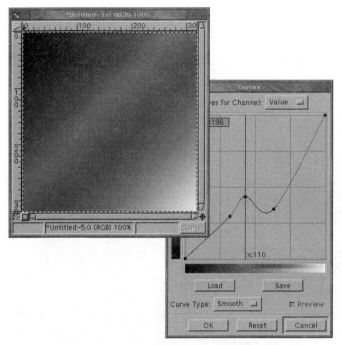

FIGURE 6-4 Same gradient, but with the curve adjusted
to either side of a central point

The next example is even simpler, but shows the power of
Levels. We'll take a desaturated photo (so that it will look well in
the grayscale print this book uses) that has poor contrast and
adjust it using the Levels dialog to bring out the detail.

1. Start with a poorly contrasting image.

2. Open the Level dialog from the Colors menu.

3. In this image the range of color is not spread where the
darkest pixels are black and the lightest pixels fully white.
Drag the left triangle more to the left and the right triangle more to the right. Click on OK.

The range contrast has been increased, thus bringing out the
details in the image.

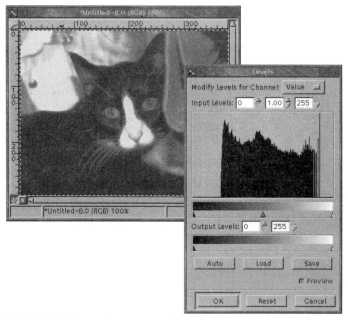

FIGURE 6-5 A poorly contrasted image

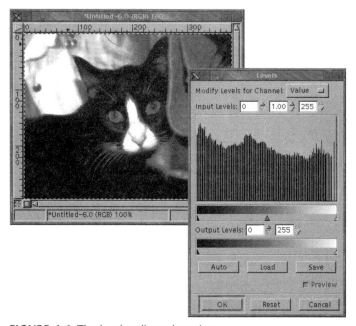

FIGURE 6-6 The levels adjusted version

◆ Brightness/Contrast

The Brightness/Contrast dialog is less sophisticated than its Curves and Levels cousins. As its name suggests, it works only on the overall brightness and contrast of an image, without respect to the colors. In other words, it works only on the value of pixels. This tool is useful for reducing the shine or reflections in an image, although for selective changes of this nature the Dodge and Burn tool is more appropriate.

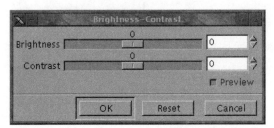

FIGURE 6-7 Brightness/Contrast dialog

◆ Hue/Saturation

Both the Curves and Levels dialogs allow you to work on specific color channels, adjusting the brightness of pixels in the chosen channel. Brightness/Contrast works the same way but without respect to color channels. The Hue/Saturation/Lightness dialog (known simply as the HSL dialog) provides the finest grain control for color adjustments by allowing you to work on seven different channels (red, green, blue, cyan, magenta, yellow, and the master channel) and providing adjustments for three different aspects of the channel selected.

Modifications to the Hue affects the visible color—reds move to orange or yellow, for example. Changes to Saturation affect how pure the color appears—from a dull, washed-out red to a vibrant red. Lightness affects how bright the red appears.

Use of the HSL dialog provides very fine grain control because it allows you to change aspects of all pixels at the same time based on how much of the original component they contain. Pixels with lots of red can be made yellow by selecting the red channel and moving the hue slider to the right. This sort of control is far more sophisticated than Curves, and is often used as the last step in a color correction process.

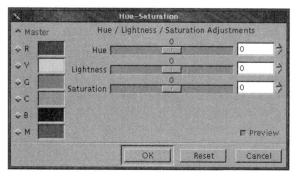

FIGURE 6-8 HSL dialog

◆ Softening Images and Bringing Out Hidden Detail

So what can you do with all of this? The normal use for Curves and Levels is to enhance the color quality of a scanned photo. But you can do more than enhance color quality—you can bring out details that are not plainly visible in the original image.

Let's try a few more real world examples. In the first, we want to bring out hidden detail in an underexposed image without overexposing the whole image. In the second example we'll show how a similar process can be used to soften the focus of an image.

Hidden Detail

We start with a scanned photo which is overexposed in the foreground, leaving the background dark and lacking detail.

1. Duplicate the original layer.

2. Desaturate the duplicate layer.

3. Use Ctrl-A to select the entire duplicate layer.

4. Use Ctrl-C to save a copy of the selection.

5. Add a white layer mask to the duplicate layer.

6. With the layer mask active, select *Edit->Paste* from the Canvas menu.

7. Anchor the floating layer. This will place it in the mask.

8. Select *Image->Colors->Invert* for the layer mask.

9. Select *Filters->Blur->Gaussian Blur IIR* and set the radius to 25.

10. Set the Layer blend mode to *Screen*.

The result is that the dark regions of the original image are now being lightened. We haven't yet used the curves or levels dialogs, though; that comes next.

1. Click on the duplicate layer (not the mask).

2. Select *Image->Colors->Levels*.

3. Adjust the sliders to increase the white level in the image.

FIGURE 6-9 A photograph with underexposed regions

FIGURE 6-10 Same image, with hidden detail brought out

What happened? The dark areas became brighter, bringing out the detail, without brightening the foreground regions. This makes the image appear as though the original photo had proper lighting. The blurred mask serves two purposes: The white regions determine which parts of the duplicate layer are added to the original (thus brightening them) and the blur makes the effect flow smoothly between the dark and light regions. You can tighten the area in the duplicate that is added (i.e., screened) to the original by changing the Curves dialog for the mask to have a more parabolic shape. You can enhance the amount of brightening by doing the same on the duplicate layer itself.

Selective Blur

We can take this effect one step further. You saw in the previous example how to isolate a region of an image by making use of the high contrast in the image. A duplicate layer was desaturated and inverted to create a mask. The same thing can be done to isolate the foreground and background of an image in order to do a selective focal blur.

1. Duplicate the original layer.

2. Desaturate the duplicate layer.

3. Use Ctrl-A to select the entire duplicate layer.

4. Use Ctrl-C to save a copy of the selection.

5. Add a white layer mask to the duplicate layer.

6. With the layer mask active, select *Edit->Paste* from the Canvas menu.

7. Anchor the floating layer. This will place it in the mask.

8. Select *Image->Colors->Invert* for the layer mask.

9. Use the Brightness/Contrast dialog to increase the contrast in the mask.

10. Use *Filters->Blur->Motion Blur* on the duplicate layer.

This is mostly the effect you want, but not completely. The problem is that the foreground was not completely deselected by the mask—dark areas in the foreground ended up becoming part of the background. Here is where you need to use paint tools to manually paint out the parts of the mask that the desaturation and contrast adjustments don't quite catch. This is an important lesson in using any tool like the GIMP: Find what gets you close to what you want so that the detailed work is kept to a minimum.

FIGURE 6-11 Selectively blurred

Selective focus is a process used to focus a viewer's attention on a specific part of the image. The trick here is to either start with an image with high contrast between the foreground and background, or duplicate the original layer and manipulate it with the Curves, Levels, Brightness/Contrast, and HSL dialogs to create such a contrast.

◆ Low Resolution Images with Posterize, Normalize, and Indexing

Although not used much these days, the LOWSRC option to IMG tags in HTML allows you to specify a low resolution image to display in place of slower loading, high resolution images. Generating low resolution images can often produce interesting effects by adding grain to an image.

To create a low resolution image, you first need to remove the color content from the image by converting from RGB to a Grayscale image (*Images->Mode->Grayscale*). Then you apply one of several possible color reduction options. In these examples I've used the Posterize and Normalize options (under *Image->Colors*). The format allows me to specify the number of colors to use. The latter doesn't. Instead, it spreads the saturation so it fits a normalized curve more closely. Finally, the image is converted from Grayscale to Indexed mode. This option also lets me specify the number of colors to use. In one example the image was reduced to five levels of gray, while two others were reduced to only three.

The differences in the images are as visually important as file size, since an image reduced to very few colors but is unrecognizable is of little use as a LOWSRC image.

FIGURE 6-12 Original, indexed to 255 colors, size = 323104

FIGURE 6-13 Indexed to five colors, size = 43371

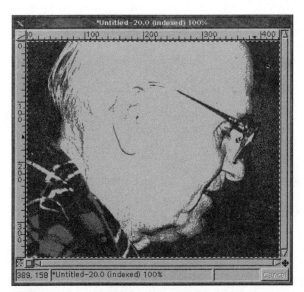

FIGURE 6-14 Posterized to six colors, then indexed to three colors, size = 28426

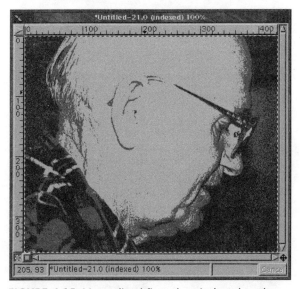

FIGURE 6-15 Normalized first, then indexed to three colors, size = 25310

◆ When Do You Adjust Color?

Color adjustments are most useful on scanned pictures. They are not generally useful for text, not even fancy colored logos. The human eye makes distinctions between ordinary images and those with distinct lines. Text usually has such lines. If the text is simple anti-aliased text with little or no color, then color adjustments will have almost no effect. If the text is a highly stylized logo with rich colors, then color adjustments can cause noticeable artifacts—noticeable due to the distinct edges and regions of solid color in the logo. Pictures of people, on the other hand, have few distinct lines and few regions of constant color. Color adjustments on images like this usually enhance the color quality. Scanned photos can also be color adjusted to create unique effects—posterizing, for example. A posterized photo looks interesting. Posterized text looks like, well, text.

RECAP

Monitors for PCs differ from Macs, a problem usually addressed by adjusting gamma. Most applications can't do much about gamma on their own; the monitors have to be adjusted manually. Web artists usually just remember that Macs display brighter than PCs.

Even though you can't do much about gamma, you can adjust color in an image in order to improve its quality, bring out details, reduce its file size and speed its download time.

PROJECTS

Find an image that has bright colors. Check its file size. Now convert it to grayscale and index it. Try to determine how many colors are required to keep it recognizable. How much disk space did you save by making this conversion?

Find an image that has high contrast between the background and the foreground. Adjust its levels and curves to bring out the detail in the background.

Try using levels and curves on a desaturated version of an image to generate a mask. Keep in mind that you may need to invert the image to mask the section you want.

chapter

7 Drawing and Painting

IN THIS CHAPTER

- Using Brushes and Patterns
- The Joys and Ills of Gradients
- Back to Banding
- Drawing
- Painting
- Paint Effects
- Working with Paths
- Recap
- Projects

One of the biggest complaints from users of the original version of the GIMP was that it lacked any reasonable drawing tools. Let's be honest here—the GIMP is no more an Adobe Illustrator style tool than Photoshop. But with the latest version, it has added quite a few tools for drawing that take it into a new realm for the Web developer. Tools for drawing straight and curved lines have been added, and the brush tools now support extended features for drawing and painting. And most importantly, support for drawing tablets is vastly improved.

◆ Using Brushes and Patterns

All drawing and paint tools in the GIMP use brushes. The Brush Selection dialog controls the shape and spacing for brushes. Brushes come in several formats: hard-edged, soft-edged (which are anti-aliased), colored, and brushpipes. The latter two are new and the last one, brushpipes, allows you to have a brush with multiple shapes, each applied according to the direction and speed of the brush tool.

The Brush Selection dialog defines the characteristics of a brush but the brush tools—Pencil, Paintbrush, Airbrush, Eraser, Clone, Convolve, Smudge, and Dodge/Burn—define how the brush is applied to the Canvas. The Pencil will apply a hard-edged brush with no anti-aliasing along the edges (no matter what the brush itself may imply) whereas all the other brushes apply soft-edged brush strokes when used with soft-edged brushes. Airbrush and Pencil apply paint based on the foreground and background colors. Clone and Convolve apply paint taken from a source image or pattern. Paintbrush is special. It can apply paint from the foreground and background colors or from the currently selected gradient.

FIGURE 7-1 Paintbrush from color

FIGURE 7-2 Paintbrush from gradient

FIGURE 7-3 Airbrush applying a brushpipe

Each brush tool has its own set of configurable options, its Tool Options dialog. All drawing tools can work with drawing tablets to different extents. You can change each tool to either accept or reject tilt and pressure input from the tablets pen, if your tablet supports it.

Selecting patterns is performed using the Pattern Selection dialog (*Dialogs->Patterns...*). Like the Brush Selection dialog, you simply click on the pattern of choice. The Bucket Fill, Convolve, and Clone tools can be used with the currently selected pattern. You can quickly access the Pattern Selection dialog through its active tool indicator button in the Toolbox.

FIGURE 7-4 Active tool indicators below the foreground/background color boxes in the Toolbox. Since the toolbox can be resized and shaped, the position of the active tool indicators can change

◆ The Joys and Ills of Gradients

Web designers have a love/hate relationship with gradients. A smooth, flowing color change, they offer fast and simple effects. The problem is that the file formats provided for the Web don't work well with gradients. If not handled properly, gradients can make an interesting site look downright childish.

Gradients are important for showing depth. For example, you can create 3D spheres very easily using nothing more than a circular gradient (one that starts in the center and flows outward) and a round selection. Let's see what you can do with gradients.

Quick Tubes

The simplest effect to make with a gradient is a tube or pipe. Start with a blank Canvas window. Make a rectangular selection that is about twice as tall as it is wide. Now click on the Blend tool's button in the Toolbox. Click anywhere to the left of the selection in the Canvas and, with the left mouse button held down, drag to the right side of the selection. This effect works best if you start right on the left edge of the selection and end on the right edge.

FIGURE 7-5 The Blend button from the Toolbox

FIGURE 7-6 Selection and gradient

What you end up with is a simple tube. This works visually because the gradient makes it appear that one side of the tube is lit more than the other. The top and bottom edges give away the trick, however. Since we can't easily make curved ends on our selection (but try subtracting and adding some elliptical selections!), it will help the effect if you hide the ends behind something else. Making the selection run the entire height of the window is one possibility.

The problem with this tube is that you can only angle the apparent lighting directly to the left or right of the tube. What if you want it to appear that the lighting is coming primarily from some angle in front of the tube? No problem. Double-click on the Blend button to open the Blend Tool Options dialog. Select Bi-

Linear from the Gradient menu in this dialog. Now reverse the foreground and background colors by clicking on the curved double-ended arrow. White is now the foreground color and black is the background color. Looking at the Tool Options dialog again you can see that the gradient is applied from foreground to background. So white is applied where you start your drag and the gradient gets dark at the same rate in both directions as you drag away from that point. To make a better looking tube, click just to the right of center inside your selection and drag to the left edge. Now that's a much better tube!

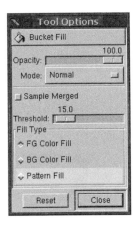

FIGURE 7-7 Blend Tool Options dialog

FIGURE 7-8 Foreground and background colors, reversed. Note the swap arrow

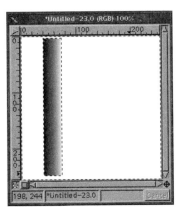

FIGURE 7-9 A much better tube!

Quick Bubbles

Another quick and extremely simple effect made with gradients are bubbles or spheres. These are simple, so we'll run through them with a step-by-step example.

1. In a new Canvas with a white background, make a circular selection. Hold down the Shift key while you drag the mouse to make the Elliptical selection tool to create a perfect circle.

2. Double-click on the Blend Tool to get the Tool Options dialog.

3. Select a Radial blend from the Gradient menu.

4. Make sure the Foreground is set to white and the background is set to black.

5. Drag from inside the circular selection, somewhere near its middle, to the outside edge of the selection.

Voila! Instant bubble.

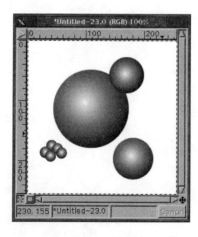

FIGURE 7-10 A bunch of bubbles

So what do you do with tubes and bubbles? By themselves they aren't all that interesting and, in fact, lose their luster moments after creation. But try adding a partially transparent Bucket Fill of some pattern, with the blend mode set to color. Let's run this example step by step.

1. Make a rectangular selection.

2. Double-click the Blend Tool to open the Tool Options dialog.

3. Select Bi-Linear in the Gradient menu of that dialog.

4. Make sure the foreground color is set to white and background set to black.

5. Click and drag from just right of center in the rectangular selection to the left edge. You'll get the black and white tube we made previously.

6. Double-click on the Bucket Fill tool in the Toolbox.

7. Select Pattern Fill.

8. Set the blend mode to Color in that dialog.

9. Click on the Pattern active tool indicator button in the toolbox. Set the current pattern to Pine. This is the default pattern so if you've never changed it before you don't need to change it now.

10. Click inside the rectangular selection once.

What happened? The wood grain pattern was applied over the tube gradient. Since the effect is based on color components of the image, we can't show it in grayscale, but it will be obvious when you try it yourself. The lightness in the gradient was combined to the pine pattern to create a pine dowel! Try this same experiment on the bubble example. You should end up with a spherical piece of pine, if all goes well. Try it with different patterns on both the tubes and bubbles.

This simple example creates only a simple effect, but it shows one important aspect of the GIMP—it isn't the individual tools but the combination of tools that creates images. Learn to combine colors, patterns, and images using different blend and layer modes. The effects can be astounding!

Why do you care about bubbles and tubes? Consider a bunch of bubbles with sky and cloud patterns applied. Now imagine them dancing around your page using DHTML layers! We'll touch on animation in a later chapter, but as always, we're building on previous experience to get to the next level. We needed to know about selections to use gradients to get bubbles so we can make animations later.

◆ Back to Banding

But beware: Gradients can also cause banding in your Web images. Banding is where distinctive lines appear in the gradient perpendicular to the direction of the gradient and in the shape of the gradient, such as round bands for circular gradients or straight-lined bands for linear gradients.

Banding problems are most evident in GIF images, though they can be a problem in JPEG images as well. With GIF images the problem is simple—there simply aren't enough colors in an indexed image (i.e., one with only 256 colors available to it) to show smooth color changes over large areas. Even so, there is a fix to get around this problem: Add grayscale noise.

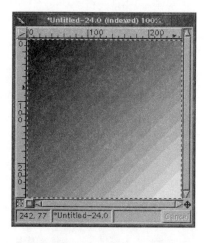

FIGURE 7-11 Indexed image with banding in the gradient

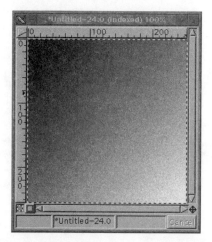

FIGURE 7-12 Same gradient with noise applied before indexing the image

What the noise does is add randomness to the gradient. This changes the gradient values along the lines where the banding would have occurred so that when the RGB image is converted to an indexed one, little to no banding is evident. The same trick can be applied to JPEG images, though these images have less problem with banding depending, at least in part, on the amount of compression you specify.

The amount of noise to add to a gradient prior to converting the RGB image to an indexed one, or prior to saving the RGB image as a JPEG, varies according to the color spread in the rest of the image. Generally, you don't need to add noise to a gradient applied to make a sphere, for example. But if you generate a background image for your page that is very large with a soft gradient running a quarter of the page in any direction, then adding some noise might improve the quality of that background.

✦ Drawing

Most of the tools available in the GIMP for drawing or painting are used much like their real-world counterparts. In fact, when used with a drawing tablet, the similarity is even more apparent.

Learning to draw lines may be one of the hardest things to do with the GIMP, so let's take it step by step. There are a number of ways to draw lines, so we'll look at quick examples of each.

Specifying End Points

The simplest way to draw a straight line is to specify its end points. The pencil, paintbrush, and airbrush tools all support this method.

1. Select the pencil, paintbrush, or airbrush tool, the foreground color you want, and the brush you'll use.

2. Click once in the Canvas.

3. Holding down the Shift key, click again somewhere else in the Canvas.

When you hold the Shift key a thin line is drawn anchored at the first point with the other end following the mouse. This allows you to see where the line will be drawn using the brush and foreground color you selected.

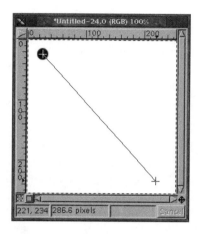

FIGURE 7-13 Selecting endpoints for a straight line

Stroking Selections

Another method that can be used to draw lines is to stroke selections. Stroking simply means to use the currently selected brush to follow the outline of the selection.

1. Choose one of the Selection tools from the Toolbox.

2. Click and drag around the Canvas to generate a selection.

3. Choose *Edit->Stroke* from the Canvas window menu.

The quality of the line generated by stroking can be altered by changing the Spacing value in the Brush Selection dialog. Often, smooth but distinct edges around corners can be created by reducing the spacing to 1 and using a relatively small brush size.

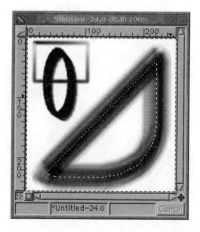

FIGURE 7-14 Examples of stroked selections

Stroking selections will produce lines of any shape, from rectangular and oval to any shape defined with the Freehand and Bezier selections. The only caveat to stroking is that since all selections are closed (endpoints are joined) all lines drawn in this way are closed as well.

Using Paths

The last method of drawing is the newest in the GIMP: paths. A path is a line drawn in much the same fashion as those made by the Bezier tool—in fact they are technically called Bezier paths. But the difference between using a path and using the Bezier tool is that the latter makes a closed selection. Paths can be ordinary lines with distinct endpoints. We'll talk more about using paths in a later section of this chapter.

◆ Painting

Freehand drawing is also possible in the GIMP—just select the tool, brush, and colors of choice and click and drag through the Canvas window to your heart's content. The drawing tools act more like real-world painting tools in this mode. With the paintbrush, for example, you can select pressure and size options for use with a drawing tablet. When the pen is pressed harder on the tablet it's like applying a firmer brush stroke on a real canvas. If you select a Fade Out amount, the paintbrush also acts like it runs out of ink the longer you paint with it, i.e., the longer you drag around the Canvas without letting go of the mouse button. Once the mouse button is released, the brush is filled with paint again, ready for your next click-and-drag performance.

The Airbrush tool behaves much like the paintbrush but has a much softer application and never runs out of paint. If you apply the airbrush over an area of the Canvas it will appear as faded paint initially (depending on the brush type, spacing, and so forth) and will darken the longer you hold the mouse button down on that spot.

The Paintbrush and Airbrush can be used to generate images on their own, or they can be used with layer masks to soften the edges of an image, making it appear to meld into the underlying layers.

A new tool in the recent release of the GIMP is the Ink Tool. This is a drawing tool not unlike the pencil, but with more control over the shape of the drawing tip. It also provides for soft edges while drawing, something the pencil does not support. The Ink

Tool was designed specifically for use with drawing tablets prior to such support being made available to all the drawing tools. While its performance is good with the tablet, you may find that outside calligraphic designs, the Ink Tool offers little that the other drawing tools do not.

◆ Paint Effects

Now that you're familiar with the basic drawing tools, let's look at some of the less obvious options for painting in the GIMP. There is, of course, the Bucket Fill tool which we've used in previous chapters. One quick way to use this tool is to click in the foreground or background icons (to select either color) and, with the mouse button still held down, drag it into the Canvas window and release the mouse button. If you have a preexisting selection then it will be filled with the color from which you are dragging. If you don't have a selection then the entire layer is filled. Be careful here: This behavior is different than the Bucket Fill tool itself. With no selection, clicking in the Canvas window with the Bucket Fill tool selected will fill the contiguous region that falls within its threshold value specified in its Tool Options dialog.

The Paintbrush was updated in the latest release to support what are known as gradient brushes. Simply put, the paintbrush paints with the currently selected gradient. The effects can be rather stunning, especially when combined with fadeout and pressure and tilt options.

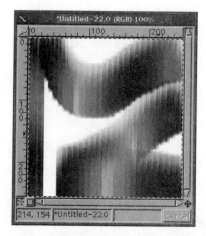

FIGURE 7-15 Gradient brush in action

Cloning is a paint tool that is often used to remove blemishes from scanned images. It works by taking a copy of a source image, in the shape of the currently selected brush, and copying it over or merging it with a destination point. By setting the opacity in the Brush Selection dialog to something less than 100, you can merge the source and destination points. Using soft-edged brushes will also help merge the source into the blemish.

To use the Clone tool, try these steps:

1. Start by opening an image you've scanned that has a small scratch or other blemish on it.

2. Select a soft-edged brush.

3. Set the opacity in the Brush Selection dialog to about 70.

4. Hold down the Ctrl key and click in the Canvas window near the blemish, someplace that looks a bit like what should be where the blemish is.

5. Now click and drag over the blemish.

The source point is copied to the destination point. The distance between the original source and destination is kept constant, so if you drag down from the destination, you get a copy of a line that starts from the source location and goes as far down as you dragged.

There are three other tools which work with the currently selected brush and the existing pixels in a Canvas: Convolver (a.k.a. Blur/Sharpen), Smudge, and Dodge/Burn. Each of these tools change the existing pixels by mixing them with surrounding pixels.

Convolver allows you to selectively clean up portions of an image using a brush shape. Brush opacity is honored, meaning that the amount of blurring performed, for example, will decrease with lower values of opacity. Similarly, Dodge and Burn work with the current brush and its specified opacity. Dodge lightens pixels while Burn darkens them. In both Blur/Sharpen and Dodge/Burn the active tool is selected by the respective Tool Options dialog.

Smudging is sort of like finger painting, where you take a blob of paint and smear it out in some direction. In this case, the shape of the smudge is determined by the currently selected brush and the length of the smudge is set using the Smudge tool's Tool Options dialog.

All of these paint tools provide interesting artistic effects, but you'll find that few of them are very useful for the Web. The reason: Images on the Web tend to be small, limited in color ranges, and distinctly shaped. While drawing lines and Bucket Fills are likely to be common practice for Web designers, it is the unusual Web graphics designer who spends much time smudging and burning.

◆ Working with Paths

Earlier we talked about drawing lines using paths, a new feature of the GIMP. A path is, technically, a nonclosed Bezier curve. In layman's terms it's a squiggly line whose ends don't meet. What's important about paths is that they are editable. If you use the point-to-point method or stroke a selection, you can't edit the line after it's been drawn. You can use Ctrl-Z to undo it and then redraw the line, but you can't edit the line directly. You have to respecify the points or the selection. With paths, you can go back and modify the line using control points and handles, just like with the Bezier Selection tool.

Working with paths can be confusing. First off, paths are kept in their own set of layers which do not correspond to any particular image layer. In this way you can draw many different paths in multiple path layers and then render (draw) them in any order, in multiple image layers, or all in a single image layer.

The best method of learning about paths is to walk through a simple example. Here we're going to make an S-shaped curve in a single path layer. The first step is to open the Layers and Channels dialog. You'll find a third option in this dialog, Paths. Click on the Paths tab. Make sure you have a blank Canvas (one with only a single, white background layer) to work on.

1. Add a new path layer by clicking on the button in the lower left of the Tools dialog. This automatically enables the Bezier Selection tool which is used to draw the path.

2. Click in the upper right quadrant of the Canvas. A control point is placed at this location.

3. Click in the middle of the Canvas. Another control point is deposited and a line is drawn between these first two control points.

4. Click in the lower left quadrant. Another control point is added, connected to the second point. Now you're ready to edit the line.

5. Click on the Edit Point button in the Paths dialog. This is the button on the far right just above the path layers display. Place the mouse over the button and you should see a ToolTip displayed stating that button's name.

6. With the Edit Button selected, click and hold down the mouse button on the last control point, then drag the mouse to the right. A curve is formed between the last and middle points. This is the bottom half of the S shape. The thing you're dragging is called a handle and is used to control the shape of the curve between two points.

7. Click on the upper right control point, hold the mouse down, and drag to the left. You've made the upper part of the S. The path is complete now. We can edit it at any time in the future, though once it's been rendered, the rendered drawing can't be edited (you have to undo the rendering or delete the image layer, neither of which affects the path).

8. Double-click on the Paintbrush tool and select the Gradient option. When you do this the path appears to go away in the Canvas window, but it hasn't. The path layer is still there, in the Path dialog; it's just not active at the moment.

9. Click on the path layer to activate it again.

10. Click on the Stroke path button at the bottom of the dialog. The path is rendered using the paintbrush tool, the current brush, and the current gradient.

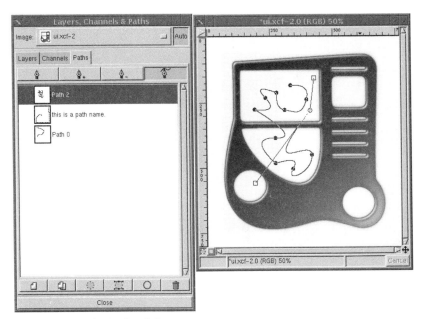

FIGURE 7-16 The Paths dialog

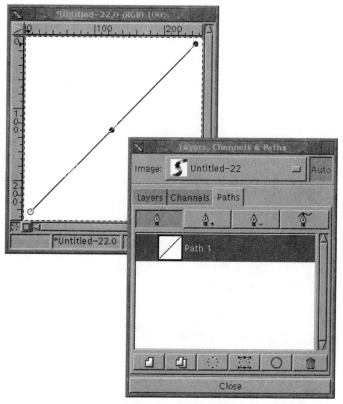

FIGURE 7-17 The three connected control points and their paths layer

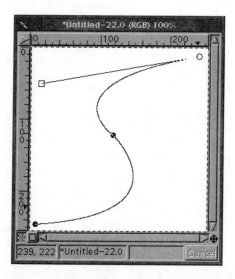

FIGURE 7-18 The S shape after editing the path

FIGURE 7-19 Rendered with the standard brush and gradient

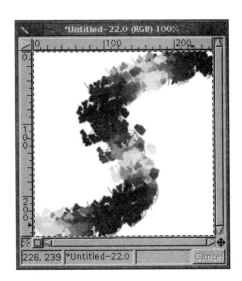

FIGURE 7-20 Rendered using a BrushPipe brush (the vine brush)

In Figure 7-20 you can see what you might get using a different brush, in this case a BrushPipe brush. In full color, using a gradient and the brushpipe brush, this effect is rather stunning in its beauty considering its simplicity.

RECAP

We came a long way in this chapter. Drawing and painting are at the core of the GIMP—it's what the GIMP was specifically designed to handle. From simple effects with gradients to the various drawing tools to working with paths, there are many options available to you as a Web artist. Taken independently, each of these tools is little more than a toy, but when combined, they give you the ability to outline images, paint them like cells in a cartoon, and edit them at your whim. As always, you build upon the features one piece at a time until you find the combination that fits your needs.

PROJECTS

Try making a tube or pipe with rounded edges. Use elliptical selections to round the ends of a rectangular selection by adding or subtracting from that selection.

Make a molecule with red, blue, white, and black atoms. Connect them with tubes. How can you rotate a tube? Try making a tube in a separate Canvas and using cut and paste to connect atoms. Pasted tubes become new layers. Look at the Transform tool for a way of rotating a layer. Hint: You need to select the layer first.

Try to cut out just the molecule. You can use Fuzzy Select to click on the background (which will work fairly well if the background is all one color). If parts of the image are not selected, hold down the shift key and try again. Ctrl-X will cut out the selection. What happens? Is the background transparent? If not, why not? Hint: What's special about the background layer? Look at the Layers menu.

After you successfully cut out the background of your molecule, add a new transparent layer above it. Bucket Fill this layer with some pattern, say leather. Try different layer blend modes on it. Try adjusting the Levels on the leather layer with each different blend mode. Notice the variation of effects just by changing the layer blend modes.

Create several different path layers. Then go back to the regular Layers page in that dialog (click on the Layers tab). Add a few transparent image layers over the background. Now, going back and forth between the layers and paths pages, render one or more paths in each of the different image layers. Try to see how the paths' layers do not correspond to specific image layers—you can render them in any layer at any time.

8 Site Design 2: Background Textures

IN THIS CHAPTER

- Goals for This Site Design Project
- Background Design Issues
- Painting the Initial Image
- Adding a New Logo
- Making It Seamless
- Using Background Images with Cascading Style Sheets
- Recap

◆ Goals for This Site Design Project

Background images are used on Web pages in many different ways. Besides their use as page backgrounds, they can also be used in tables and DHTML layers. Designing a background image is as much a matter of knowing where the image will be used as what the image should contain.

In this chapter we'll explore our second Site Design project. In Chapter 5, "Site Design 1: Logos," we looked at logos for the Wilbur Widgets company. The company has now asked that we design some background images to be used along with the logos on various pages of the Web site. They want to add more pizazz to the site.

Our first instinct is to find out if background images is what they really need. A background image is nothing more than fluff on a page—it provides no navigation and normally has no information that would be of any real use to a visitor to the site. While they can provide some form of corporate identity, they generally are not used in this way. So do they really want the fluff? "Yes," they say. "We live for fluff." So be it.

The next thing we'll consider are the three types of backgrounds you can use on a Web site: page backgrounds, table backgrounds, and DHTML layer backgrounds. A page background is connected to a specific page and scrolls with the page. It is bound by the rendering rules of the browser, which often leaves small gaps between the page background and the browser border. Page backgrounds are also tiled over the full page (unless they happen to be larger than the page).

Table backgrounds come in three flavors: table, row, and cell backgrounds. There really isn't much difference in these three other than the area of the table covered by the background image. The problem with table backgrounds is that using an image with anything other than tileable patterns seldom works right. The size of the table (or row or cell) doesn't take into account the size of the background image. You can't force a cell, for example, to be the size of the background image without clever tricks using multiline text or clear images as spacers. Additionally, a tiled image used as a row background is not guaranteed to be tiled from row to row; it's only guaranteed to be tiled within the row it is being used. So, the effect you're looking for is often much harder to find using tables than, say, DHTML layers.

DHTML layer backgrounds are not really tied to a page, but to a layer in that page. That means the visibility of the background can be changed with JavaScript, the image can be set not to scroll, and the position of the layer can be more precisely set than a normal page background. DHTML layer backgrounds are more flexible than ordinary page backgrounds, but with flexibility comes complexity. Where a page background will nearly always be fully displayed, a layer background's visible regions are dependent on a properly sized layer.

Since we've not yet talked about DHTML, and since most of the issues that surround layer backgrounds are similar to ordinary page backgrounds, we'll limit our project to normal page backgrounds and table-based backgrounds.

◆ Background Design Issues

As we just noted, page backgrounds are usually tiled to fit the displayed page. The exception to this is if the page is smaller than the actual background graphic. Although it's possible to create such large images for backgrounds, their file size generally prohibits their use in this way (it would take too long to download it). Therefore, most page backgrounds are designed as tiled images.

Because they are generally tiled, background images need to be seamless. If you're not familiar with this term, it means that the left and right edges could be placed next to each other and you couldn't see the edges (ditto for the top and bottom edges). Seamless tiles are not all that difficult to create, but it helps if you keep the images fairly bland—too much imagery makes seams harder to hide.

Most corporate Web sites tend to avoid background images, but the few that do use them try to keep them from being the focus of attention on the site. Gaudy patterns and pastel colors are generally avoided. Light gray or highly faded colors are used instead. The point of the background is to add to the corporate identity of the site, not to distract from the true content.

As with colors, contrast is of high importance with background images. If the background is dark and the foreground is dark, the focus of the site (and in fact the entire visibility of the site) can be lost. The background should contrast significantly from the foreground text and images. Most sites prefer to use light colored background images with dark text and foreground imagery.

◆ Painting the Initial Image

In order to make the page background we want to start with a solid background. This is the simplest means of making sure we have a tileable image, although we'll look at a trick later to verify this. We'll fill a 512 x 512 Canvas window with black, then use the Curves dialog to move the black end of the curve way up, creating a light gray background.

Next, we add just a little noise to the gray background. This isn't necessary, but it adds a little texture to the image. Most of the noise will be lost later when we lighten the image, but the results of blending the layers of this image will be affected to some extent by a little noise.

FIGURE 8-1 The noisified gray background

◆ Adding a New Logo

Now let's add a quick logo from scratch. In Chapter 5 we created some simple logos using the Basic I and Cool Metal Script-Fu logo scripts. What we want here, however, is so simple and effective that it deserves a special look.

In the upper right corner of the image we're going to add an oval shape. Inside of this we want to add a large letter W, and the letters "ilbur" and "idgets." These two bits of text will sit next to the W, vertically placed from one another. The text and the oval are all to be made to appear as three dimensional.

Let's work on the oval first. Start with a new layer.

1. Use the elliptical selection tool to create an oval selection.

2. Choose a soft-edged, round brush that isn't too thick. I'm using the Circle Fuzzy 17 brush.

3. Stroke the selection in the new layer.

4. Turn off layer transparency.

5. Duplicate the layer twice.

6. Gaussian blur the first layer by 8 pixels in both X and Y.

7. Gaussian blur the second duplicate (topmost oval) layer by 3 pixels in both X and Y. The middle oval layer should not be blurred.

8. Offset the top oval layer by –3 pixels in X and Y.

9. Offset the bottom oval layer by 5 pixels in X and Y.

10. Select the top oval layer. Open the Curves dialog and drag the curve to the upper left square. This will brighten that layer but leave it a modest gray.

11. Change the top oval layers blend mode to Addition.

This same technique—duplicate, blur, curve adjust, and blend mode to addition—will be used on the text as well. The only differences will be the radius of the blurs and the amount of offset for each layer. You can also leave off the middle layer of the text. Its only purpose in the oval is to darken the shaded areas. In the example images the middle layer was not used with the text. A scalable Times font was used in this example.

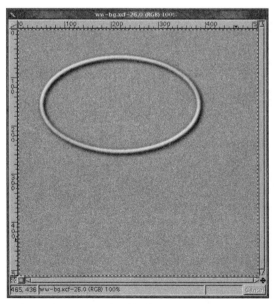

FIGURE 8-2 3D oval added to image

FIGURE 8-3 3D text added

Once the text has been added you can go back and darken the background. This is necessary because the overall image needs to be lightened to reduce the shadows in the 3D areas. If we start with a light background, then the lightening will just make the background completely white. We want a little gray in there, so we now darken it prior to flattening the layers and lightening the full image.

◆ Making It Seamless

The image we've created so far is already tileable. We know this for two reasons:

1. The original background color was a solid gray.

2. The noise filter does not create seams along the edges.

However, what if the image wasn't seamless? We can see how to fix this by adding a black border to the image. Use Ctrl-A to select the entire image and then stroke the selection using a small brush. Then choose *Image->Transforms->Offset*. In the dialog box, click on the button labeled Offset by (x/2), (y/2).

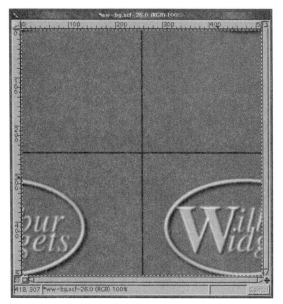

FIGURE 8-4 Seams in the image

To fix the seams use the Clone tool from the Toolbox. Make sure you have a soft-edged, round brush selected. While holding the shift key down, click on the background anywhere but over the seam. That selects the source from which you will be cloning. Now click and drag over the seam. The distance from the source to the mouse location is kept constant as you drag, so you get a nice smooth covering over the seam. If it doesn't look quite right, try reducing the amount of opacity in the Brushes dialog.

FIGURE 8-5 The updated version, with seams removed

Adjusting Contrast

Referring back to the original image (before we stroked the selection to show how to fix the seams), we now need to flatten the layers and lighten the overall image. Choose *Layers->Flatten Layers* from the Canvas menu. Then open either the Curves or Levels dialog. Either will work to lighten this image.

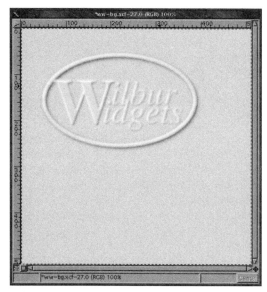

FIGURE 8-6 The final version

Adding the Original Logo

The only thing left to do is apply this to a Web page. Figure 8-7 shows the Web page with the tiled background image and our original logo. The original logo has been placed in a table, right-justified, and a few table cells have been added with generic text, just so we can see the layout.

We haven't talked yet about page layout issues using HTML. That will come in Chapter 10, "Gallery Images." For now, just take a look at the HTML used to generate this simple front page.

```
<html>
<body background="ww-bg.jpg">
<table width="100%" border="0">
<tr>
  <td colspan=2 align=right>
   <img src="logo1.jpg" border=1><br clear=both><br>
  </td>
</tr>

<tr>
  <td>This is some stuff.</td>
  <td width="90%" align=right>This is some other
stuff.</td>
</tr>
</table>
</body>
</html>
```

FIGURE 8-7 The Wilbur Widgets logo and page background in a Netscape browser window

◆ Using Background Images with Cascading Style Sheets

DHTML layers are a relatively recent addition to most Web browsers. As such, they are not supported to the same degree by all browsers. The official DHTML specification allows for page designers to specify if a background image is to be scrolled (like a page background) or anchored. Anchored background images don't move as the rest of the page is scrolled up and down or left and right. Unfortunately, this feature is not fully supported by all browsers at the time of this writing.

Background images can also be addressed as objects in a Document Object Model (DOM) using JavaScript. This feature is also not well supported. In general, use of background images in layers should be considered similar to ordinary page backgrounds with the exception that they are confined to the boundaries of the layer.

Layers can be any size but not all browsers will honor the full size request. Some browsers will only display as much of the layer as is necessary to display objects within the layer. This does not include the background, however. So the background image can be cut off at a strange point if the layer's contents don't extend far enough down the layer to expose the full background. It's a tricky problem and, for the time being, you're best off leaving background images out of layers until either the browsers properly support the DHTML specification or you find a way to create a background that looks fine no matter how much of it is actually visible.

RECAP

Background images should be tileable and provide a soft contrast to the focal elements of a page. Background images do not provide navigation for a Web site but can provide additional corporate identity to each page. While it is possible to have a single image cover an entire background, this technique is seldom used because the file size of the background slows the loading of the page.

Generating 3D effects on the background is simple to do. Using 3D effects can make the background more than a flat color or noisy pattern. It can also turn generic texture into corporate identity.

In general, the use of background images is discouraged in tables, rows, and cells since the tiling of the image is not guaranteed to span rows or cells. Background images are also discouraged in connection with DHTML layers until browsers have evolved enough to properly implement the DHTML layers specification.

Web Imaging

The GIMP is a great tool for doing all sorts of graphics work, but Web-based imaging has some specific needs. Compatibility with older systems leaves you with limited color choices for your images. Transparency support in existing browsers also leaves you with little choice. In this chapter we're going to look at some of the issues that are most important to working with the two most widely supported image formats, GIF and JPEG, as well as compare them to the newest addition, PNG, the Portable Network Graphics format.

◆ RGB versus Indexed

When you work on images in the GIMP you will usually work in RGB mode. This mode provides 8 bits of color information for each color channel: red, green, and blue. Even on systems which

115

can only display 256 colors, an RGB image in the GIMP still has all 24 bits of color information while you work in RGB mode.

But the GIMP also provides two other modes in which you can work. The first is called Indexed mode. This mode reduces the number of colors you can use to a palette of 256. The color of each pixel in the image is represented by an index into that palette. Initially, the palette has two colors—black and white. As you add colors more entries are added to the palette until it reaches 256 colors. After that, you either replace entries or use an existing one.

The third mode GIMP provides is called Grayscale mode. This is essentially the same as RGB mode but the colors are desaturated. If you use the Color Chooser you'll see three channels displayed but with each channel showing the same value for any given pixel. The scale runs from fully black to fully white. You don't often work in this mode for images on the Web, though you may find very specific need of it from time to time.

Two image file formats have been supported by most browsers almost since the beginning of the Web: GIF and JPEG. GIF is an indexed format providing only 8 bits of color information to be shared among all the pixels in the image. JPEG supports 24 bits of color, 8 bits for each color channel. These formats are very different and each should be used for the types of images for which it is best suited.

JPEG Format

The JPEG format retains color information in a manner that is suited to what the human eye can handle. This means that JPEG images can often be reduced in file size much more so than GIF images without losing the quality of the image itself. JPEG is most often used with real-world images, like scanned photographs. Image galleries are usually produced using JPEG images. You can reduce the file sizes quite a bit and still display a large number of images on a single page without forcing the user to wait a long time for the page to load.

Where JPEG doesn't work well is with images with distinct edges. If you rasterize a vector drawing, for example, and then save it as JPEG you won't get quite as good results as you would with GIF. Additionally, JPEG has no support for transparency. All JPEG images are fully opaque.

JPEG does not support animations, so if you try to save a layered GIMP image to a JPEG file you'll get an error. You need to reduce the number of layers to one by either flattening the image or merging the visible layers and removing hidden layers. Flattening will convert any transparent pixels left in the final layer to the current foreground color, while merging layers will keep transparency. However, since JPEG doesn't support transparency, flattening the layers is usually your best bet when you want to save your image as a JPEG file.

GIF Format

GIF files are widely used on the Web because of their limited color requirements. Where JPEG does not limit an image to a specific palette of colors, GIF images are required to use a limited palette. Additionally, since the colors are indexed from this palette, you can make all images on a page use the same palette, ensuring that all images on a given page on any browser will show up pretty much as you intended them to. This is not the case with JPEG. Web designers also use GIF palettes to guarantee that certain color schemes are adhered to on a given Web site.

JPEG images don't work well with distinct lines in an image, but GIF does. In fact, GIF works much better with text in an image than JPEG does. If you have an image which will have text in it, chances are good your image will appear better as a compressed indexed GIF file than as a compressed JPEG file. The trade-off here is that JPEG images compress better than GIF images. A photograph reduced to 35% quality with 35% smoothing in JPEG will be significantly smaller than the same image converted to Indexed and saved as a GIF file. The question remains, however, which one visually displays better.

GIF also supports transparency. A single entry in the palette can be specified as transparent and any pixel in the image that has that index will be transparent. This is known as 1-bit transparency and is the only widely supported method of using transparency in an image on the Web today.

One caveat to using the GIF format: The GIMP doesn't like to try to figure out if a layered image is supposed to be a GIF animation, if you just want to save a single layer as a GIF file, or if you want the layers merged before saving. It does make some guesses, but your best bet is to make sure you know beforehand what you're saving—is it a layer, an animation, or the whole image? If it's the latter, you need to flatten the image first (or merge the visible layers and delete any hidden layers).

PNG Format

PNG came on the scene about two years ago and is designed specifically to deal with limitations in the GIF format. The first limitation is the 1-bit transparency in GIF files. PNG supports 256 different levels of transparency by providing an 8-bit Alpha channel, similar to the 8 bits of color for each of the red, green, and blue channels it supports. PNG is also free of the licensing issues inherent with GIF, a problem that arose long after GIF had been widely adopted for use on the Web.

The largest obstacle to PNG is browser support. At the time of this writing neither of the two most popular browsers, MS IE and Netscape Navigator, supported the 8 bits of transparency available in PNG. This leaves PNG as a poor replacement for GIF at this time. But over the next few years PNG will become much more widely supported. GIF's days are numbered.

◆ Indexed Color Conversion

Most of the image editing work you'll do directly in the GIMP will be done in RGB mode. In order to save your work as a GIF file you have to first convert it to Indexed mode. Converting an image with up to 24 million colors down to one with only 256 colors (at the most) is fairly painless, though it's not completely automatic.

Let's walk through another example. Here we want to start with any 24-bit image, say a JPEG or TIFF image you have on file somewhere.

1. Open the 24-bit image. You'll be in RGB mode in the GIMP.

2. Click on *Image->Mode->Indexed* in the Canvas menu.

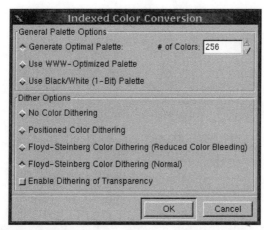

FIGURE 9-1 Indexed Color Conversion dialog

At this point you now have the Indexed Color Conversion dialog open. This dialog is used to select the method of converting your many-colored image to one with a limited color palette. You'll notice that there are several palette and dither options available. The palette options allow you to specify either a maximum number of colors, a specific palette to map the image to, or to use a 1-bit palette to convert the image to a black and white (not grayscale!) image. The dithering options provide a number of methods for determining how to map pixels in the image to entries in the indexed palette.

1. Select *Use Custom Palette* from the General Palette Options, then choose the Web menu item for that option.

2. Select *Floyd-Steinberg color dithering*.

This will cause the pixels to be mapped to colors that are considered Web safe (more on this later). The default dithering method is a good bet for most images, but you have to experiment to see which method will work best for any specific image. Remember that after you've converted an image to Indexed mode you can use Ctrl-Z to undo it. From here you can try different dithering options.

This example works well to convert any image to a set of Web-safe colors. If you need to reduce the number of colors down even further you can specify the maximum number of colors using the Generate Optimum Palette option. This will reduce the image to the best possible image with no more than the specified number of colors. However, those colors might not be considered Web safe.

To fix this problem, you can do your conversion in multiple steps. First, index your image to the specified number of colors. Then, convert it back to RGB mode by selecting *Image->Mode->RGB*. Don't use Ctrl-Z! Use the menu option instead. Now you have an RGB image that has only the specified number of colors you asked for the first time you converted to indexed mode. Now convert the image again, this time using the Web custom palette. Voila!

One important tip: Make the conversion to Indexed mode the last step of your image processing. Performing a rotational transform with smoothing, for example, will change the palette. Rotations on indexed images are also likely to cause stairstepping along edges and seriously degrade the quality of the image.

◆ Transparency

By now you're quite familiar with the GIMP's layers system. It's quite useful for building an image and allowing you to experiment at various stages of your work. One important aspect of layers is transparency. The pixels of each layer can be marked as having some level of transparency, or more accurately, to have some level of opacity, the opposite of transparency. If a pixel is 30% transparent, then it is also 70% opaque.

All layers in the GIMP automatically support transparent pixels except the original background layer. If you want to create a transparent GIF image for the Web, then you need to make sure you've added transparency to the background layer using the *Add Alpha Channel* option of the Layers menu.

The problem with using transparency on the Web is that only one widely supported format, GIF, currently supports it. What's worse is that GIF only understands two levels of transparency—all or none. As stated earlier, pixels in an RGB image can be partially transparent. When the image is converted to indexed mode, pixels are checked for their level of opacity. Anything above 50% becomes fully opaque. Anything below becomes fully transparent. This can lead to all sorts of jaggies (stairstepping) in your image along the transparent edges. This problem will remain until browsers fully support the PNG format.

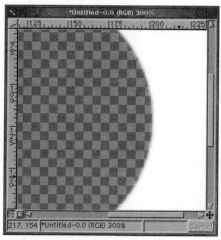

FIGURE 9-2 RGB Transparency

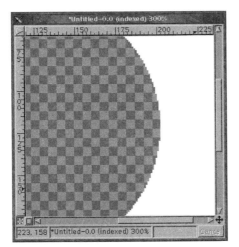

FIGURE 9-3 Stairstepping from indexing

Although this problem is annoying, there are some things you can do to get around it. First, stick with straight edges in your GIF. Curved edges are where the jaggies show up. Second, flatten your image (reducing it to a single layer) before you convert to indexed mode. This will permit some blending of pixels between your image and the background color. As long as the background of your Web page matches the background of your image, then visitors to your site won't notice the problems. Finally, use a filter before converting to indexed mode. This filter will use the current foreground color to fill in the regions along the edges of transparency. This works well if your image will end up on backgrounds of different colors, but you'll have to make versions of the image for each background using this method.

Working with transparency becomes important when you start working with animations. In the GIMP, you can create multiple layers, one each for a new frame in an animation which is placed over a constant background image (there are even better ways, but this is how it works with the GIMP). You can generate a series of frames in a single XCF file which will then be turned into an animation. But a more interesting option will be the movement of images using DHTML layers. Transparency will allow you to move images around the screen without making it look like spastic squares are running wild.

◆ Web-Safe Colors

Earlier we talked about the use of Web-safe colors. You might have heard of these referred to as the Netscape color cubes. This is a palette of colors which Netscape designed in order for browsers to work well on color-limited systems. At the time browsers were starting to become popular, most desktop computer systems were limited to displaying a maximum of 256 colors. In order to display images and still let your computer display windows, buttons, and icons correctly, Netscape created a palette of 216 colors for use in Web pages. The other 40 (out of 256) are left for the rest of the system to use.

Web designers would index all their images using Netscape's color palette. By doing so, the designers would be guaranteed that the images would display the same on any system. Images that had colors outside of this palette that were displayed on 256 color computers would get dithered by Netscape itself. If you were lucky, Netscape did a good job of this. Most of the time, however, you weren't lucky.

How do you know if a color is Web safe? Use the Color Picker tool to look at its hex value. This value has six characters, two each for the red, green, and blue components of that color. Each two-character value should be a multiple of three. Since most people's ability to multiply in hex is limited, just remember that every character in the six-digit hex string should be one of the following: 0, 3, 6, 9, C, or F. If any hex digit is not one of these, that color is not Web safe.

◆ JPEG Options

While GIF images are used extensively for images with simple text or animations, JPEG images are used for showing photographic detail. For example, JPEG images are often used as backgrounds or in product galleries. JPEG will retain visual cues in an image while still allowing large amounts of image compression. Good Web designers will reduce a large background image as far as it can go to reduce load times for visitors by using the JPEG format for that image.

Saving an image as a JPEG file requires that you've reduced the layers to one, either by merging them or flattening. Once you've done this, select *File->Save As...* and specify a filename with a ".jpg" extension. The GIMP recognizes extensions like this and will use the appropriate format. If you don't want to use the .jpg extension, then simply choose the format type from the Options menu provided.

When you press the OK button in the Save As dialog you'll get another window, the Save As JPEG dialog. Here you can specify how much compression to use, whether smoothing should be performed, and whether JPEG should be progressive or not. This latter option is like interlacing a GIF image, allowing the image to be displayed progressively instead of waiting until it's completely downloaded.

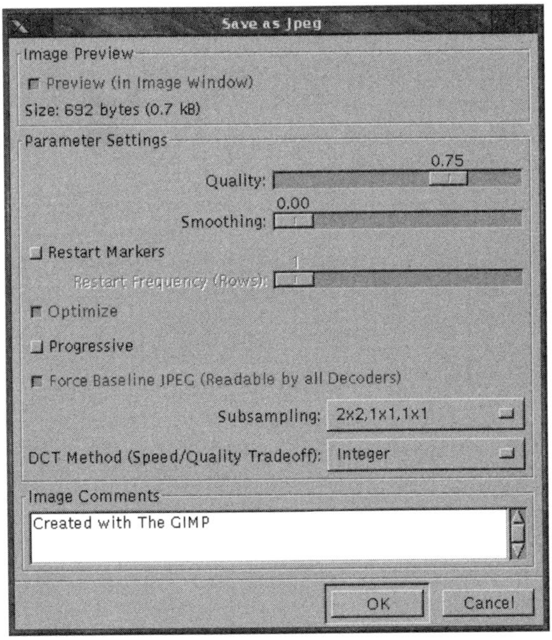

FIGURE 9-4 Save As JPEG dialog

The most interesting part of this dialog is that it will preview the image using the settings you use as a new layer in the Canvas. As you specify lower levels of quality (which is the same as increasing the amount of compression), the image is updated in the Canvas. At the same time, the size of the file that will be saved is displayed at the top of this dialog. By playing with different settings you can choose the smallest file size with the least acceptable level of image quality. Once you're satisfied, click on the OK button in the Save As JPEG dialog.

◆ Image Information and HTML Syntax

Up to now we've focused on the GIMP and how to use it to make images destined for the Web. But we've not really tied this together with how you actually get those images into a Web page. Well, now you're ready to start putting your pages together.

The first thing to be aware of is that HTML is a text-based language. Despite the numerous tools available (this author uses Netscape's Composer quite often even though it doesn't completely conform to all HTML standards), you still need to know what HTML looks like to understand how to use it properly. Later, when you're digging in deep with your WYSIWYG editor, you'll thank yourself for understanding just what that editor is asking for when it requests things like alignment and spacing.

To specify an image URL using HTML you use the following general syntax:

```
<IMG SRC="/path/to/image">
```

This is the most simplistic format of this command. We won't go into detail on specifying URLs—the /path/to/image—since that is a topic for a book on its own. What you should recognize is that the IMG tag tells a browser that an image is to be loaded and that it can be found where SRC points.

There are many options to this, not all of which are useful. One option that you will want to make use of is the image dimensions. To specify the height and width of your image in your HTML, you would use the following syntax:

```
<IMG SRC="/path/to/image" WIDTH=100 HEIGHT=100>
```

Here we're specifying the image has a height and width of 100 pixels in each direction. But how do you know what values to use here? Simple. Use the *View->Info Window* option in the Canvas menu. This window shows all the relevant information about your image, including the height and width.

Browsers use the height and width options in the IMG tag to determine how much space to reserve for an image. If you don't specify the height and width, then the browser often has to load the entire image in order to properly align the rest of the page. That delays the display of the page to your visitors. If the size you specify is not the size of the image, browsers will automatically resize the image to fit the requested space. This little trick can lead to some ugly side effects.

First, if you specify a smaller size for the height and width, the browser still has to load the whole image. If you need a smaller size, a thumbnail, then resize the image to the size you need. We'll talk more about thumbnails in the next chapter.

If you specify a larger size than the actual size of the image then the browser will scale your image to fit. This enlargement generally causes image degradation, particularly in GIF images which do not retain enough information from their original RGB format to provide for quality enlargements.

The trick is to specify the exact image size. The purpose of the height and width options is to help the browser speed display of the page. Don't use the browser as an image processing tool—that's what the GIMP is for! Use the GIMP for creating, managing, and updating your images and let the browser handle page display.

One other option to the IMG tag is BORDER. This option tells the browser how large to make the colored border around images that are used as links. For example, the following HTML tells the browser to use a default width for this border:

```
<A HREF="/path/to/page"><IMG SRC="/path/to/image" WIDTH=100
HEIGHT=100></A>
```

With Netscape you'll get a 2-pixel-wide border in the color of the link (active or inactive). With most images, you don't want this border. So specify your image links in this manner instead:

```
<A HREF="/path/to/page"><IMG SRC="/path/to/image" WIDTH=100
HEIGHT=100 BORDER=0></A>
```

Recap

Web designers need to recognize where and when to use the right image file format in their site designs. We've talked about GIF, JPEG, and PNG in this chapter, noting how GIF is good for small text-based images while JPEG is good for larger, photographic galleries. Image conversion from normal RGB mode to Indexed mode is required for any work bound for a GIF file, while JPEG images need to be flattened or merged before saving. And although the Web has limited support for transparency, it is an area limited to the GIF format until PNG is better and more widely supported. Finally, indexed images are normally mapped to existing color palettes and most, though not all, end up being mapped to Web-safe colors.

PROJECTS

Open an RGB image, say a TIFF or JPEG image, and convert it to a GIF. Make sure it has been mapped to the Netscape colorcube (i.e., mapped to the Web palette).

Undo the image mode, reverting the image back to RGB. Make a circular selection and use Ctrl-X to cut out that selection. What happened? Should there be transparency there? Why or why not?

Add an alpha channel to that image (we assume here that you still have only one layer in it). Make the cut in the image again. Now change the foreground color to blue. Choose *Filters->Colors->Semi-Flatten*. What happened to the edges of the cutout? Undo this. Now change the color to red. Apply the same filter. Now what happened to the edges?

Select *Dialogs->Palette...* (this will open the Color Palette dialog) and pick a color palette. These are the same as the options you have in the Indexed Color Conversion dialog. Choose one of these palettes, then try converting a set of four or five images to the same palette by selecting *Image->Mode->Indexed*. After you've made all the conversions, look at the Color Palette dialog and verify the colors. Now, try editing one of the entries in the Color Palette dialog for one of the images! This wasn't covered in this chapter, but it leads to how you can create your own palettes!

Use a WYSIWYG editor, such as Netscape's Composer, to create a simple Web page with a single image. Then use a text editor or word processor to read in the HTML file produced and look at the syntax in the file. What does the IMG tag look like? How does it relate to the other tags in the file (position between other tags and their matched closing tags)? Add a horizontal line beneath the first image and then another image below that line. Look at the page source again. How did things change? Become familiar with the format of an HTML file. You'll thank yourself later!

10 Gallery Images

IN THIS CHAPTER

- Thumbnails and Galleries
- Creating Thumbnails
- Speeding the Download
- Photo Retouching
- Photo Effects
- HTML Revisited
- Using Tables
- Recap
- Projects

There are many kinds of images that Web designers will use in a site design: buttons, banners, logos, background images, thumbnails and galleries, separators, etc. In previous chapters we touched on logos, backgrounds, and buttons. In this chapter we're going to take a look at thumbnails and gallery images. Where buttons are textual, backgrounds are dim, and logos sit solitary on any given page, thumbnails tend to be photographic, sharp, and numerous on one or more pages. Knowing how to generate thumbnails and when to use them will increase your site's value to any visitor.

◆ Thumbnails and Galleries

A thumbnail is simply a smaller representation of a larger image, usually a scanned photograph, though not necessarily so. Normally, you create thumbnails to give "sneak peeks" to visitors, enticing them to stay and view the more detailed (and longer to download) versions. Thumbnails are often grouped together, creating what are known as galleries. If you've ever picked up a roll of film after developing and found a single sheet with small versions of all the photos on it, that's a contact sheet. Galleries are like online contact sheets.

Galleries are useful for displaying artwork and collections of items, but thumbnails can also be used to display sets of products for a company. A toy company, for example, might want to show photographs of a Lego box set, its contents, and a constructed creature. Visitors can then click on the thumbnail to place an order, get more information, or see a close-up of the photograph.

FIGURE 10-1 Original image and its thumbnail

Creating thumbnails, in general, is fairly easy. They are, after all, just smaller versions of a larger image. The problem is maintaining sufficient image quality to let the viewer know what the thumbnail represents. In the Lego example you are fortunate that the Lego pieces are fairly easy to recognize, especially if you show something built with them. But a photograph of a stack of blue jeans reduced to thumbnail size might not be so obvious. It's a trade-off between proper planning in the photo session and Web site design issues.

◆ Creating Thumbnails

Although creating thumbnails is pretty straightforward, there are a few things you should keep in mind. The first is the aspect ratio of your original image. Aspect ratio is the ratio between the width and height of an image. When you select *Image->Scale Image* from the Canvas menu you'll get a dialog allowing you to specify the new width and/or height or change the ratio of the x and y dimensions. The latter option is specified as a decimal number, essentially the percentage of the new image size to the old, with 1.0 being the current size.

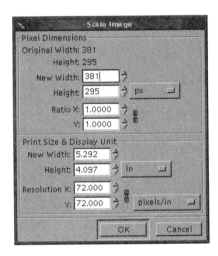

FIGURE 10-2 The Scale Image dialog

The default behavior of this dialog is to maintain the aspect ratio of the current image. The height and x fields on this dialog are tied to width and y fields. A change to the height, for example, will update all the other fields in order to maintain the aspect ratio. You can change this default behavior by simply clicking on the small chain link icon to the right of the ratio fields. Clicking on this icon will change it to a broken link, allowing you to make changes to the width, for example, without modifying the height.

Why is aspect ratio important? Well, you may want to maintain the ratio when creating your thumbnail so that the image stays as close a representation to the original as possible. However, if you're generating a gallery of images you may find that a uniform appearance be maintained—perhaps you want all the thumbnails to be square. Alignment of thumbnails on a product page may be important as well. Keeping all the images the same width, for example, may make alignment a simpler issue when generating your HTML.

Note that you can also change the resolution of the image with this dialog, but you shouldn't do so. Images bound for the Web should stay at 72DPI. Resolution changes are usually only necessary when dealing with images destined for print. Web images make poor print images and chances are if you want high-quality print versions of your images (such as prints of your gallery artwork), you'll maintain much larger versions of the image, (with proper print resolution specified) offline.

Another issue to consider when creating your thumbnails is image sharpness. Scaling an image down tends to cause the image to blur slightly. To bring out details you'll want to apply some level of sharpening to the image. There are two ways to do this in the GIMP: the Sharpen filter and the Unsharp Mask filter.

Sharpen, found as *Filters->Enhance->Sharpen* in the Canvas menu, is the simpler of the two to use and is better suited for the limited sharpening you can do on thumbnails, especially if they're smaller than 125 pixels by 125 pixels. The interface is simple and interactive. You simply preview the changes and click on OK when you're satisfied.

FIGURE 10-3 The Sharpen dialog

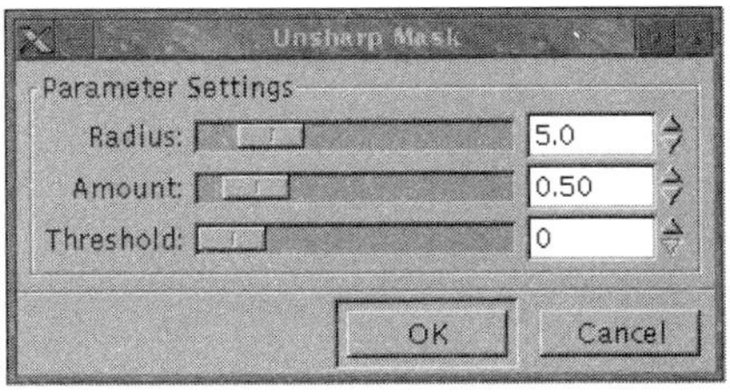

FIGURE 10-4 The Unsharp Mask dialog

Unsharp Mask, despite its name, actually performs the same function as Sharpen but using a different method. There is no preview with this dialog, which you access using *Filters->Enhance->Unsharp Mask*. The three sliders allow fine-tuning of the effect, but its use is mostly a trial and error affair. In the case of thumbnails, you may find that its use is overkill. Unsharp Mask tends to work very well on large images, bringing out very subtle details. It can produce fairly good results on smaller images, like thumbnails, using small values for the radius and amount and setting the threshold to 0. But, in general, you'll find that you don't need the clarity that Unsharp Mask provides.

◆ Speeding the Download

One of the advantages of using thumbnails is to reduce the amount of download time required to get that sneak peek. Smaller images have smaller file sizes, generally, and so take less time to load. There are several ways to reduce the download time beyond just resizing the image, however. Knowing which one, or which combination, to use takes practice.

The first speedup comes from reducing the number of colors in the image. If an image has three colors instead of 123, it will compress much better using the JPEG format. It may reduce the size of the GIF slightly, though not as much as with JPEG. You can reduce the number of colors by dithering the image down to the specified number of colors using the Indexed Color Conversion dialog. When you save an indexed image as a JPEG, the GIMP will ask you to export the image, which essentially converts it back to RGB mode using the lower color count. With fewer colors you can probably reduce the quality level in the JPEG file, possibly as low as 10 or 20 percent, without overly distorting the image. This will get you a smaller image than with an indexed GIF image.

In a similar vein, you can try using the *Image->Colors->Desaturate* or *Image->Colors->Threshold* options to reduce the amount of color in the image. Both of these remove all the color, but Desaturate leaves the image in a grayscale appearance (though it's not a Grayscale image, it still has its RGB components). Threshold converts the image to black and white, producing what looks like a pencil drawing of the original. This image will compress very well with JPEG. Again, keep in mind that such compression is optimal for gallery and thumbnail images, but not for images which contain and/or emphasize text. JPEG also can't be used if your thumbnail is intended to have any transparency.

Often times you can reduce an image in dimensions just so far before it really isn't recognizable as a thumbnail. In these cases you might be better off carving a smaller version out of the original and then reducing that. For example, if the image is a full body pose of a women standing in front of a fountain, a thumbnail might be just her face and shoulders. The trick is to find the subsection of the original that is fully representative of the original. Should the fountain be included in this example? It depends on how important it is to the original image. In either case, the image file size is already reduced, without reducing image quality at all, by simply reducing the amount of the original you show in the thumbnail. We'll talk more about carving up images in the next chapter.

◆ Photo Retouching

The whole purpose of a page of thumbnails, the galleries, is to provide access to larger, more complete versions of images. If you're going to be scanning in photos for these galleries, you're probably going to have to do some image retouching to clean up scratches from film developing and smudges or lint on your scanner's glass top.

Photo retouching in the GIMP follows a fairly standard process, though the amount of time and effort spent in each step varies greatly. The basic steps are:

1. Scan the image.

2. Color correct the scanned image. This involves running Auto-Levels and possibly applying Curves and Hue/Saturation/Brightness adjustments as well.

3. Sharpen it. This is almost always necessary for any desktop scanner. Even good scanners can have poor glass scanning beds.

4. Apply cloning to remove the blemishes.

5. Convolve if necessary.

Walking our way through a simple example is the best way to demonstrate this. A photograph of an airplane in flight was scanned but the resulting image is very dark. We could spend some time adjusting the Gamma options in the *xscanimage* plug-in, but it's easier to deal with this using the Levels dialog. We run Auto Levels on it (from the *Image->Colors->Levels*), then adjust the levels again to lighten the overall image.

FIGURE 10-5 Original airplane image and the Levels adjusted version

As you can see in Figure 10-5, the original image had a poor distribution on the white point side of the levels histogram. An auto levels stretched the white and black points across the full range and a second levels adjustment shifted the weight towards the white point. This can also be seen in Figure 10-5.

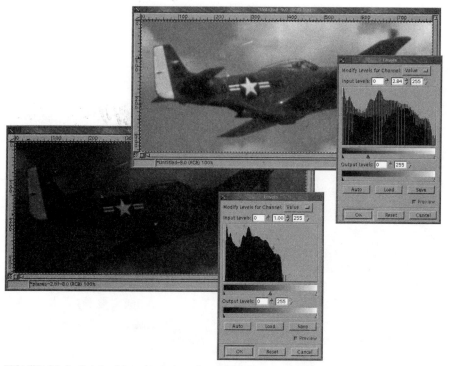

FIGURE 10-6 Original Levels and updated Levels

The only thing left to do is to fix up some minor scratches in the image. One long white streak sits just above the plane in the clouds. Scratches like this are easy to fix because the cloud layer (and sky scenes in general) has no uniform shape. A scratch along the body of the plane would be a little more difficult to fix, but would follow the same basic process.

First, zoom in on the scratch to make it easier to work with. Next, pick a small soft-edged brush. The width of the brush should be a little larger than the width of the scratch, though you may have to determine this with a little trial and error. Remember: Ctrl-Z is your friend!

Now, select the Clone tool from the Toolbox (the icon looks like a rubber stamp). Click near the scratch with the left mouse button while holding down the Control key. This sets the source point. Now left-mouse click over the scratch and drag a little. The source point is overlaid on the scratch. You can vary the effect by changing the source point periodically. Also, by setting the Opacity for the Clone tool to something less than 100 percent, you can make the source blend more smoothly with the area surrounding the scratch.

FIGURE 10-7 Visible scratch

FIGURE 10-8 Fixed scratch

This was a very simple example, but it does show how easy it can be to quickly clean up a gallery image before placing it online.

◆ Photo Effects

To this point we've talked about the basic process of generating thumbnails and galleries, but we've not really discussed how to spice them up. The GIMP comes with a large collection of filters that you can use to apply both simple and artistic effects to an image.

A few of the more appropriate filters for image galleries are the Film, Slide, and Old Photo filters. Film, found using *Filters->Combine->Film*, will add the perforated edges found in a roll of film to the top and bottom of an image. More than one image can be added to a roll of film, with each image taking up a single frame. Each frame can also be numbered. This filter was used, along with *Filters->Distorts->Ripple*, to generate the cover image for the annual graphics issue of a popular Linux related magazine.

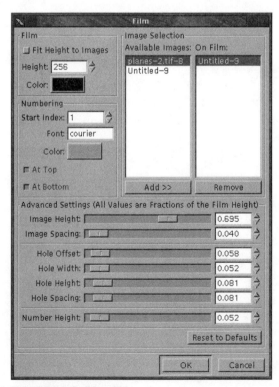

FIGURE 10-9 Film dialog

FIGURE 10-10 Roll of film example

Slide is a simpler version of Film which can only produce a single frame. It does provide the ability to add text to the edges of the slide, something the Film filter does not. Both allow you to add frame numbers. Slide also uses the built-in Text Tool to select a font. Film currently requires you to specify a font name as it is known to the X server. Oftentimes, specifying a font name such as "Helvetica" should work, if it's a very common font (Times, Helvetica, and Lucida are probably fairly safe options).

Old Photo takes an image and applies a colorization and faded border to make it appear as if it were taken at the turn of the 20th century. This filter is actually a Script-Fu script and can be found in the Canvas menu under *Script-Fu->Decor->Old Photo*. The effect could be used, for example, on a set of thumbnails in order to present a more uniform color scheme to a thumbnail gallery.

FIGURE 10-11 Old Photo dialog

FIGURE 10-12 Old Photo example

◆ HTML Revisited

In the last chapter we talked about how to specify the HTML to add an image to a Web page. Remember the tips on specifying size in the HTML? A properly formatted IMG tag might look like this:

```
<A HREF="/path/to/page"><IMG SRC="/path/to/image"
WIDTH=100 HEIGHT=100 BORDER=0></A>
```

Remember that the height and width should be the actual height of the image. It might be tempting, if you're lazy and in a hurry, to not resize an image when using it as a thumbnail and simply specify a smaller size in the HTML. This would work; the browser would resize the image on its own, but you force your visitors into long waits to download large images they can't even see! If you want return visitors, use the actual image size in the height and width options to the IMG tag.

With thumbnail galleries you have to consider your page layout. Will there be a specified number of images per row and/or column? If so, how do you force this layout? How do you align the images on the page? The answer is usually to use tables, but it's not the only way. Let's first look at what you can specify in the IMG tag to align text around an image. The following syntax aligns an image so text is to the right of it:

```
<A HREF="/path/to/page"><IMG SRC="/path/to/image" WIDTH=100
HEIGHT=100 BORDER=0 ALIGN=LEFT></A>
```

The text placed after the link will be displayed aligned with the top and to the right side of the image. It will continue down along the right of the image until it can wrap around under the image. To add 2 pixels of space between text and the right side of the image and 4 pixels between the bottom of the image and the wrapped text, you would use something like this:

```
<A HREF="/path/to/page"><IMG SRC="/path/to/image" WIDTH=100
HEIGHT=100 BORDER=0 ALIGN=LEFT HSPACE=2 VSPACE=4></A>
```

The hspace option specifies the horizontal space between the image and text, and the vspace option specifies space between the image and text above and below it. If you need to force text to stop aligning to the left or right sides of the image, you can force a break below the image, as the following example shows.

```
<A HREF="/path/to/page"><IMG SRC="/path/to/image" WIDTH=100
HEIGHT=100 BORDER=0 ALIGN=LEFT></A><BR CLEAR=both>
```

This sort of alignment and spacing works well for images placed in the middle of a lot of text, but most pages really don't have that much text around images. In fact, they have mostly other images and only a limited amount of text. Because of this, most Web page designers tend to use tables to lay out a page with thumbnails.

◆ Using Tables

Early on in the development of the Web, content developers realized that page layout was not easily managed using ordinary HTML. Because of this, the World Wide Web (a.k.a W3) Consortium adopted the use of tables in HTML. Tables are simply a row/column mechanism used for alignment of text and images. Though not as sophisticated as the newer CSS (Cascading Style Sheets) that you'll find in the new HTML 4.0 specification, tables were adopted quickly by Web browser manufacturers and have been used extensively since the very early days of the Web.

Using a table is simple. You have to first define the table, then define a row and the contents of each cell (i.e., column) within that row. A simple table might look like this:

```
<TABLE>
<TR>
<TD ALIGN=right>This is some text</TD>
<TD ALIGN=left>And this is an image: <IMG
SRC="/path/to/image"></TD>
</TR>
</TABLE>
```

The table has one row (the TR tag) and two columns (the TD tags). The second column has an image in it. Notice that we aligned the cell contents using the ALIGN option to the TD tags, but we didn't specify any alignment using the IMG tag.

You can add space in cells, as in the following example:

```
<TABLE CELLPADDING=2 CELLSPACING=4>
<TR>
<TD ALIGN=right>This is some text</TD>
<TD ALIGN=left>And this is an image: <IMG
SRC="/path/to/image"></TD>
</TR>
</TABLE>
```

The only change here is in the TABLE tag itself. The CELL-PADDING option adds breadth to the walls of the table. The CELLSPACING adds breadth between the walls and the contents of the cell. Often, you won't want the cell walls visible, so the CELL-PADDING will be set to zero and spacing between cells is managed with the CELLSPACING option. The following example uses this method and turns off the table borders (i.e., the cell walls):

```
<TABLE CELLPADDING=0 CELLSPACING=4 BORDER=0>
<TR>
<TD ALIGN=right>This is some text</TD>
<TD ALIGN=left>And this is an image: <IMG
SRC="/path/to/image"></TD>
</TR>
</TABLE>
```

There is quite a bit you can do with tables and images. Cells do not have to be the same width and you can have cells which span multiple rows and columns. Content developers will often cut up an image to fit into multiple cells of a table in order to allow the page to load more easily and to create unusual effects that would otherwise be too difficult to do with generic square cells.

Recap

Thumbnails help Web designers display visual information while limiting the expense of download times. In this chapter we looked at how galleries of thumbnails can be used to provide quick views into an artist's full-sized online portfolio or to a storefront's product list. Image retouching should be used on all scanned artwork and photos given the quality and problems in working with desktop scanner systems. Finally, we showed how thumbnail galleries can be spiced up using standard filters available to the GIMP.

Image alignment can be handled both through HTML IMG tags and by using HTML tables. Alignment is used for page layout of galleries but can also be used in more sophisticated ways with image carvings.

Projects

Open any color image and attempt to sharpen it using the Sharpen filter. How far can you take it before the image becomes distorted? Try a second image. Can you go as far? Can you tell what Sharpen does to edges in either image?

Now try Unsharp Mask on the same two images. What values do you need to use for the Amount and Radius to get similar results as found with the Sharpen filter? What happens when you increase the Threshold value? Hint: Increase the threshold in large amounts to exaggerate the effect, then undo, reduce it, and try again until its effect becomes clearer. If you can't tell what it's doing, try another image, preferably one with fewer gradients or color variations. The effect is not obvious, but essentially Threshold softens the sharpening, effectively reducing its effect.

Pick any color image and try to reduce its file size through indexing, thresholding, and desaturating. Combine your changes with Sharpen and Unsharp Mask. See if you can find an optimal size that has a file size that is both less than 5000 bytes and is recognizable and reasonably representative of the original at no more than 100 pixels in width and height. When might a black and white thumbnail be preferable to a color one? Hint: Think color schemes.

Open three images and scale them to the same size. Use the *Filters->Combine->Film* filter to put them all into a single image roll. Try to add some text to the film border after it has been created. Use what you've learned about layers and text to add a date and company name to the film. Save it as a JPEG. What do you need to remember to do before you can save the complete image as a JPEG?

11 Image Maps and Carvings

IN THIS CHAPTER

- Introduction to Image Maps
- Why Not Buttons Instead?
- The GIMP's Solution—The Image Map Filter
- Special Effects—Nonlinear Page Layout
- Carving Up An Image
- Interactive Cuttings with Perl-o-tine
- Recap
- Projects

HTML wasn't designed as a full-featured page layout specification. In order to get some of the special effects you find on the better designed Web pages you need to play a few tricks. Two of these tricks, image maps and image carvings, are used in tables. The former is used in conjunction with JavaScript, an interpreted language for programs embedded right in your HTML page. Image maps let you specify nonrectangular regions of an image as links.

An image carving is simply an image that has been cut up into pieces so that it can be placed within various cells of a table. The use of tables for page layout, while crude and not very pleasant at times, is one of the most common means of applying rollover and Java-enhanced portions of an image. It is also the most common means of creating nonlinear page layouts.

◆ Introduction to Image Maps

One of the first features introduced to make the use of images more pleasant in Web pages was the image map. An image map is nothing more than HTML tags which specify regions of an image to use for a link. The regions are specified in pixels and can be rectangular, oval, and even polygonal in shape. In this way you can create a single image to represent multiple links instead of having to generate a bunch of images. It also allows you to create an image with links that are not aligned horizontally or vertically. You could, for example, add icons in a diagonal across an image and use image map tags to specify each icon as a link. This would be much simpler to do than trying to guarantee the diagonal alignment with tables.

Before we can get into how the GIMP can generate image maps for you, we need to look at the general format for HTML image map tags. The following example specifies a simple image map with rectangular regions for links:

```
<MAP NAME="fred">
<AREA SHAPE="RECT" COORDS="43,20,44,21"
HREF="http://some.place.com">
<AREA SHAPE="RECT" COORDS="55,98,56,127"
HREF="http://another.link.org">
<AREA SHAPE="RECT" COORDS="216,98,264,127"
HREF="ftp://ftp.home.org">
</MAP>
```

Each image map has an opening tag which names the map. In this case, the map name is "fred." It can be any name, and the name will be used later to associate some image with this map. The image map is closed using the </MAP> tag. Everything between the opening and closing tags is part of the map.

After the opening tag comes one or more AREA tags. These tags must exist between the open and close MAP tags or else the browser will ignore them. Each AREA tag includes the shape of the area (in our case all the areas are rectangles), the coordinates which define the region, and an HREF option which associates some URL with that region within the image. The shape can be oval, rectangular, or polygonal and the format to the COORDS option depends on which shape you use.

The open and close MAP tags, along with the AREA tags that go between them, can be placed as a group anywhere in an HTML document after the BODY tag. As a rule, they are often placed right after the BODY tag so that they are easier to find later on.

After defining what the map looks like, we need to associate it with an image. This is done by adding the USEMAP option to the IMG tag:

```
<IMG SRC="/images/file.gif" WIDTH=265 HEIGHT=128 BORDER=0
USEMAP="#fred">
```

The browser now knows to check when the cursor is over this image and to provide a link to the appropriate URL when the cursor is over a region defined in an AREA tag.

There are different types of image maps you can use, including maps that are managed on either the client side or the server side. The GIMP provides a convenient tool for developing client-side maps, which we'll be covering in a moment.

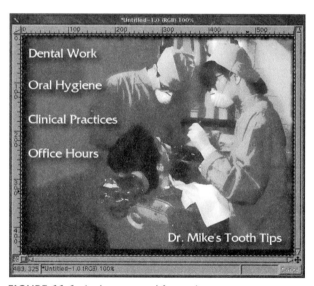

FIGURE 11-1 An image used for an image map

◆ Why Not Buttons Instead?

The decision to use an image map over single images for each link depends on both your intended navigation and page layout needs. An image map cannot easily handle rollovers, images which change when the mouse is placed over them. Rollovers are handled though the use of JavaScript and require two images: one to display by default and one to display when the mouse is over the link. An image map is a single, static image. Image maps are usually much larger than simple rollover images. Technically, you could make the image map a rollover by providing a separate image for it, but since the images are larger than normal rollover images, they require more download time and, as such, slower page viewing by your visitors. Additionally, the rollover would swap between two images, but your image map may have many links. You can't have a different image for each link in the image map.

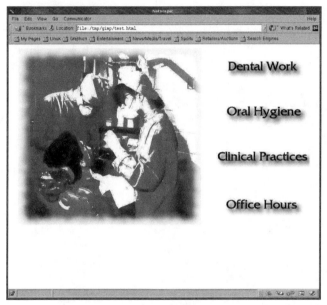

FIGURE 11-2 Images used as text links

On most pages images provide either navigation or visual appeal. Image maps provide both. Often, text links are replaced by graphic images using special fonts because not all browsers handle the use of interesting fonts the same way (CSS attempts to rectify this, but it's not widely used yet). These images are nicer looking than their text-only counterparts, but the image *is* the link. In an image map, the space between links is filled with other images— visual cues or pizazz that add character to your page. In this way you can lay out the complete navigation and page design in a single image—but at the cost of a possibly long download time. The use of image maps, then, is often combined with single images and tables to create a full front-page navigation for a Web site.

◆ The GIMP's Solution—The Image Map Filter

The quick and easy way to generate an image map in the GIMP is with the Image Map filter, found in the Canvas menu under *Filters->Web->Image Map*. This utility works on the currently active layer of any Canvas window and allows you to zoom in and out on that layer. A point and click interface provides oval, rectangular, and polygonal selections in the image. Each selection is converted into the appropriate AREA tag and the necessary HTML is produced automatically, ready for you to cut and paste into your HTML text file.

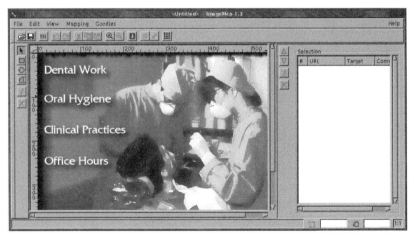

FIGURE 11-3 The Image Map filter's dialog box

Once opened, the Image Map dialog shows a preview of your image on the left (in a scrolled window if the image is large). To the left of this are a set of buttons. Clicking on one of these will allow you to draw selection outlines in the preview window. As you click and draw a selection in a preview, you are prompted for information about that selection: the link settings, selection settings, and even JavaScript references for various JavaScript event types.

Once a selection has been defined completely, it is listed in the white box on the right of the Image Map dialog. Each entry in this box can be double-clicked to open up the appropriate Settings dialog. Besides the Settings dialog, you will also find dialogs for general preferences, general map information, and grid settings.

Selections can be cut, copied, and pasted. Selections have a hierarchy. When one selection overlaps another, the image map

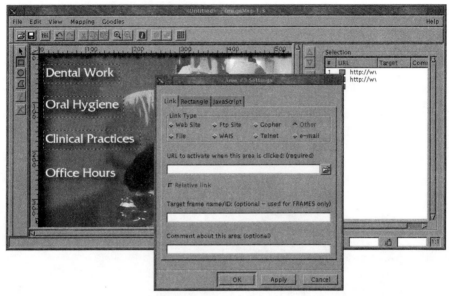

FIGURE 11-4 Setting the URL for a region

that is generated causes the browser to see the top level selection in the overlapping area. The lower selection is lost in the overlap region. This doesn't seem like much, but it allows you to place an image map link (remember, it can be just about any shape) inside another one—a smaller circle inside a square, for example. This trick isn't used often, but that may be because no one has been clever enough to think of something interesting to do with it yet.

FIGURE 11-5 The View Source dialog box

The Image Map plug-in has an option to view the source code it will produce from the selections you have created. Choosing *View->Source* from the Image Maps menu bar will open up a window showing the code. Since Image Map won't update the text automatically when you make changes, you'll want to close the View Source window after looking it over and before making any new changes.

An interesting feature of the Image Map plug-in is that the menu and icon bars are detachable—you can click on their grab bars (thin regions on the right of each) and drag the bars off the window. This is useful if you have a small display area, such as on a laptop, and need to rearrange the Image Map dialog to make things fit a little nicer.

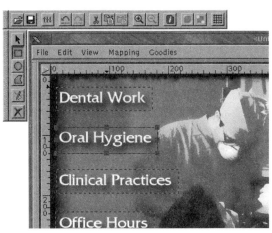

FIGURE 11-6 Drag-off menu and icon bars make working on laptops a little nicer

◆ Special Effects—Nonlinear Page Layout

There are a couple of problems with using image maps. The first is that they tend to be large, requiring large download times for your visitors. The second is that they are static. Images which change to reflect some static information are more desirable. Imagine a large square image map with a central icon—say, a picture of a computer—that you want to change to show the icon plus some text when the mouse is over it. This would be done with a rollover. But how can you keep that nonlinear layout that the image map provides? The solution: build a large, single image with all your components and then carve it up and place the pieces in a properly formatted table.

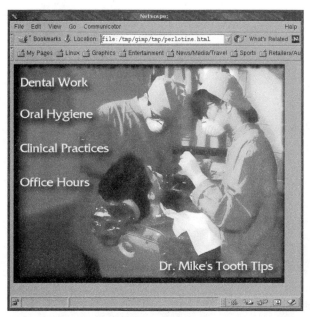

FIGURE 11-7 A page with a carved up image in a table

◆ CARVING UP AN IMAGE

HTML tables are made up of one or more rows and columns. Each row/column pair identifies a specific cell of the table. Cells can have varying widths and heights. This makes it possible to overlay an image onto a table, adjusting the table cell dimensions, and placing the appropriate parts of the image into their corresponding cells. By doing this, the individual cells can be managed independently using JavaScript code for things like rollovers or pop-up menus.

The GIMP provides two methods of carving up an image: Guillotine and Perl-o-tine. Both do basically the same thing: cut up an image based on the position of guides. Guillotine creates a new Canvas window for each region defined by the intersection of guides. This can get messy if you have a lot of guides. Perl-o-tine is geared specifically for carving an image for use in a table. You'll need to have a working GIMP Perl installation in order to use Perl-o-tine, but that's something you'll want anyway since many useful filters and plug-ins are now being written in Perl.

◆ Interactive Cuttings with Perl-o-tine

You'll find the menu entry for Perl-o-tine under *Filters->Web* in the Canvas menu. Once selected (and as long as GIMP Perl is enabled on your system) you'll see the Perl-o-tine dialog.

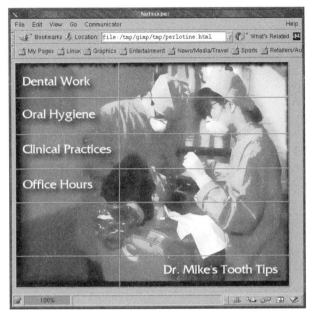

FIGURE 11-8 Same page with table borders turned on

The dialog is fairly straightforward to use. First, make sure you have some guides placed within the Canvas (click on the left or top ruler and drag into the Canvas area). Basically, you're creating a set of rectangular regions which will become separate images that will be used in your HTML table. The Save Path is the directory into which the individual images will be saved along with the HTML code snippet. The HTML Filename is just the name you want to use for the file that will hold the HTML code. Since the code generated is just a table definition—it doesn't include the HEAD, BODY, or any other tags—you can name it anything. You're going to have to either edit it by hand later or import it into another HTML document.

The image base name is the name to use for each image cutting. Each cutting gets this name as a prefix followed by the row and column numbers and the image type as a suffix. If you want the images to be placed in a directory called "images" under the Save Path, click on the Separate Image Dir button. You can also change the name to use for the image's directory in the Relative Image Path field.

The Capitalize Tags option will force all the HTML tags to be capitalized. This makes reading the code a little easier (if you do your HTML coding by hand). HTML tags are case-insensitive, so aside from making the code easier to read, this doesn't change the generated table.

The last option is probably not useful. It will add some padding in the cells between the cell walls and the images you place in them. But unless the edges of all the images created from the carving have the same color as the background of the page, the cell padding won't help much. It can create a moderately interesting effect by breaking up the image a little, however,

Once you've made all your choices, click on the OK button. The image is automatically carved up along the guides and the separate images stored in the specific directories. The HTML for the table that will hold the images is saved into the file name specified. Again, you'll need to import this into your real HTML page. Perl-o-tine doesn't generate a complete, stand-alone page for your carving.

Once you've created the carving, you can then make changes to the original image and generate a second carving. For example, you can change the color of some text in the image. After you generate the second carving (be sure to use a different directory!) you'll have two images that can be used with JavaScript rollover code. Be certain to use a different image base name for the second carving.

Recap

In this chapter we've looked at two different ways of using images as links: image maps and carvings. Image maps are useful for creating nonlinear effects on your page as long as you don't need visual interaction. They're simple to create and easy for your Web site visitors to use, but they tend to be bulky and slow to load.

Carvings allow you to use large images with JavaScript to create visual changes based on user input. Using tables and Perl-o-tine allows you to create a single image with all the visual elements you need at once and then automatically break it up into component pieces for alignment using the table.

PROJECTS

Create an image map which can be used to link to pages with contact and download information. Make it simple; just create an image with the words "Contact Info and Download Info" offset from each other slightly. Then use the Image Map plug-in to generate the HTML code for using this image. What other work will you need to do in order to integrate this page into your Web site? Will you need to adjust any relative or absolute links?

Use Perl-o-tine to cut up an image into nine parts. Change the middle image to a different color. Now, using the HTML output from Perl-o-tine, attempt to create a complete HTML page that shows the nine image cuttings as a single, unbroken image. Can you figure out how to use JavaScript to make the middle image switch to the color-changed version when the mouse is over it in a browser window?

chapter

12 Animations

IN THIS CHAPTER

- Animation Primer
- What the Web Can and Can't Do
- GIF Animations
- DHTML Layers
- Streaming Media Support with GAP—GIMP Animation Plug-ins

The GIMP can perform all the basic processing necessary for static images on the Web. But the Web is anything but static, and animation plays a big role on many major Web sites. The GIMP has very strong support for the most common animation format used today on the Web—GIF animations. The 1.2 release also ships with a wide range of more advanced animation tools, collectively called GAP (GIMP Animation Package) which is a set of Plug-ins for generating MPEG formatted animations.

◆ Animation Primer

Animations are, essentially, just a series of static images played very quickly one after another. Playing these images would seem fairly simplistic, amounting to nothing more than flipping the pages of a book quickly. But digital images take time to load across a network and take up lots of disk space, so a number of methods have been developed to make transfer, storage, and display of animations easier.

The most widely used animation format on the Web is GIF animation. This format is just like the flip book analogy, where a series of GIF images (known as *frames*) are played successively. Tools for creating GIF animations usually provide a means of determining what to do with each frame after it's been displayed (clear it or leave it displayed) and the amount of time to display each particular frame. Because it is based on the GIF static image format, a GIF animation uses indexed images for the frames and the frames can each use the same indexed color map or install a new color map for each image. Not all GIF animation tools provide support for changing color maps, however.

While most animations of this format on the Web use frames of the same dimensions, the GIF animation format also supports the use of *sprites*. A sprite is a small image that can be overlaid on a background and then removed when the next frame is displayed. The use of sprites greatly reduces the amount of data that has to be transferred or stored for an animation.

The GIF format is used extensively in banner ads and as attention grabbers on Web sites. The problem with the GIF format is that it is not very efficient. Long play animations can take quite a bit of time to load, even when the animation makes good use of sprites. Alternative formats, therefore, are needed for long play animations or, as we know them better, streaming video.

One of the more popular formats for streaming video is MPEG. The specification of this format is publicly available, so support for it in the format of content generators and content players is fairly widespread. MPEG, like GIF, is concerned with frames of content. But MPEG is designed to compress the frame content down to the point of providing a throughput of up to 1.5 Mbits per second. MPEG also includes support for synchronized audio, which the GIF animation format does not.

◆ What the Web Can and Can't Do

Despite the apparent wealth of graphics on the Web today, most browsers have a very limited set of graphics formats that they support natively (i.e., without external programs). While GIF, JPEG, and (to some extent) PNG are supported for static images, only GIF is supported for animations by nearly all browsers. All other formats require external programs to display them. This becomes an important factor when determining whether you want all visitors to your site to view the animation or only those who specifically request it and have the appropriate display program.

Visitors to your site that want to play MPEG content will be required to configure a MIME-type for the .mpg extension and install an MPEG player. Similarly, other streaming video formats available on the Web, such as QuickTime, AVI, RealVideo, or Windows Media Format, will also require external players. Generating content in GIF and MPEG formats can be done using the 1.2 version of the GIMP fairly easily. Due to the proprietary nature of most other formats, you will need to acquire commercial products to produce animations in those formats and to play them back.

Animations in GIF and MPEG formats use raster-based (sets) pixels for their frames. A popular alternative to this is *vector graphics,* which require less data to be transferred for longer animations. One example of a vector-based animation format is Macromedia Flash. Unfortunately, the GIMP was designed specifically as a raster-based design tool and as such does not lend itself well to generating vector format animations.

The GIF animation has many limitations. First, the animation is bound by the dimensions of the animation, that is, the farthest edges of the various frames of the image. You display this animation in its own block on the page and nothing else can overlay it, nor can it interact with other parts of the display. Also, GIF places the animation control within the image file itself (as does MPEG, but in a much more sophisticated way). What is more desirable in the browser world is to have an image that is managed externally through the use of, for example, JavaScript.

An alternative to using the GIF format to produce an animation is to use the layers and scripting features of DHTML—Dynamic HTML. This is a relatively new definition added to standard HTML that includes scripting features. DHTML can, for example, be used to place an image in a layer of the same size as the image, then move that layer around the screen. The image stays static, but where it is displayed moves. This technique has been popularized by the interesting (if not quite annoying) flying bees that infest many DHTML pages today.

◆ GIF Animations

It's easy to generate GIF animations in the GIMP. Since GIF animations are nothing more than a series of frames, the GIMP uses a multilayered image for the animation where each layer is a different frame. The layer name is used to determine the period to display the frame and its disposition when moving to the next frame. There are also tools for testing the animation, running filters on multiple frames, and optimizing the sequence.

To show you how simple this whole process is, we'll walk through a quick example. We want to show a text dissolve: showing a text string and then causing it to dissolve until it's not visible anymore. The goal is to generate this dissolve using a 20-frame animation. To do this we start with a new Canvas window with a white background. Add a text string to this. Note that adding a text string will create a floating layer. Be sure to anchor this into the background layer. Next, duplicate the layer nine times making a total of ten layers.

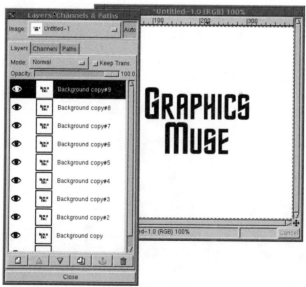

FIGURE 12-1 The ten-layered image

The bottom layer is the first frame of your animation. We could apply filters to each layer one at a time, but there is a faster way—the *Filter All Layers* option in the Filters menu. We'll use this option to apply two filters, Shift and Motion Blur, using slightly varied amounts of each to each layer automatically. Select *Filters->Filter all Layers* from the Canvas menus. This will open a window similar to the PDB Browser and allow you to select a function to apply to all layers. Click on *plug-in-shift* to select it, then click on the Apply Varying button.

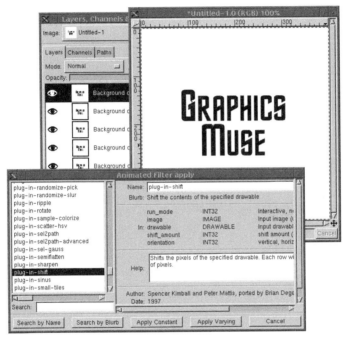

FIGURE 12-2 The Filter All PDB selection dialog

This will open the Shift dialog so you can enter the plug-in parameters for the first frame. The Shift filter offers the choice of Horizontal or Vertical shifts along with a user-specified length. For this example we've chosen a Horizontal shift that will range from 5 to about 150 pixels.

Once you've entered those values, Filter All runs the filter on the first frame and then prompts you to enter the parameters for the filter on the last frame. It then runs the filter again for the last frame and computes appropriate parameters for all the intermediate frames and applies the filter to them.

FIGURE 12-3 Filter All finishes the first frame and asks to continue

FIGURE 12-4 After Filter All requests and applies the filter parameters to the last frame, it then prompts to run the filter on all intermediate frames

After Filter All completes you can test the animation by selecting *Filters->Animation->Animation Playback*. This option opens a dialog with three buttons for playing and stopping the animation, stepping through the frames, and rewinding back to the first frame. An interesting aspect of this dialog is that you can click and drag the display window out of the dialog and lay it over another window, like a browser window for example. This lets you see the animation in action over your Web page before having to edit it and add the HTML syntax!

FIGURE 12-5 The Animation Playback dialog

Now that you've applied the Shift filter, try doing the same thing with the Motion Blur filter. This time you want to select the *plug-in-mblur* function in Filter All's PDB browser window. Select the Zoom option in the Motion Blur dialog and allow it to range from 5 to 200 in length (the angle doesn't matter) for all the frames.

Now there are two more frames to add—a new first frame and a new last frame. The Filter All Layers option does just that— applies a filter to all the layers in the image. But that means the Shift and Motion Blur filters were applied to the first frame, the one we wanted with crisp, unmodified text. So we need to add a new first layer of text plus a blank top layer that acts as the last frame of the animation.

We'll handle the last frame first. Click on the top layer to select it. Then click on the New Layer button in the Layers and Channels dialog and select a white background to match our other layers. That should do it for the last frame.

To add the first frame we first need to add an Alpha Channel to the first layer. Without this the first layer cannot be moved on top of any other layer. Click and hold the right mouse button over the first layer's name to open the Layers menu. Select *Add Alpha Channel*. You won't notice any changes, but if you open the menu again for that layer that menu option should be unselectable.

Now add a new white layer. With the bottom layer selected the new layer should be added right above it and become the active layer. Just click on the down arrow button to move the new layer below the first layer. Now you're ready to add text to the new layer; do it just like you did originally, making sure you anchor the floating selection to the new bottom layer.

While this is sufficient for a simple animation, there are some other options you can add to your layers to change the way the animation is played. The first is to set the timing for each frame. The second is to set the disposition of each frame. Both of these are set in the layer name for each frame, and both are done by enclosing them in parentheses. For example, to set the first frame to be displayed for 150 milliseconds and to be left in place when the second frame is displayed, the layer name would look like this:

```
Frame 1 (150ms)(combine)
```

The timing value can be any number of milliseconds and must be in the form of XXXms, where XXX is the number of milliseconds. Any other timing format is ignored.

The second option is the disposition. There are three possible values here: replace, combine, and default. The latter value requires no setting in the layer name. The words "replace" and

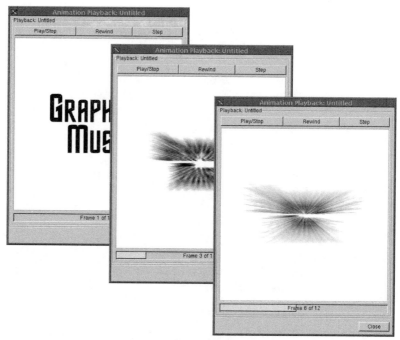

FIGURE 12-6 A number of frames displayed in multiple versions of the Animation Playback dialog

"combine" should always be in lowercase. Replace causes each frame to be cleared before the next one is displayed so no part of the first frame is left in place when the second frame is displayed. With combine, the first frame is left in place and the second frame is displayed over it. In our example, since every frame has an all white layer with black text, the two options would have the same visual effect, so it doesn't matter which one you choose. If your layers were of different sizes or contained any amount of transparency you would want to choose one or the other.

To smooth the appearance of the animation, we made the first and last frames display for 250ms and all intermediate frames for 75ms. This gives a slight pause at the start of the animation as it loops, and provides a less jumpy appearance than the default timings of 125ms.

Saving the Animation

Now that you've got an animation ready in the GIMP you need to save it to a GIF file for use in your HTML. The first thing to note is that GIF files are indexed. Since you've been working in an RGB image you need to convert it to indexed before saving (you can actually do this as you save the file, but it's less confusing to do it manually first).

Select *Image->Mode->Indexed* from the Canvas menu. The Indexed Color Conversion dialog window will open, allowing you to choose how to do the conversion from RGB to indexed colors. Using a WWW optimized palette is generally preferred since this will map your images to the Netscape Color Cube, making it display pretty much the same in any browser. Since our example used only black and white, we could use an optimal palette of only a few shades of gray but that won't really reduce the size of the GIF file all that much. So stick with the WWW optimized palette for this example.

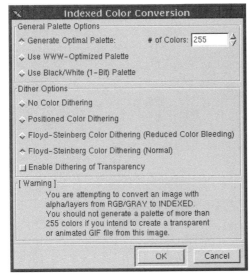

FIGURE 12-7 Indexed Conversion dialog

The other options in this dialog allow for some manual control over the way the colors are mapped. Dithering means to do the mapping, and the various methods shown all do it in slightly different ways. Since trying each one is quick (and since Ctrl-Z will undo the conversion quickly as well), you can experiment to see how the colors are affected by each option. Again, because of the black and white nature of this example we really don't care that much which method is used so we just use the default.

Once the conversion is complete you can test the animation again to verify that the conversion didn't distort the frames of the image in an unacceptable way. Just use the Animation Playback tool to view the animation again.

Now that the image has been converted to an indexed format, we're ready to save it to a file. Simply select *File->Save As* from the Canvas menu. In the file selection dialog type in the file name with a .gif extension, such as animation.gif. When you click on OK the *Export File* dialog appears. Select the *Save as Animation* option and click on the *Export* button. After this you'll get the *Save as GIF* dialog where you can set a few GIF file options. The Comment field is useful for adding your own personal identification to the file. In the Animated GIF Options section you set the animation to loop forever (which is the default). Turning this toggle option off will set the animation to play a single time and then stop.

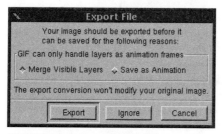

FIGURE 12-8 Export File dialog

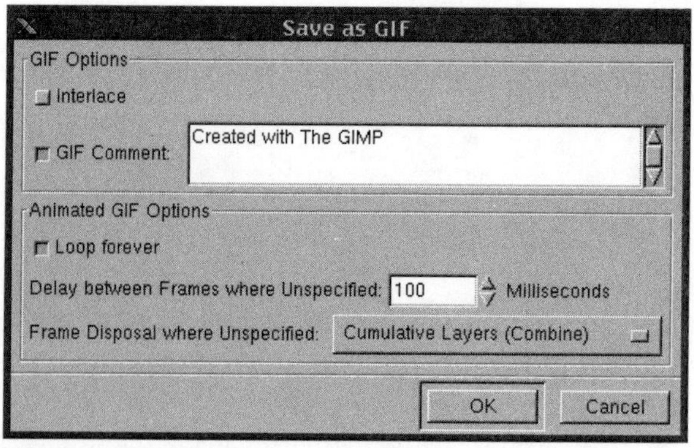

FIGURE 12-9 Save As GIF dialog

Below this you have two more options: the default frame timing and the default disposition. If you set the timings for each individual frame you won't need to worry about the default tim-

ing value. You can use this field if you want to set the same timing for all frames and don't want to manually edit some or all
frames timing. The same is true for the default disposition,
although if you set any frames to *combine* manually then you
should choose *combine* here as well. Don't leave this option set to
I don't care if you manually set any frames to *combine*!

Once you've done all this you can click on OK and the animation will be saved as a GIF file, ready to be included in your
Web page's HTML.

The GIMP's support for animated GIFs is good, but not complete. One thing you can't do is change the color map on a
per-frame basis, which the GIF animated format allows. It also
doesn't support the Netscape extension that allows specifying the
number of times to loop through the animation. And while the
Animation Optimize feature will reduce the size of the animation,
it doesn't quite provide the support for sprites that GIF allows.
Finally, the Filter All Layers feature only allows the application of
plug-ins of a certain type, essentially those you find under the
Filters menu. It won't, for example, allow you to apply Levels and
Curves processing to each of the frames. PDB functions do exist
for these, so you could write your own Perl script to handle this
manually, if you'd like. See Chapter 17 for details on scripting.

◆ DHTML Layers

A recent addition to the HTML language provides an alternative
to GIF animations. Dynamic HTML, known more commonly as
DHTML, provides many new features that tie in closely with the
use of JavaScript. One of these features is called *Spans*, with a
Netscape alternative called *Layers*. Layers are like little browser
windows embedded within the main browser window. These little
windows can be moved around the screen, hidden, raised and
lowered above other layers, and manipulated in all sorts of ways
using JavaScript. Because of the tie-in with JavaScript, it's possible
to use these layers with images and text to generate animations
with far more control.

While the GIMP doesn't provide any special features to help
with DHTML itself, you can use it to generate the images you
place in your layers. Remember that layers are like small browser
windows—anything you can do with an ordinary image in a
browser window you can do in a layer. The only difference is you
can use JavaScript to manipulate an image's position and display

characteristics. For example, you can change the image's size on the fly, which means you download only a single image and let the client manage the fade-out effect.

Since the GIMP doesn't do anything specifically to aid in working with DHTML, we'll skip a discussion on that. A good place to get more information on DHTML is to read *Essential CSS & DHTML for Web Professionals* by Dan Livingston and Micah Brown, a companion book to this series.

The main drawback to DHTML is that support in newer browsers is questionably consistent, and it's nonexistent in older browsers (certainly prior to Netscape 4.0 and probably prior to Netscape 4.5).

◆ Streaming Media Support with GAP—GIMP Animation Plug-ins

Both GIF animations and DHTML are natively supported by the most recent browsers from Netscape and Microsoft, which explains their widespread acceptance and use. But both methods are fairly limited by the image formats they use (GIF in GIF animations and GIF, JPEG, and PNG in DHTML). These formats are simply not designed for long play animations, known more commonly as streaming media. Because of this limitation many organizations, both private and public, are working to provide alternative solutions for streaming media products.

One format that has public specifications and controlling committees is MPEG. This format is supported by many external players, allowing users to install the player of choice and configure their browsers to launch those applications using the MPEG MIME type. The GIMP provides a set of animation tools, collectively known as GAP, for generating MPEG animations. You've already seen some of these tools, the Animation Playback and Filter All Layers features. Now it's time to look at some of the other options available.

GAP tools are found in the Canvas menu under the *Video* option. There are options associated with exporting and importing, navigating through frames, and managing individual frames. The primary tool of interest will be the Move Path tool, which provides features for automating movement of an object through frames.

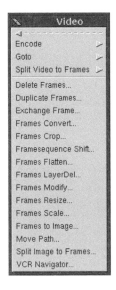

FIGURE 12-10 GAP Animation (aka video) menu

Terminology

Before getting too deep into GAP we need to understand a little terminology. In the earlier discussion on GIF animations, each layer in an image was an animation frame. Using GAP to produce MPEG formatted animations goes further. Individual multi-layered images are frames, each of which conforms to a special naming convention. Each frame uses a project followed by a numbered suffix of the form "_xxxx," where "xxxx" is the frame number. Each file name must also end with the *.xcf* extension, such as *spaceship_0001.xcf*. Here, the project name is "spaceship" and this file is the first frame (of up to 9,999 frames in this case). The .xcf extension is required in order to maintain layer information for each frame. The GAP tools will automatically flatten individual frames when previewing the animation without altering the frame's XCF file.

Moving about the frames is called navigation and is handled by a number of different GAP tools that let you step through frames or jump to specific frames in the animation. There is also a tool for moving ranges of frames around by shifting them forward or back in the sequence.

Move Paths are the most important aspect of a GAP animation. These paths define the motion of an object (an image) through your frames. Most of your work involving GAP will come in the form of manipulating Move Paths with the Move Path tool (*Video->Move Path*).

While the Animation Playback tool was used for GIF animations, GAP animations require the use of the *VCR Navigator* (*Video-
>VCR Navigator*). This is because GAP needs to flatten the layers of
individual frames in order to play them. You'll notice that the
VCR Navigation tool looks a bit like a VCR console, but that the
actual animation display tool turns out to be the familiar
Animation Playback dialog launched when you hit the Play button on the VCR Navigator.

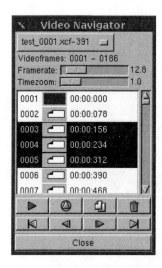

FIGURE 12-11 The VCR Navigator

Starting an Animation

Let's do a simple animation, a horizontal text scroll. The first
thing we need is to open the first frame of the animation. We'll
make it 600x200 and 51 frames in length—short by streaming
media standards, but useful as an example. Open a new Canvas
window with a white background. Save the file as anim_0001.xcf.
You've now prepped the first frame, but we need to duplicate it 50
times to get our animation started. Select *Video->Duplicate Frames*
and set the bottom slider—the one labeled *N times*—to 50. Click
on OK. You won't see much happen, but you've just duplicated
the image 50 times on disk. Look in the directory into which you
saved the first file and you'll see the other new files.

As an alternative you can also import an animation using
Video->Split video to frames->Any Xanim readable. This option uses
the external *xanim* program to read and split animations in various formats into frames. However, before you can use this, you
must acquire the exporting edition of Xanim from http://hero-

ine.linuxbox.com/toys.html. Since we're starting from scratch, we'll skip this option.

The next thing we need to do is create an object to move across our frames. In this example the object will be a block of text. Open a new 40x100 Canvas window with a transparent background. Select the Text Tool and place some new text in this window. Try and center it using the Dynamic Text Tool. You don't need to save this unless you want to keep a copy handy for reuse later. You're now ready to use this as an object in your animations.

Move Paths

Objects in GAP move along paths traced from one frame to the next. Setting up a path is done using the Move Paths dialog, *Video->Move Paths*. This large dialog controls the path of the text object we just created through all frames, not just the currently displayed frame. It is broken into a number of sections: Source Select, Move Path Preview, and layer/frame. The last is not labeled, but includes the set of sliders and two toggles buttons at the bottom of the dialog.

The *Source Select* section allows you to choose a Canvas window and layer from which to take the object that will be moved along the path. In this case, we are using the Dynamic Text layer in the Canvas window we just created. The path we'll create will be based on control points which we'll define after we take a brief tour of this dialog.

The *Mode* is actually a blend mode. For our purposes we use *Normal*, but we could have the text blend with the background if we had something other than plain white with which to blend. The *Stepmode* determines how the animation will play: in loops, one time through, ping-pong style, and so forth. For this simple animation we'll select *Once* so the animation plays one time through. Finally, the *Handle* option determines how the object layer is aligned with the control points you'll set that define the move path. For example, *Center* (which we'll use) means to align the center of the object over the control points. *Top Left* means to align the top left corner of the object layer with the control point. Note that this option is what makes it clear that the object should fill the layer it's in as much as possible or else you'll have over-hangs and/or unexpected delays in your animation.

In the *Move Path Preview* section you have a set of sliders that specify how each control point will be placed and managed. The X,Y coordinates can be set or changed manually using the top two sliders. The width/height sliders allow you to resize the object at a given control point while the opacity slider changes the object's opacity. Rotation of the object is handled by the rotate slider. Keyframing allows you to set a control point to a specific keyframe.

The set of buttons below the slider and to the right of the preview window are used to add, delete, insert, and navigate through control points. We'll use these in a moment to add a few control points.

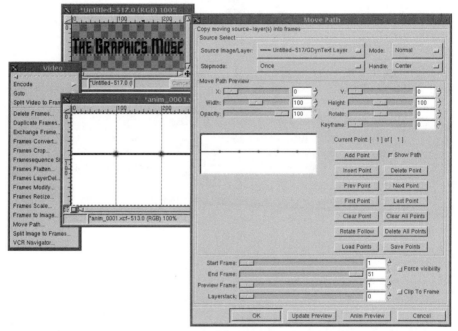

FIGURE 12-12 The text object, Move Path dialog, blank first frame, and Video menu

The sliders at the bottom are used to specify where to apply this path, from the specified start frame to the specified end frame. The *Preview Frame* slider determines which frame to use for the preview window, and the *Layerstack* slider determines which layer to apply the object to in each frame. Leaving this slider at 0 will cause the object to be placed on top of all layers. The *Force Visibility* toggle forces the layer to be visible, even if partly obscured by other layers. Finally, the *Clip to Frame* toggle will clip the object layer to the frame it is being applied to if, at the control point, the object layer overhangs the frame's boundaries.

Let's add a control point every 10 pixels starting on the right. That should give us 51 control points. Just click on the right side and then set the X slider to 500 and the Y slider to 100 (all the way to the right, halfway down). Then click on Add Point. Now change the X slider to 490 and click on Add Point. Repeat this step, reducing X by 10 each time, until you get to 0. Now you've created a neat, little, straight line path. Ready to see it in action? Click on OK to apply the path to your frames. Note that your start and end frames defaulted to the first and last frame we created in the first part of this example. If you need to apply a path to a smaller set of frames, you could do so now by adjusting the appropriate sliders.

Tip
If you aren't sure what the path should look like, you can add a layer to your first frame with a freehand drawing of the path and then open the Move Path dialog as I've done in this example. This will cause the drawn path to be visible in Move Path's preview window, allowing you to plot your control points more accurately. After the path is applied you can remove that layer from the first frame.

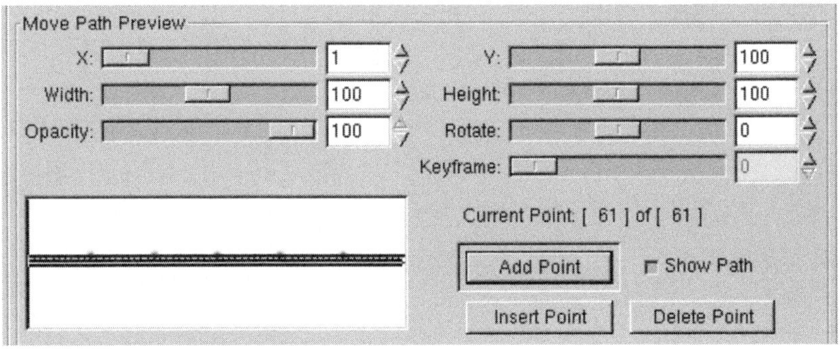

FIGURE 12-13 The completed path

Oops! We actually created 61 control points. When we hit OK, GAP tells us we have too many control points. In this example the fix is easy: Use the First Point and Last Point buttons to jump back and forth to the ends of the path and delete the points. Do so in pairs (first and last points) until you've deleted five pairs. Then you're ready to try the OK button again.

Depending on the speed of your computer and the amount of memory you have, GAP will take some time to process all the frames. While it works you'll get the familiar stopwatch icon flashing. When it's done, the flashing mouse pointer will return to its normal shape and the first frame (which you have open) will be updated to show the object added to it. Since GAP works on multiple files, all the updates are saved automatically. That means there is no Undo operation for this type of animation work. Be certain of your changes before you apply them!

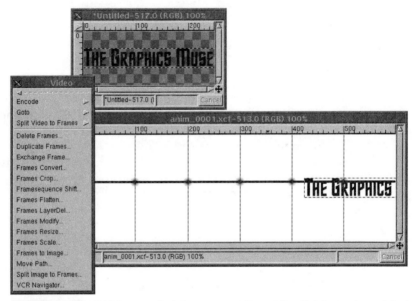

FIGURE 12-14 GAP has applied the move path and the first frame is updated

Now select *Video->VCR Navigator* to view the animation. If you have multiple Canvas windows open, be sure the one with the first frame of the animation is active (just click on one of its rulers) before opening the navigator. Once it opens, you can just click the play button to start the preview. Since the navigator has to open and flatten each frame file, it can take some time to start. If you move the mouse pointer over a Canvas window you'll see the mouse pointer flash to the stopwatch periodically—that's GAP processing the frames. Once it's done you'll get a new Canvas window and the Animation Playback dialog will display. Just hit play and watch it go!

The VCR Navigator is also useful for jumping around your frames. Double-clicking any of the frames listed will open that frame for editing. Right-mouse click on a listed frame and you'll get a menu for cutting and pasting frames right within the Navigator!

There many other options in the Video menu. Once your animation is completed you can export it to MPEG using the *Encode* option (though this does require some external programs to be installed). You can convert your frames to JPEG, TIFF, or some other GIMP-supported format using *Frames Covert* (a process required for generating MPEG files). You can even convert all your frames into a single image displayed in a Canvas window using *Frames to Image*. This process allows you to then convert that new image to indexed and save the animation as a GIF animation. Why would you create a GIF animation this way? To allow you to work with multiple layers per frame. In our example, we wouldn't convert the animation to a GIF animation for two reasons: (1) a 600x200 animation of 50 frames would take forever to download on a slow link and (2) big GIF animations are just plain clumsy on a Web page.

If you want to apply a filter to all your frames you need something a little more sophisticated than the Filter All Layers option we used with GIF animations. For GAP animations, you would use the *Frames Modify* option in the Video menu. This dialog allows you to process frames in many ways, including the option *Apply Filter on Layers*. The process works just like it did with *Filter All Layers*, but the *Frames Modify* acts as a frontend to apply this to multiple files.

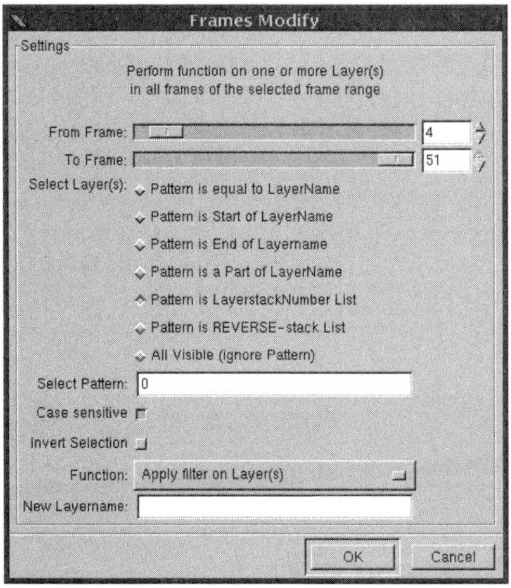

FIGURE 12-15 *Frames Modify* dialog

There are other features in the GAP toolset, far too many to cover in this short text. However, as long as you have the power to play back the animation we just created, you can experiment with all of them at your leisure.

RECAP

Animations on the Web come in two basic formats: GIF animations and streaming media. The GIMP provides easy-to-use tools for developing simple GIF animations based on the use of layers, including the ability to preview the animation on a browser window. More complex animations can be produced using the wide variety of tools in the GIMP Animation Package (GAP). This includes multilayered frames, multiframed filter applications, and more. Frames and animations can be converted to various image formats, including GIF and MPEG formatted animations.

PROJECTS

Play with the VCR Navigator a bit. See if you can figure out how to cut four frames from one location and paste them into another. Hint: Look for the frame menu discussed in this chapter.

Remake the animation made with GAP in this chapter. Apply the Shift filter to frames 10 to 25 that increase, and then again to frames 26 to 41 that decrease. Note that because the text layers were added with the Keep Transparency set, you need to merge all layers in all frames before applying the Shift filter or you won't see the effect of the shifting. The key here is to make the animation just like we did in this chapter, then merge the layers using Frames Modify. Finally, apply the shifting by using Frames Modify again. The trick is to figure out what settings to use in the Frames Modify dialog to accomplish this. If you aren't sure, try the same project using only five frames so testing the animation won't take so long.

13 Site Design 3: Site Navigation

IN THIS CHAPTER

- Goals for This Site Design Project
- Navigation Planning
- Page Layout
- Image Map Design
- Rollover Design
- GIF Animation
- The Web Page HTML Code
- Recap

Once again we take our experiences into a real world example. In this chapter we'll use our knowledge of image formats, animation, and image maps to create a page of services for our dental example from Chapter 11 "Image Maps and Carvings." We'll look at page layout considerations that provide easy-to-use navigation for your visitors and integrate an animated banner that provides insight into the office and its services.

◆ Goals for This Site Design Project

In this Site Design project we want to produce a navigation page that presents a series of services for an imaginary dental office.

There should be simple rollovers that take visitors to parts of the site unrelated to services offered, an image map for the services provided by the office, and a GIF animation that displays office hours, doctors' names, and upcoming events. We want the page to load quickly, which means keeping the image sizes small. We also want the animation to loop. No particular color scheme has been requested (which is good, since this is a black and white example), which makes the job all that much simpler.

◆ Navigation Planning

Before we start this we need to do a little planning. This page contains primarily navigational aides, with the only real informational content coming in the form of the GIF animation. There are two types of navigation here: external links to pages unrelated to the doctors' services and those specifically linked to the information on services provided.

In order to properly plan for navigation through the site, we've interviewed the doctors and asked them what they want visitors to know about their offices. The doctors listed the following items:

- Doctors' names and credentials
- Oral procedures covered
- Orthodontia services
- Office locations
- Insurance plans
- Dental terminology
- Clinical practices
- Dental hygiene information

The oral procedures needed expanding, and the doctors offered the following:

- Gum cleaning
- General teeth cleaning
- Teeth whitening
- Molds and casts
- Caps
- Extractions
- Root canals

Now we have the information we need for this page. Dividing these up into our two categories, we come up with the following:

Services Provided	External Links	Banner Information
Gum cleaning	Office locations	Doctor's names and credentials
General teeth cleaning	Insurance plans	Office hours
Teeth whitening	Dental terminology	
X-rays	Clinical practices	
Molds and casts	Dental hygiene	
Caps	information	
Extractions		
Root canals		
Orthodontia services		

That's enough information for a single page—almost too much for an average user. Ideally, when you have so many links you tend to leave out the cute rollovers or image maps, but we're learning how to design and make a big page work well for visitors. This will be a good test of your skills up to this point!

◆ Page Layout

The information provided for navigation is sufficient to start work on the page. We're going to make the external links into rollover buttons that change slightly using JavaScript. The image map with links to services is just like the one we made in Chapter 11, but this time we need to break the image up into pieces to accommodate a left side full of rollovers. Sounds tricky, but it turns out to be pretty simple using standard GIMP tools.

Following the design most commonly used on the Web today, we'll provide the external links on the left side of the page, the image map links to service information in the center, and the animation across the top. It's a simple design, and one that is easy to follow and uncluttered. The banner should be no more than 400 pixels across and 50 pixels high. That should make the page fit well on any monitor without requiring the visitor to scroll up or down.

Using the example from Chapter 11 is a good way to jump into this project. The first thing we notice from Figure 11-1 is that it used a black border around an image map. That's fine—we can use a black background on the page. The page layout is split into three sections: the top banner, the left-side rollovers, and the middle image map. While there are many ways to handle this, we'll just set the left side and middle sections in a table and center the table on the page horizontally. The top banner will be above the table and also centered. This allows us to easily set the width of the table cells and be fairly certain they'll be maintained on any browser.

Using a table also has one other advantage: We can add more space, filled with black, to the left side of the original image and then split it near the edge of the original image. This permits some of the original image to be used as a background in the table cell where the rollovers will be placed. In effect, it makes the image used in the image map appear to be partially set under the rollovers.

◆ Image Map Design

We're going to start with the dental office image we used in Chapter 11 (a photo taken from a royalty-free stock photo collection and run through a few filters to generate the special effects). We want to generate a similar fuzzy-edged border then add some space on the left side filled with black. To do this we generate our special effects first (some selective motion blurring along with Curves and Level adjustments) and then apply the Fuzzy Border filter (*Script-Fu->Decor->Fuzzy Border*).

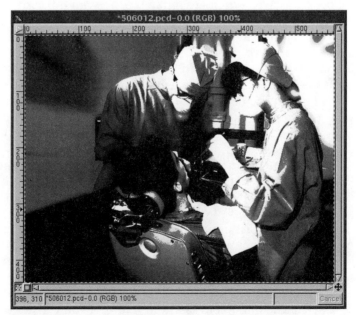

FIGURE 13-1 The original image, filtered and ready to be expanded

Now we want to split this image into a right and left side. The right side will be used in the image map and the left side as the background for the rollovers. The GIMP makes this cut simple—just drag out a guide from the left-side ruler and position it where you want the cut. Then choose *Image->Transforms->Guillotine*. This will chop the image into two pieces, opening two new Canvas windows. Save the left side to a JPEG file named *rollovers-bg.jpg*. We want to concentrate on the image map side now.

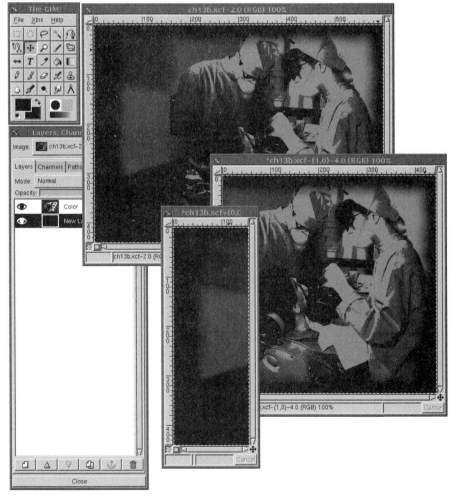

FIGURE 13-2 The original image and its cut-out left and right sides. We still have to set the text fields for the links prior to applying the Image Map plug-in to it

Open up the Image Map plug-in (*Filters->Web->ImageMap*) on the right side image. Use rectangular mappings around each text field in the image and set a URL for each link. We set each link to point to *services/item.html*, where *item* is the name of the service. This is just an easy way to manage the files on this site, but the real naming conventions are another part of full site design and are beyond the scope of this project.

One note on using the Image Map plug-in: Be careful on how close together you set your links. If the rectangular (or other shaped) regions overlap it may cause problems, possibly even causing the plug-in to exit unexpectedly. The trick is to leave just a little extra space between your text so those link regions don't overlap.

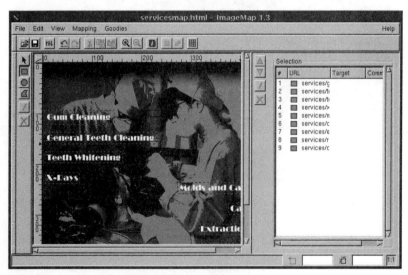

FIGURE 13-3 The GIMP's Image Map plug-in

That's all there is to the image map part of our page. Now we want to generate the rollovers. It turns out these are pretty easy to do using the GIMP layers.

◆ Rollover Design

Rollovers are something new we're adding to your knowledge in this chapter, but it turns out all they require is some basic GIMP knowledge. A rollover is nothing more than a set of two images, usually colored differently, that are displayed under different conditions. The first image is the normal image and the second, the active image, is displayed when the mouse is placed over the image. The switch between the two images is handled by fairly simple JavaScript code.

In our design we found we needed five rollovers, which means ten total images. Each image is simply a text image generated in the GIMP. The trick is to make exact duplicates of the normal and rollover images. The GIMP makes this easy by using layers.

Let's start with our first external link—"Office Locations." The steps for a simple rollover are as follows:

1. Open a new Canvas the size of the text image you need. In this case, the background layer turned out to be 156 pixels wide, so we'll make the text images a little smaller, say, 150 pixels. We can center these in the table cell later.

2. Set the foreground color to the normal state color. We'll use a gray color for this.

3. Create a text layer in the font you desire.

4. Set the foreground color to the active state color. We'll use white.

5. Duplicate the text layer.

6. Select all of the duplicate layer. Make sure Keep Transparency is set.

7. Use the Bucket Fill tool to fill the duplicate layer with the new foreground color. This should color just the text.

8. Convert the image to indexed (so we can save them as GIF images).

Now you have all the pieces you need to make the two images for the first rollover. To save the two images, follow these steps:

1. Save the image with the layers intact to an XCF formatted file.

2. Delete the top layer.

3. Flatten the image.

4. Save this as *offices-normal.gif.*

5. Type Ctrl-Z twice in the Canvas window to undo the flatten and layer delete.

6. Delete the original text layer.

7. Flatten the image.

8. Save this as *offices-active.gif.*

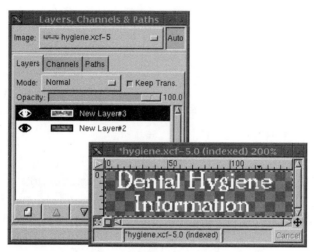

FIGURE 13-4 A two-layer example of the rollover images

JavaScript

That takes care of both images. Now we're ready for the JavaScript code. While we can't get into a detailed discussion of JavaScript here, there are a few things you need to understand before we get to the actual code. First, JavaScript deals with *events*—something a user does over the browser window, like move the mouse or click on something. You tell JavaScript to look for a particular event at a particular place, and when it sees that event, it runs the JavaScript code you associated with that event.

Second, you need to understand how JavaScript references images on a Web page. JavaScript is *object-oriented*, meaning anything you want to attach JavaScript code to is referred to as an object. JavaScript references images as objects and as such treats them just like any other JavaScript object. Links, frames, and browser windows are examples of other JavaScript objects. The trick to rollovers is to update the correct image—in some cases the image to update is not the image over which the mouse currently rests (though it will be for this example). Image objects in a document (documents are HTML pages) are referenced using names, such as *document.dog.src.* This name might reference the normal state image for a picture of a dog, while *document.dog.active* might reference the active state image. The *document* means the current document (page), the *dog* references the NAME= tag given to the image, and the *src* refers to the name of the image, such as "dog-1.gif." Let's look at the code that handles this.

First, let's look at the HTML definition for our first rollover—the Office Locations images:

```
<A HREF="javascript:void(null)"
  onMouseOver="mouseIn('offices', 0); return true;"
  onMouseOut="mouseOut('offices', 0); return true">
  <IMG SRC="images/offices-normal.gif" NAME="offices"
  BORDER=0 HEIGHT=25 WIDTH=150>
</A>
```

Notice the name of the image: NAME="offices." This gives JavaScript the object reference it needs to access the correct image. You can also access images using a document's images numeric index, but that's a somewhat haphazard method and a bit harder to use. Use the NAME tags for rollovers.

A few other things we should note about this bit of HTML:

1. There are event handlers for when the mouse enters the image area (onMouseOver) and for when the mouse leaves the image area (onMouseOut). These are JavaScript keywords for specific events. We'll discuss the values we associate with each of these in a moment.

2. The event handlers are placed in an anchor with an HREF tag. The HREF points to a JavaScript function called "void," which is a simple method for doing nothing. In this case we want only the event handlers to cause work to be done and the anchor to do nothing.

3. We've set the border width to 0 for the image so that no border will be placed around the image. If we didn't do this a border would be added that used the link and visited-link colors because the image is wrapped in an anchor tag. This way, the image doesn't really look like a link. That's good, since it's not really a link to anything.

The onMouseOver and onMouseOut events call two different JavaScript functions: mouseIn and mouseOut, respectively. These function names were our choice, and their JavaScript code looks like this:

```
<SCRIPT LANGUAGE="JavaScript">
<!- Hide script from older browsers
```

```
numitems=5;
ActiveImages = new Array(numitems);
NormalImages = new Array(numitems);

// Initialize two arrays used for the images.
for (i=0; i<numitems; i++) {
ActiveImages[i] = new Image();
NormalImages[i] = new Image();
}

// Establish the Active image objects we want to use.
ActiveImages[0].src="images/offices-active.gif";
ActiveImages[1].src="images/insurance-active.gif";
ActiveImages[2].src="images/terms-active.gif";
ActiveImages[3].src="images/practices-active.gif";
ActiveImages[4].src="images/hygiene-active.gif";

// Establish the Normal image objects we want to use.
NormalImages[0].src="images/offices-normal.gif";
NormalImages[1].src="images/insurance-normal.gif";
NormalImages[2].src="images/terms-normal.gif";
NormalImages[3].src="images/practices-normal.gif";
NormalImages[4].src="images/hygiene-normal.gif";

docObj = 'document';

// Event handler called for onMouseOver event
function mouseIn(item_name, index)
{
    docname  = eval(docObj + '.' + item_name);
    docname.src = ActiveImages[index].src;
}

// Event handler called for onMouseOut event
function mouseOut(item_name, index)
{
    docname  = eval(docObj + '.' + item_name);
    docname.src = NormalImages[index].src;
}

// End of hidden script -->
</SCRIPT>
```

We first allocate and initialize two arrays that will hold the names of our images. We then define a variable called *docObj* which we'll use to build the name of the object (i.e., image) to update on each rollover event. After that comes our two event handling functions, *mouseIn* and *mouseOut*. Both of these take a name and an index number for the image to update. The name is actually the object name to use, which we use in building the object name in the variable *docname*. Then we set the object to the new image and we're done.

Remember that this code gets called when the appropriate event happens for any given image that has the JavaScript code attached to it. Each event is also set up to pass in the appropriate values. In our first example, the Office Locations code, we set the *item_name* to "offices" and the *index* to 0 since the first image in our indices are the office location images.

For this example you are safe in placing this bit of code inside the *<HEAD>* section of your HTML. Although it accomplishes what we want, it's not very efficient code and could easily be shrunk to even fewer lines of code. That task, alas, is for another book.

Note: This JavaScript code is designed for use on Netscape 4.x. To make it work on any browser (including MS Internet Explorer) requires more complex code, and such programming is beyond the scope of this book.

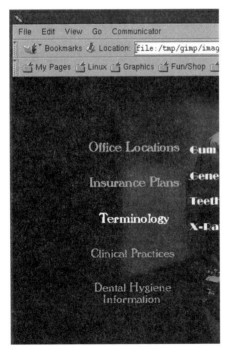

FIGURE 13-5 The rollovers in place on the Web page

◆ GIF Animation

The image map and rollovers are done, so we just need to generate a GIF animation and place it over our table and our page will be complete. The doctors asked for their names, office hours, and special events to be placed in this animation. However, if the special events change often, then this image would have to be modified often and that's more work than you want to do. The solution is to leave another spot for the special events on the page (usually another row in the table that is just text or maybe an image) and just include the names and office hours in the animation. In our case, we'll just leave out the special events.

The first thing we want to do is define the dimensions of the animation. We originally specified this to be 400 pixels wide by 50 pixels high. That should fit nicely above the table we've made without overpowering it. We'll use a black background in our frames, too, so it appears that the animation is nonrectangular. We'll add transparent layers with text over black background layers and combine them, using different timings to stagger the display a little. And we'll fade the text in.

Although we could use the Filter All Layers feature to produce some of these effects (like the fade in of the text), you'll find that manually creating the text layers, duplicating them, and then adjusting their Brightness/Contrast is easier to do by hand. What we end up with is:

1. A black background frame.

2. A frame with the first doctor's name (we'll assume two doctors here) to replace the background.

3. A set of frames that fade in, stating this doctor's experience level. These are transparent except for the text, so we'll set these to combine with the doctor's name.

4. A black frame to replace the first doctor's name.

5. The next doctor's name on a black background, also set to replace.

6. The transparent frames with text that combine with the second doctor's name to describe her background.

7. A black frame to replace the second doctor.

8. A black frame with "Office Hours" set to replace the last frame.

9. The Monday, Wednesday, Friday hours, combined with the last frame.

10. A black frame with "Office Hours" set to replace the last frame.

11. The Tuesday, Thursday hours, combined with the last frame.

12. A black frame with "Office Hours" set to replace the last frame.

13. A Saturday hours (by appointment) frame, combined with the last frame.

Don't get confused by the content of the frames; we made up the names, experience, and office hours to use for this example. The thing to note here is the process we used—combining black backgrounds with transparent layers that contain some text, then replacing those with the next set of frames.

We set the timing different on each of these. The first frame gets a modest length of about 350ms. That's the buffer between the end of the last animation and the start of the next loop. The last frame of text for each doctor gets a very long time—1500ms —so that their information can be ready clearly. And the same time, 1500ms, is given to each of the frames for the office hours.

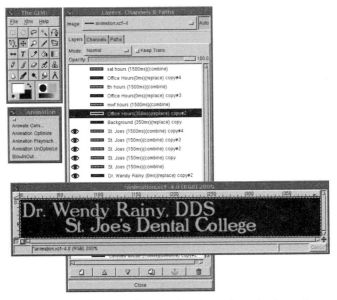

FIGURE 13-6 The completed animation. Note the layer timings and disposition of each layer (combined or replaced)

◆ The Web Page HTML Code

Those are all the little pieces that go into the page. Now you need to put them all together. It's easy to do, really. Here is one possible version. Just remember that with the Web, alternatives always abound!

```
<HTML>
<HEAD>

<SCRIPT LANGUAGE="JavaScript">
<!— Hide script from older browsers

numitems=5;
ActiveImages = new Array(numitems);
NormalImages = new Array(numitems);

// Initialize two arrays used for the images.
for (i=0; i<numitems; i++) {
   ActiveImages[i] = new Image();
   NormalImages[i] = new Image();
}

// Establish the Active image objects we want to use.
ActiveImages[0].src="images/offices-active.gif";
ActiveImages[1].src="images/insurance-active.gif";
ActiveImages[2].src="images/terms-active.gif";
ActiveImages[3].src="images/practices-active.gif";
ActiveImages[4].src="images/hygiene-active.gif";

// Establish the Normal image objects we want to use.
NormalImages[0].src="images/offices-normal.gif";
NormalImages[1].src="images/insurance-normal.gif";
NormalImages[2].src="images/terms-normal.gif";
NormalImages[3].src="images/practices-normal.gif";
NormalImages[4].src="images/hygiene-normal.gif";

docObj = 'document';

// Event handler called for onMouseOver event
function mouseIn(item_name, index)
{
   docname  = eval(docObj + '.' + item_name);
   docname.src = ActiveImages[index].src;
}

// Event handler called for onMouseOut event
function mouseOut(item_name, index)
{
```

```
    docname   = eval(docObj + '.' + item_name);
    docname.src = NormalImages[index].src;
}

// End of hidden script —>
</SCRIPT>


<MAP NAME="map">
<!— #$-:Image Map file created by GIMP Imagemap Plugin
—>
<!— #$-:GIMP Imagemap Plugin by Maurits Rijk —>
<!— #$-:Please do not edit lines starting with "#$" —>
<!— #$VERSION:1.3 —>
<!— #$AUTHOR:Michael J. Hammel —>
<AREA SHAPE="RECT" COORDS="2,93,145,121" HREF="services/gum-
cleaning.html">
<AREA SHAPE="RECT" COORDS="3,136,230,159"
HREF="services/teeth-cleaning.html">
<AREA SHAPE="RECT" COORDS="4,175,162,197"
HREF="services/teeth-whitening.html">
<AREA SHAPE="RECT" COORDS="5,216,75,238"
HREF="services/xrays.html">
<AREA SHAPE="RECT" COORDS="273,236,431,258"
HREF="services/molds-casts.html">
<AREA SHAPE="RECT" COORDS="377,277,429,299"
HREF="services/caps.html">
<AREA SHAPE="RECT" COORDS="317,318,429,339"
HREF="services/extractions.html">
<AREA SHAPE="RECT" COORDS="313,356,429,380"
HREF="services/root-canals.html">
<AREA SHAPE="RECT" COORDS="232,398,432,422"
HREF="services/orthodontia.html">
</MAP>

</HEAD>



<BODY bgcolor=#000000>


<!— Banner goes here —>
<CENTER>
<IMG SRC="images/animation.gif" WIDTH=400 HEIGHT=50 BOR-
DER=0>
</CENTER>


<!— A 2-celled table for navigation — >

<table align=center cellpadding=0 cellspacing=0 border=0>
```

```
<tr>
<td width=156 background="images/rollovers-bg.jpg">

<A HREF="javascript:void(null)"
onMouseOver="mouseIn('offices', 0); return true;"
onMouseOut="mouseOut('offices', 0); return true" >
<IMG SRC="images/offices-normal.gif" NAME="offices" BORDER=0
HEIGHT=25 WIDTH=150></A>

<br clear=both>
<br clear=both>
<br clear=both>

<A HREF="javascript:void(null)"
onMouseOver="mouseIn('insurance', 1); return true;"
onMouseOut="mouseOut('insurance', 1); return true" >
<IMG SRC="images/insurance-normal.gif" NAME="insurance" BOR-
DER=0 HEIGHT=25 WIDTH=150></A>

<br clear=both>
<br clear=both>
<br clear=both>

<A HREF="javascript:void(null)"
onMouseOver="mouseIn('terms', 2); return true;"
onMouseOut="mouseOut('terms', 2); return true" >
<IMG SRC="images/terms-normal.gif" NAME="terms" BORDER=0
HEIGHT=25 WIDTH=150></A>

<br clear=both>
<br clear=both>
<br clear=both>

<A HREF="javascript:void(null)"
onMouseOver="mouseIn('practices', 3); return true;"
onMouseOut="mouseOut('practices', 3); return true" >
<IMG SRC="images/practices-normal.gif" NAME="practices" BOR-
DER=0 ></A>

<br clear=both>
<br clear=both>
<br clear=both>

<A HREF="javascript:void(null)"
onMouseOver="mouseIn('hygiene', 4); return true;"
onMouseOut="mouseOut('hygiene', 4); return true" >
<IMG SRC="images/hygiene-normal.gif" NAME="hygiene" BORDER=0
></A>

</td>
```

```
<td width=444>
<IMG SRC="images/servicesmap.jpg" WIDTH=444 HEIGHT=441 BOR-
DER=0 USEMAP="#map"></td>

</td>

</tr>
</table>

</BODY>
</HTML>
```

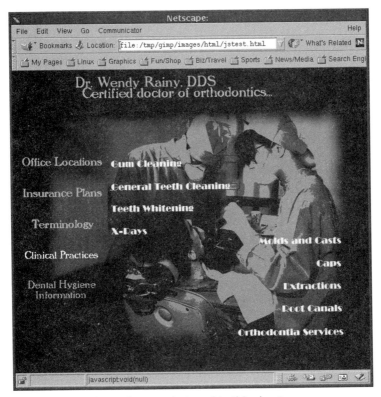

FIGURE 13-7 The Web page designed in this chapter

RECAP

Congratulations! You've made your first fully functional Web page—well, almost. The links still have to be resolved to real pages, so there would be lots of other work to do. But you can see how quick and easy making pages can be using the many features the GIMP has to offer!

14 Scanning and Digital Cameras

IN THIS CHAPTER

- Getting Images into the Computer

- Scanner Support

- Using the xscanimage Interface

- Lines and Details

- Gamma Again

- After the Scan

- Digital Cameras

- Recap

By now you already know enough about the GIMP and page layout to run off and generate your first few attempts at a Web site design. You could stop here in this book, but there are a few more issues that will give you the strong background needed to take you from an average designer to a great one. These include the use of specific filters and dealing with the GIMP's scripting interfaces. We'll cover these items in later chapters. In this chapter we'll look at another of the more obvious expert issues: getting an image into the GIMP.

◆ Getting Images into the Computer

One of the first problems you'll face while working on image design for your Web sites is where to get stock images from. Stock images are usually just collections of photos (although other artwork could be included here) used by other artists in their image processing work. There are many ways to get a hold of these: Scan photos and other images yourself, get them on disks from friends or acquaintances, grab them directly from a digital camera, download them from the Net, or buy a stock photo CD from a commercial vendor. Any of these methods work but most often you will probably scan your own work and grab images directly from a digital camera.

Desktop scanners are cheaper than printers these days, which means they are easy to get and even simpler to use. Although the GIMP doesn't include direct support for image input devices like scanners or digital cameras, it does work well in conjunction with them. In fact, an external plug-in exists to link the GIMP directly to the generic scanner interface for Linux known as SANE. We'll get to SANE in a moment. First we need to cover some scanning basics.

When preparing to work with scanners you need to consider the hardware you'll be using. Many flatbed scanners on the market today come with their own proprietary SCSI card. These cards are generally not designed to have many devices connected to the SCSI cable. Avoid these cards. Get a good SCSI card that meets the latest SCSI specifications. Linux seldom supports the proprietary versions very well (if at all) and allowing a single device connected to the cable defeats the purpose of the SCSI design anyway.

Avoid unshielded cables or cables that are too long. Modern SCSI cards (usually referred to as SCSI-2 or SCSI-3 compliant) allow up to 18 feet of cable. Older cards (SCSI-1) allow only up to six feet. If the cable is too long the last device on the cable may not be seen or work improperly. Additionally, older SCSI-1 hardware needs to be at the end of the SCSI cable. SCSI-2 devices placed after a SCSI-1 device will prevent the SCSI-2 device from being seen by the device drivers.

Once you have an appropriate SCSI card and cable you can connect the flatbed scanner to it. Be sure the last device on the cables is terminated. Most devices (scanners, Jaz drives, external hard drives, and so forth) come with a terminator that can be plugged into the device.

The next step is to clean the glass properly. Simple glass cleaner and a soft, lint-free cloth are appropriate. Any fibers left by the cloth will degrade the scans, so try to find a cloth that won't shed.

Paper towels will work, but coarse towels can begin to scratch the glass over time.

One thing to keep in mind when prepping for scans bound for a Web site is resolution. Desktop scanners today can easily scan at 600 DPI and far beyond. However, scans at that high resolution will be far too large for Web images. You can usually get away with 100 DPI scans instead. These will be faster to generate but will lack some detail. Then again, that detail wouldn't be seen at the 72DPI display resolution of ordinary monitors anyway. Save yourself some time and lots of disk space—scan at low resolutions.

◆ Scanner Support

The GIMP doesn't include scanner drivers with its basic installation. In order to make use of scanners with the GIMP you need to get a separate package, known as SANE (which stands for Scanner Access Now Easy). This package installs a set of drivers for a wide range of scanners as well as a graphical interface to those drivers. This interface will allow you to use the scanner and have the scanned images passed directly to the GIMP. From your point of view, the whole thing looks like you're working in the GIMP alone.

The SANE package is downloadable from its Web site at http://www.mostang.com/sane/. Binaries are available for versions of Red Hat Linux on various hardware platforms as well as the Debian distributions.

Installation of SANE is beyond the scope of this text, but it comes with reasonably good documentation that explains the process to build and install from the source code. Once installed, you'll need to add a symbolic link from wherever the xscanimage program is installed (usually, /usr/local/bin) to your $HOME/.gimp/plug-ins directory in order for the GIMP to use the scanner interface.

◆ Using the xscanimage Interface

The interface between SANE and the GIMP is called xscanimage. This is a fairly simple graphical interface that allows you to specify regions of the scan surface to use, set Gamma values, and enable advanced features for specific scanners.

FIGURE 14-1 The Device Dialog from the GIMP

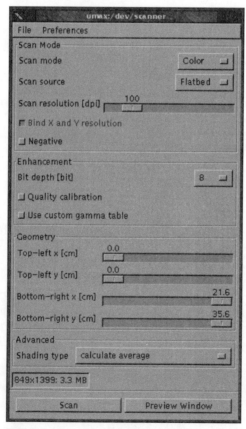

FIGURE 14-2 The Main Dialog for xscanimage

Once the SANE drivers and xscanimage are installed you'll access the interface from the Device Dialog found under the Toolbox's *Xtns->Acquire Image* menu. Selecting the /dev/scanner connected device should be sufficient if SANE was properly installed. This will open the Main Dialog window for xscanimage, which looks something like Figure 14-2. The exact layout of this window depends on the scanner you installed. This example shows a UMAX 1200S scanner.

The first step in scanning is to preview the images on the flatbed. This is done by clicking on the Preview button at the bottom of the Main Dialog. The Preview Window will open (Figure 14-3). Click the left mouse button in this window and drag it to create an outline around the region you wish to scan. The exact dimensions of the outline can be adjusted with the geometry sliders in the Main Dialog.

FIGURE 14-3 The Preview Window

◆ Lines and Details

Depending on the features of your scanner, xscanimage may provide options for scanning in color, grayscale, or as line art. The last option will scan in black and white only, sort of like scanning in full color and then applying the Threshold filter to the results. Line art scans are useful for scanning hand and mechanical drawings, diagrams, and other artwork that is simply a set of outlines. Once scanned, the images can be colored (like coloring in cells from an animation) or imported into a vector tool to be cleaned up.

◆ Gamma Again

The gamma settings for your monitor are not related to the settings from the scanner, so xscanimage provides you the option of adjusting the gamma of the scan. This feature is not visible in the default Main Dialog, however. To access gamma correction features, click on the *Use Custom Gamma Table* button in the Enhancements box. This will open the gamma correction features section of the dialog.

Set the gamma for your monitor using the gamma curve displayed. You can adjust the overall gamma or each of the red, green, or blue channels individually. If you know the exact numerical setting for the gamma of your monitor, you can click on the button on the lower right and type in that value.

It is highly likely you won't know your gamma setting or what appropriate value to use. Trial and error will be your rule of thumb. However, it will be fairly obvious when to adjust the gamma. Any image that is too dark, too light, or too faded usually benefits from some gamma adjustments. The downside is that making such adjustments requires an additional scan. That can be time-consuming if you have to do much experimenting. You may find that scans that are fairly close to accurate are more easily adjusted using the Levels dialog after the scan instead of experimenting with minute changes to the gamma setting and rescanning.

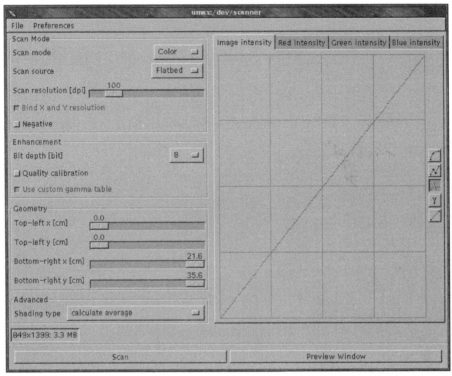

FIGURE 14-4 The Main Dialog with advanced options and Gamma options

◆ After the Scan

Most desktop scanners provide good scans, but the quality of the glass bed will vary greatly. This means that nearly all scans require some amount of sharpening and color correction. For small scans, that is, scans of 100 DPI or smaller, the regular Sharpen filter (*Filters->Enhance->Sharpen*) will provide a slightly more harsh sharpening of the image but works fairly well on images bound for the Web. Large images and those that require higher quality on the Web should probably use the Unsharp Mask filter (*Filters->Enhance->Unsharp Mask*). The difference between the two is just in the algorithms used in computing the sharpening effect. Unsharp Mask is a bit cleaner on larger images.

After sharpening you will probably want a little color correction applied, even if you intend on desaturating the image later. The Levels dialog is normally used after sharpening. The Auto-Levels option of this dialog does an excellent job on most scans, although you may find that manual adjustments to lighten or darken the overall image are also needed.

◆ Digital Cameras

Although much of your image input will probably be from scanners, another fast growing tool for Web designers is the digital camera. Many of these devices provide their images directly in JPEG format, making it an easy transition from the camera to the Web via the GIMP.

Linux supports digital cameras through a number of products. One of the most popular, and the one with support for the most number of cameras, is called *gPhoto*. It has a graphical interface based on the popular GTK windowing interface which was originally developed for use by the GIMP project and supports connecting devices to essentially any device port.

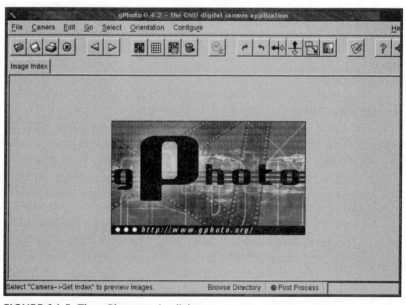

FIGURE 14-5 The gPhoto main dialog

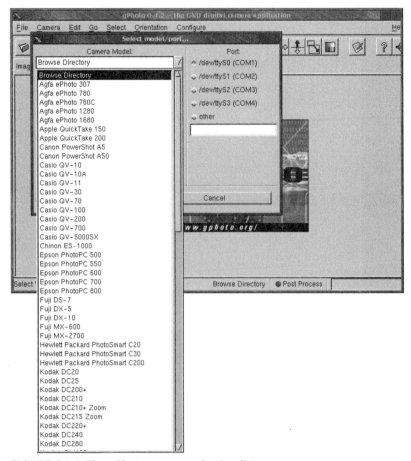

FIGURE 14-6 The gPhoto camera selection list

GPhoto supports cameras from Agfa, Casio, Epson, Fuji, Hewlett Packard, Kodak, Nikon, Olympus, Ricoh, Sony, and many other manufacturers. Although not directly connected to the GIMP—you need to run gPhoto separately—the output formats produced by gPhoto (normally JPEG) can easily be imported into the GIMP. You can also do a limited amount of image processing in gPhoto, such as rotation and flipping the orientation of the image. For cameras that support it, gPhoto will also download thumbnails of all images stored in the camera, allowing the user to view the images before downloading them from the camera.

The main Web site for gPhoto is http://www.gphoto.org.

RECAP

In this chapter we looked briefly at the two main methods of image input that Web professionals will use with the GIMP: flatbed scanners and digital cameras. Flatbed scanners are integrated directly into the GIMP via the SANE package and the xscanimage plug-in. Most scans need only be done at 100 DPI. Scanners are easy to use and offer a simple means of grabbing image data for Web pages.

Digital cameras are not directly supported in the GIMP but are supported by Linux using the gPhoto package. Images from digital cameras are normally stored as JPEG images right to disk, making it easy to import them into the GIMP for further processing.

15 Effects and Filters

IN THIS CHAPTER

- Why and When
- Blur and Noise
- Image Enhancement
- Lens Flares
- Distortion Filters
- The Right Filter for the Right Image
- Recap

While much discussion has been made about general use of the GIMP for Web image processing, little has been said about what special effects are possible. Blurring photos, using noise to generate clouds, and adding lens flares to images are all examples of effects generated by the GIMP standard filters. In this chapter we'll look at various classifications of special effects filters and what they offer to the Web image professional.

◆ Why and When

Image processing in the GIMP is handled almost exclusively using small programs called plug-ins. Everything from adjusting colors to blurring to distorting and warping images can be accomplished with one or more filters. Filters can be used to add eye-catching effects for buttons, image maps, and Web page logos, or they can be used to meld images into their solid color page backgrounds.

The majority of effects filters can be found in the Canvas Window menu under the *Filters* option. A few color options can be found under *Image->Colors* in the Canvas Window menu while a few more can be found under the *Script-Fu* option. Web professionals will want to become familiar with a certain subset of these effects filters. This subset includes blur and noise filters, general image enhancement filters, lens flares, and distortion filters. While most of these provide special effects that add pizazz to your Web images, some are essential for quality page layout issues, especially the blur and enhancement filters.

FIGURE 15-1 Various distortion effects applied to a sample scan

◆ Blur and Noise

Blur filters come in a variety of flavors. The IIR Gaussian Blur works best on scanned images, though computer-generated images (say 3D images) are better processed by the RLE Gaussian Blur filter. Motion blur provides variations on simulating motion in an image. The Selective Gaussian Blur can be used to simulate depth of field by blurring the apparent background in an image, though this filter takes some practice to recognize which sections of an image are likely to be blurred and which are not. In more simplistic use, this filter will smooth an image by not including neighboring pixels that are outside the specified Max Delta range. The effect is to smooth an image without losing any significant detail.

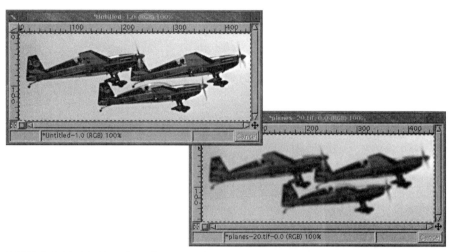

FIGURE 15-2 IIR Gaussian Blur example

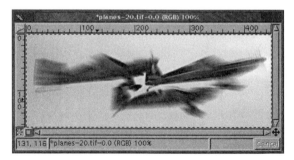

FIGURE 15-3 Motion Blur example

Noise filters produce random patterns in existing layers of an image. These range from scattered points, to streaks of feathered white blobs, to surveillance camera style visuals. The Noisify filter will add scattered points to an image with user-defined amounts of red, green, and blue points. Gray points are used if the channels are kept at equal amounts. This filter is often used to break up a gradient prior to conversion to indexed format in order to prevent color banding.

The Spread filter removes focus from the image. Think of it as adding a glass sheet between you and the image, with an unsmooth (in fact, extremely bumpy) surface on the glass.

The Xach Vision filter is actually a Perl script that converts an image to a grainy image filled with horizontal lines commonly seen on video surveillance cameras.

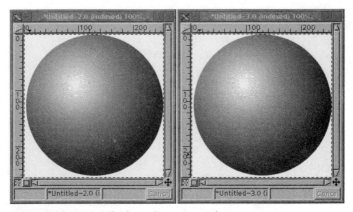

FIGURE 15-4 Noisified gradient example

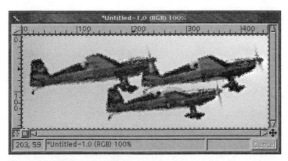

FIGURE 15-5 Spread example

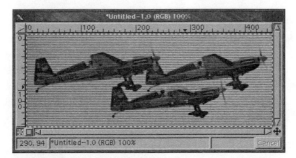

FIGURE 15-6 Xach Vision example

◆ Image Enhancement

While there are a number of image enhancement filters (*Filters->Enhance*), the two of most interest to Web developers are the Sharpen and Unsharp Mask filters. Both of these are used to clean up the quality of images and bring out details.

Sharpen is the more interactive of the two filters, providing a small preview window in which to view the effect of the current sharpen setting on the current image or layer. The effect is fairly simple: the contrast between adjacent pixels is increased, causing some pixels to brighten and some to darken, irrespective of the apparent values. What matters here is the existing contrast between adjacent pixels.

Unsharp Mask doesn't provide an interactive preview but does provide a finer granularity in setting the way the sharpening effect is applied and the places where it will be applied. The effect creates a darkening to one side of a selected pixel and lightening to the other which, when applied across the image, increases the general contrast of the image and improves the visibility of edges.

In the Unsharp Mask filters dialog, the Threshold value determines the difference in neighboring pixel values necessary before the sharpening is applied. The Radius determines the width of the effect from any given pixel. The amount increases the effect—higher values mean greater contrast and sharper edges. This is essentially the same as Sharpen except that the amount of sharpening and breadth of its application can be determined by the user. The results are generally better than the standard Sharpen filter, though on smaller images destined for the Web the difference may not be clearly noticeable.

FIGURE 15-7 Sharpen example

FIGURE 15-8 Unsharp Mask
example

◆ Lens Flares

A lens flare is the circle of light produced by reflections in a camera lens when photographing a brightly lit scene with the light source in front of the camera. The GIMP provides two standard lens flares along with a few others that produce effects similar to lens flares, all of which are accessible from the *Filters->Light Effects* option of the Canvas Window menu.

The original lens flare filter is called FlareFX. This is a fairly unsophisticated filter that produces a reddish flare with multiple, smaller-colored reflections centered over a specified region of the current layer. The dialog for this filter allows interactive placement of the flare but not color settings, diameter, number of reflections, or any other parameters.

A more sophisticated lens flare can be produced using the GFlare filter. The dialog for this filter is much more interactive and provides a true preview of the effect. Clicking inside the preview will move the center point for the main flare, around which multiple reflective flares are added. The main dialog provides an editing feature for the overall effect as displayed in the preview window. However, GFlare provides more advanced editing features that allow you to change the shape of the flares, the number of reflective flares, and spokes that emanate from the main flare's light source.

FIGURE 15-9 FlareFX example

FIGURE 15-10 GFlare example

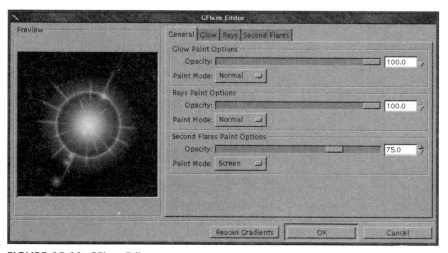

FIGURE 15-11 GFlare Editor

An alternative style of flare can be created using the SuperNova filter. This filter doesn't really produce a form of lens flare, but it does produce a light flare. The flare can be colored and positioned, with the radius and number of spokes that emanate from the center also configurable.

FIGURE 15-12 SuperNova example

◆ Distortion Filters

The distortion filters (*Filters->Distort* and *Filters->Map*) can add depth to an image, bend and smear it, scratch it, and warp it in ways that boggle the mind. These filters are all for special effects— you don't use these plug-ins to clean up an image, you use them to mess one up.

Most of the distortion filters can be found under *Filters->Distorts,* while another group lives under *Filters->Map*. Two filters, Emboss and Bump Map, are very similar but work on different types of layers. Emboss (*Filters->Distorts->Emboss*) will only work on background layers with no transparency. Bump Map (*Filters->Map->Bump Map*), which produces nearly identical effects, will work on any layer. Both add depth to an image based on pixel lightness. Figure 15-13 shows an example of the same layer processed by both filters. The direction of the light source is set using the Azimuth value. Elevation changes affect the contrast in the effect, adding to the illusion of the effect's depth. The Depth setting does essentially the same thing, though in a different manner internally. These slider settings work the same in both Emboss and Bump Map. Bump Map has many other options: The source image to use for the embossing can be changed, the image brightness can be increased, and the ambient light can be increased. In general, you'll find working with Bump Map is preferable to using Emboss.

Ripple and Waves, both of which can be found under the *Filters->Distorts* menu, add wave forms to an image. The main difference between the two effects is that the Ripple filter works either vertically or horizontally across the image while Waves applies its effect starting in the image center and radiating outward.

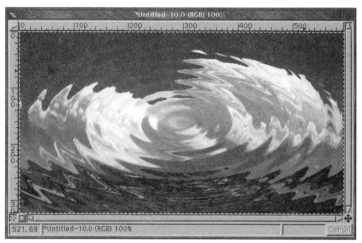

FIGURE 15-13 Ripple example

FIGURE 15-14 Waves example

One of the many new GIMP Perl scripts added to the 1.2 release is the Scratches filter (*Filters->Distorts->Scratches*). Since it uses the Perl interface it doesn't have a preview option. The filter smears the image along thin lines that flow within a range of a user-specified angle. The effect looks something like what might be produced by lightly brushing a whisk broom over an oil painting. A similar filter is Wind, which will smear an image in a user-defined direction much in the manner sand drifts with the wind. Note that the Wind filter differs from the Windify Perl-based filter (also found under *Filters->Distorts->Scratches*), with the Wind filter producing a generally better effect.

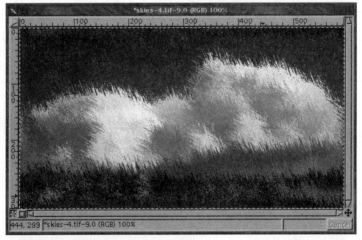

FIGURE 15-15 Scratches example

FIGURE 15-16 Wind example

IWarp (*Filters->Distorts->IWarp*) is one of the more interesting special effects filters. It provides an interactive preview where you can drag regions of an image around to enlarge, shrink, rotate, and otherwise warp the image. The interface includes simple animation features, though you aren't likely to use this filter to create animated GIFs. The Adaptive Supersampling toggle and associated options are used to increase the quality of the warping. Higher values will take longer to process and are really seldom necessary with Web-based imagery.

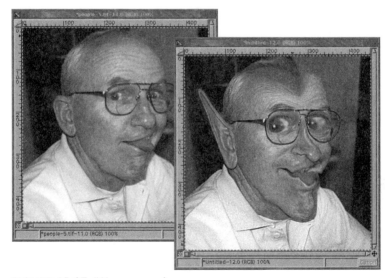

FIGURE 15-17 IWarp example

Similar to IWarp, the Whirl and Pinch filter (*Filters->Distorts->Whirl and Pinch*) moves sections of the image around. The main difference between IWarp and Whirl and Pinch is that the latter works from the central point of the current selection or layer, while IWarp allows you to interactively select where the effect is applied. Both filters provide options for setting the amount of distortion. Be careful with Whirl and Pinch, however. If you distort far enough out to reach the edges of the image, you may end up with transparent regions where you didn't expect them.

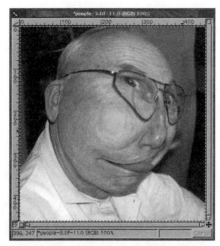

FIGURE 15-18 Whirl and Pinch example

The Page Curl filter (*Filters->Distorts->Page Curl*) simulates the curling of the corner of a page based on the current selection. There are options for determining the corner of the selection (or layer) to curl and the direction to curl. This filter does not do antialiasing along the angled edges of the curve, so you may have to play with the settings to find a selection that works without showing excessive stairstepping.

FIGURE 15-19 Page Curl example with stairstepping

The last effects filter that is easy to use and very useful to Web developers is the Map Object (*Filters->Map->Map Object*) filter. The dialog for this filter allows users to map a rectangular selection or entire layer to a plane, box, cylinder, or sphere. Options include the ability to set the location, type, and color of a light source, reflectivity and intensity levels, and the orientation of the image on the object.

FIGURE 15-20 Map Object example

◆ The Right Filter for the Right Image

Not all filters work on all images. The Page Curl filter, for example, isn't likely to work well with GIF images because its curled edge effect has a nonnoisified gradient and the edge itself will appear jagged without some antialiasing of the edge and its background. It also doesn't work on background layers unless an alpha channel has been added.

Whirl and Pinch will pinch the Canvas edges of an image and leave transparent regions (or regions filled with the background color) in the emptied space. You can't prevent this by making a selection first since the edge of the selection will have the same problem. The only way to avoid the issue is to keep the pinch effect from stretching out to the edges of the image or selection. The Ripple filter has a similar problem.

In the case of the IWarp filter, the stretching and moving of the pixels can cause color variations that, when indexed, will not be of acceptable quality for your Web site.

The point here is that you often have to experiment with the filters to find both the right settings for the effect you want as well as to determine if that effect works well as a GIF or JPEG image.

RECAP

While most effects filters in the GIMP are of little direct benefit to generating HTML or navigation features in Web site design, they all provide a means for adding style and pizazz to your Web imagery.

Blur and Noise filters are often used to clean up images or make them better suited for indexed images. Image enhancement filters are also used to clean up the quality of images, especially scanned images. Lens Flares are pure fluff but add a photographic effect to generally bland color images. Distortion filters are often the most creative of these filters. Though not used on a regular basis, they can be used to make otherwise generic images more eye catching.

16 Rendering Filters

IN THIS CHAPTER

- Why and When
- QBist
- Flame
- Clouds, Gas, and Flames
- IFSCompose
- GIMPressionist
- Sphere Designer
- Recap

In the last chapter we looked at some of the effects filters that are available to Web designers in the GIMP. While those filters are designed mostly to affect existing images and layers, rendering filters are designed to create new images or layers. Where effects filters add spice to existing images, rendering filters are spice in and of themselves.

In this chapter we'll look at a small subset of filters that generate images irrespective of existing image data. While the filters discussed here are some of the more interesting of the lot, they are in no way the complete list of rendering filters.

◆ Why and When

Rendering filters are designed to create images of their own, with little or no respect for the existing image. Because of this, Web designers will often use rendering filters early in the image design process as starting points. Effects filters, on the other hand, are used throughout the image design process, from initial image to final touch-up.

One of the reasons you'd want to use rendering filters for Web design is that they create unique patterns that can (though often don't) resemble more familiar objects. The Flame filter, for example, generates wisps of color that can resemble a flame using the default settings. The IFSCompose filter can be used to produce images that resemble watercolored trees and shrubs. But both filters can go way beyond the familiar into the artistic and stylistic.

Although these filters generally work in full RGB color, you may find it useful to desaturate the designs you create with them for use as background images.

FIGURE 16-1 The far out, as rendered in the GIMP

◆ QBist

There is no real way to describe this creative toy other than to say it's fast and easy to use. The dialog provides nine designs from which to choose. Clicking on any of them will move the selected design to the middle button and update all the others with new designs. Once you find a design of interest, click on OK and the design is rendered in the current layer and scaled to fit.

The designs generated by QBist (*Filters->Render->Pattern->QBist*) can be rather wild and colorful; however, there is no user control over either the design or colors used. You can save designs and reload them later, but other than that QBist is mostly a random chance design tool. Note that the colors used can often be too wild for use as backgrounds, so desaturating the design will likely be necessary. If desired, you can always do a Bucket Fill in Color mode to colorize the desaturated design and match the colors in your Web pages.

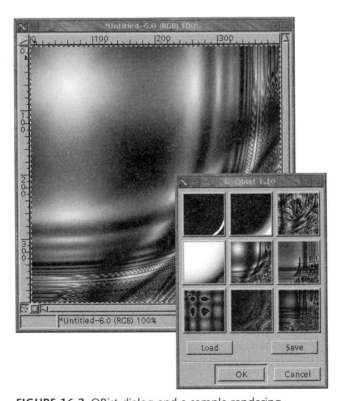

FIGURE 16-2 QBist dialog and a sample rendering

◆ Flame

The Flame filter (*Filters->Render->Nature->Flame*) is more configurable than QBist, though it still uses random generation to produce the nine design options from which the user selects. Flame's dialog presents a default design preview along with options for editing the colors, brightness, gamma, and contrast. Minimal control over the design shape is possible with the Sample Density and two spatial-oriented sliders. The design shown in the preview can be moved by adjusting the Camera slider settings at the bottom of the dialog. What you see in the preview will be rendered in the current layer. Note, however, that the background color of the preview—black—is not rendered. Only the design is rendered, and it overwrites the adjacent pixels in the existing layer, so be sure you want this change or have a blank layer to work in before running Flame.

The default design can be changed by selecting the Edit option of the main dialog. This opens a dialog similar in style to QBist's, but with the option of setting the form to use for the design—from Linear to Spherical to Horseshoe. These options aren't really the shape that is produced, but more the shape used in the algorithm that produces the renderings you see. In any case, clicking on one of the designs shown in the Edit dialog will move the selection to the center button and update the rest of the options accordingly.

Unfortunately, the real value in the designs generated by the Flame filter can hardly be appreciated in black and white images. Part of the fascination you'll have with this filter will be in selecting the right gradient to use with the designs. Using the default renderings, pure white can produce ice crystal styled designs, while the default gradient (the smooth German Flag gradient) produces very firelike designs.

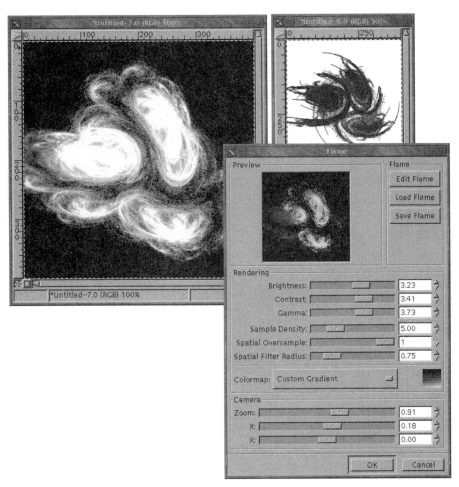

FIGURE 16-3 Flame dialog with rendered samples

◆ Clouds, Gas, and Flames

One effect that can be used in many different Web site designs is a soft cloud or gas shape. The GIMP doesn't provide any tools for directly creating clouds or gases, but it does provide two filters that can be used in a simple multistep process for rendering such shapes.

The first filter, and probably the one to use for more realistic-looking gas and flame formations, is called Plasma (*Filters->Render->Clouds->Plasma*). This filter creates a colored gas cloud that, when desaturated, looks very much like smoke. By running this image through the Levels and Curves dialogs, including making different adjustments to the individual color channels, you can produce very realistic-looking flames and explosions (which we can't show here since the effect is lost in black and white images). By keeping the rendered image desaturated and increasing contrast, you can reduce the high smoke appearance to low level smoke such as that seen in cigarette and cigar smoke. In any case, this filter is only a starting point. The rendered image will usually require some minor additional work with the GIMP's color and contrast features to produce the desired effect.

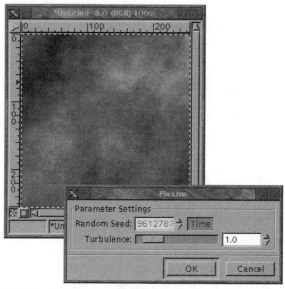

FIGURE 16-4 Plasma dialog and smoke

The Solid Noise filter (*Filters->Render->Clouds->Solid Noise*) renders an initial image that is more like clouds in the sky than clouds of smoke. Like the Plasma filter, the dialog for Solid Noise is fairly basic. Both dialogs allow the user to set the seed value for random number generation—an important step in reproducing a specific shape. The amount of turbulence in the shape can also be set for both filters. The primary difference in the dialogs for these two filters is that Solid Noise allows you to stretch the shape in the X or Y directions. This makes Solid Noise much more useful in generating clouds as they appear in the sky.

The image rendered by Solid Noise appears as soft white streaks or blobs on a black background (note that like Plasma, Solid Noise overwrites the pixels of the current layer or selection). Because of the soft edges on these streaks the image can appear to be out of focus, but that's as expected. To enhance the image you once again run it through the Levels, Curves, and Brightness/Contrast filters. The amount of processing required to get a good cloud shape is completely situation-dependent. Trial and error is your friend here.

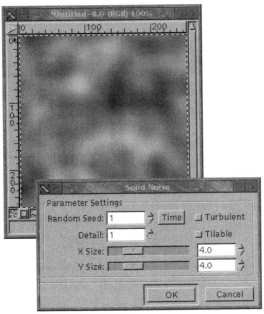

FIGURE 16-5 Solid Noise dialog and sample rendering

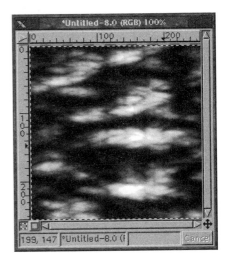

FIGURE 16-6 Rendered Clouds

◆ IFSCompose

IFSCompose (*Filters->Render->Nature->IFSCompose*) is a fractal-based filter which, although a bit difficult to master, can produce very interesting renderings. The interface to this filter can be a bit confusing and definitely takes some practice. The triangles in the upper left can be moved, rotated, and scaled by clicking on them and dragging. Each triangle represents a set of points, known as a *transformation*, to be rendered in the preview window. Moving triangles change the flow of the rendered transformations. Each triangle can also have its color set manually, or you can set the background color to the color of choice prior to adding a new triangle. You can add as many triangles as you'd like, though you can only delete triangles down to the last two.

IFSCompose will use the current foreground color for the color of the initial transformation triangles and will rescan that color when any other triangles are added. The background color is used as the background of the rendering. Keep in mind that IFSCompose will overwrite all pixels in the current image or selection. While this filter will scale its rendering to fit into a complete layer, it will not scale the rendering to fit into a selection.

Because of its fractal nature, IFSCompose is good at producing tree- and leaflike images. Because the colors can be set manually for the image, IFSCompose renderings can be made to match the color scheme of any page. However, the detail of the renderings may be lost in smaller images. Larger renderings should probably only be used as background images.

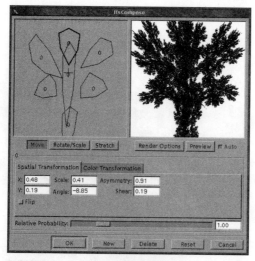

FIGURE 16-7 IFSCompose dialog

FIGURE 16-8 Samples of IFSCompose renderings

◆ GIMPressionist

The last two filters we'll discuss in this chapter are easily the two most creative filters added to the 1.2 version of the GIMP. The first is called GIMPressionist (*Filters->Artistic->GIMPressionist*). This filter takes an existing image or layer and allows you to distort it using variable brushstrokes and types. Think of it as taking an oil painting that's still wet and running a brush over it. This is similar to the Scratches filter, but with far more options and variations possible. In fact, once you learn the real power of GIMPressionist, you'll see that images can not only be modified but effectively mapped to new shapes using the same color variations of the original image.

The dialog for this filter is fairly easy to follow. First, the preview window is always visible and can be updated after each configuration change. Pages are available to configure the brush shape, size, stroke density and orientation, and the paper type on which brush strokes are simulated. All options have tips that provide brief explanations on their purpose, though not all are particularly helpful. Brushes in GIMPressionist are not the same as the standard brushes used by the GIMP. The aspect ratio (width to height) can be changed for GIMPressionist brushes as well as the brightness of the brush.

Brush orientation is a major part of the GIMPressionist effect. The Orientation page in the dialog allows for the selection of predefined orientations that can follow the hue, change based on distance from image center, and so forth. Beyond this, the Manual option (via the Edit button) allows the user to set the flow characteristics using any number of angled and strength-measured vectors.

GIMPressionist comes with a large range of presets, that is, configurations, to produce various types of effects. Because the filter has so many options, and because it's not always clear how to use all those options or what they affect, users will often want to start with one of the presets and modify to suit their needs. For an interesting look at what GIMPressionist is capable of, try running the Ballpark preset on any image, then spend some time adjusting the maximum and minimum sizes in the Size page of the dialog. Remember to hit the Update button after each change to see the changes applied in the preview window.

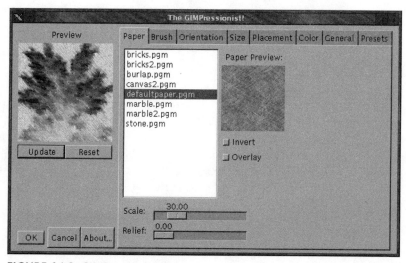

FIGURE 16-9 GIMPressionist dialog

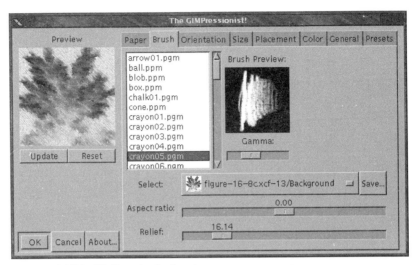

FIGURE 16-10 GIMPressionist brushes

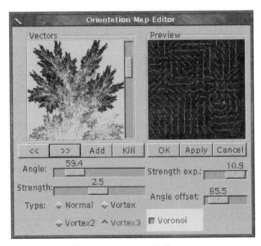

FIGURE 16-11 Orientation Editor

FIGURE 16-12 Sample renderings

◆ Sphere Designer

Sphere Designer (*Filters->Render->Sphere Designer*) comes to the GIMP from Vidar Madsen, the same fellow who brought us GIMPressionist. In this filter, the user is given the opportunity to design a 3D sphere using variations on lighting and layered surface textures. The sophistication of this filter is levels above nearly all the other GIMP filters in both ease of use and number of features. While the need for planetlike spheres may be minimal in general Web design, it can be paramount in 3D simulation and animations, both of which are fast becoming Web-based technologies.

If you've ever used any 3D tools with a texture editor you'll have little trouble learning to use Sphere Designer. A series of textures, each of which is given a wide range of properties, is applied to a sphere. The textures are layered, with the one listed first in the Textures list being on the bottom. Textures can be either a true texture (which would be like an image mapped to the sphere), a bump map (which would add limited depth to the textures above it in the list), or a light source.

Although you can achieve various effects with light sources below texture and bump map layers, you will generally want light sources listed last in the Textures list in the Sphere Designer dialog. Since this filter was still under development at the time of this writing, you may find slight changes to your version. Currently, layers cannot be easily moved and new texture layers are added at the end of the list, which means you need to do some planning ahead of time. The default texture and light source layers cannot be moved, so you'll need to duplicate them to move them around in the list.

Textures start with a set of predefined types ranging from a solid color to marble and wood types. The patterns generated by the default settings for each type can be changed using the various sliders in the dialog. Adding turbulence will change the straight lined wood texture to something more organic. Amount and Exp will change the effective transparency and reflectivity of the texture. A preview window allows you to view changes, though this is not updated automatically. Click on the Update button to view the changes.

Sphere Designer, like most of the other rendering filters discussed in this chapter, overwrites the contents of the current layer.

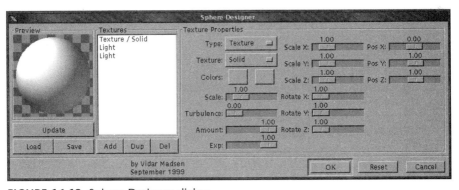

FIGURE 16-13 Sphere Designer dialog

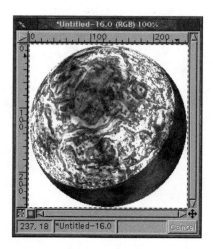

FIGURE 16-14 Example of a Sphere Designer rendering

RECAP

The GIMP's rendering filters generate new images with little or no respect to existing image pixels. Most of the rendering filters are best for adding light fluff to the background of pages, though they can be used to create eye drawing effects as well.

17 Scripting

chapter

IN THIS CHAPTER

- Perl versus Scheme versus Python
- Perl Requirements
- Script Basics
- Sample Program
- Recap

One of the early design requirements for the GIMP was to include a script-able interface—a way for users to automate common tasks. For example, wouldn't it be nice to be able to run a Selective Blur on multiple images without having to open them all manually? Or maybe cut a set of images into identical pieces for use in HTML tables? Scripting allows you to do this type of work.

While the early versions of the GIMP came with just a Scheme-based inter-face, the 1.2 version of the GIMP offers direct and indirect support for up to three different scripting languages: Scheme, Perl, and Python. A fourth language, Tcl, had an external package available for 1.0, but at the time of this writing its support for 1.2 was questionable.

In this chapter we assume a basic knowledge of Perl since a discussion of the language itself is beyond the scope of this book.

◆ Perl versus Scheme versus Python

Of the three scripting languages supported, only Scheme comes without external requirements. Scheme, a Lisplike language, was added early on to the GIMP and was a favorite within developer circles. However, the language itself was not well accepted by non-technical users and information on programming with it has been limited. The Scheme-based interface for the GIMP is referred to as Script-Fu and a few example scripts using this language are provided in its base distributions. Although Script-Fu is a complete scripting interface (with limited error handling), most script writers have migrated to the more powerful Perl interface to the GIMP.

Python is an up-and-coming scripting language that has wide support in many developer environments, including group programming for the Web. While the language is younger than Perl, it has a very vocal user community with many printed manuals to help aid new users learn its structure. Despite this, while Python support exists for the GIMP, it is not widely used yet. Most scripts provided with the base GIMP distributions are provided as Perl scripts.

By far, the most widely used scripting interface for the GIMP is the Perl interface. Perl support is included in the GIMP, but to make full use of it you may need to install some additional Perl modules. Without these additional modules (which are extensions to Perl, not the GIMP itself) many of the Perl scripts provided won't work properly.

Before we get too far into this, a little terminology lesson is in order. Script-Fu is the name of the Scheme-based scripting interface in the GIMP. Scripts written in SIOD, the Scheme subset that the GIMP uses, are known simply as Script-Fu scripts. That part is easy enough to understand. The Perl interface to the GIMP has two of its own modules: GIMP-Perl and GIMP::Fu. GIMP-Perl is the name of the Perl module that knows how to talk to the GIMP. It is, therefore, the primary interface between Perl scripts and the GIMP. GIMP-Perl, however, does not include easy access to a user interface—the GUI features of the GIMP—nor does it make the Procedural Database (PDB) easy to use. User interfaces and PDB abstraction are more properly handled by GIMP::Fu. Some people collectively refer to Perl scripts that use the GIMP-Perl and GIMP::Fu modules simply as Perl-Fu scripts. It's a little confusing, having so many names applied to the Perl-to-GIMP interface, but there are reasons for it all. After a little practice, it will all seem second nature to you anyway.

◆ Perl Requirements

A complete GIMP 1.2 installation will include the necessary modules on the GIMP's side of the Perl interface, but you may need to install a few additional Perl modules manually. Most recent Linux distributions are being shipped with a fairly complete Perl installation, but there are literally thousands of Perl modules available so they can't all be installed with every Linux distribution. The two that are essential to complete the Perl interface to GIMP are the PDL and GtkPerl modules. These can be retrieved from the CPAN archives at

```
http://www.perl.com/CPAN-local/README.html.
```

PDL, the Perl Data Language, allows unique methods of data manipulation which you will want if you need to manipulate individual pixels in your scripts. Since many of the scripts provided in a basic GIMP distribution make use of PDL, you will want this module to access those scripts.

GtkPerl is absolutely essential if you expect to provide a user interface to your scripts. While it's possible, and even desirable in some cases, to run scripts without a user interface, you need GtkPerl in order to get buttons, labels, menus, and so forth. Note that GtkPerl is actually the Perl binding for the GTK+ widget set and can be used on its own for application development outside of the GIMP. GIMP-Perl also provides some additional features that allow you to use some of the GIMP's built-in user interface features, but you still need GtkPerl in order to use those.

The best way to verify that all your bits and pieces are in place is to install PDL and GtkPerl first, then install the GIMP 1.2. When you start the GIMP, look under *Xtns->Perl* for the *Control Center* option. This will start a small window with three buttons. Clicking on *View Perl Status* will open a window showing which features are available. Look for *gimp-1.2, gtk-1.2,* and *pdl* to be listed as present (a Yes entry in the Present column). If they are, you should be ready to work on your first GIMP-Perl script.

Since Scheme has fallen out of favor and Python has few example scripts to work from, we'll limit our scripting focus from here on to Perl scripts for the GIMP.

◆ Script Basics

All scripts interact with the GIMP through the use of the Procedural Database, known simply as the PDB. The PDB contains information about all publicly known functions accessible to scripts (and C-based plug-ins too, for that matter). This information can be viewed directly from the GIMP using the PDB Browser, *Xtns->DB Browser*. This window provides a scrolled list of functions, their input and output parameters, and any help text associated with them. Functions can be searched on using the Search field. Any function which contains the specified string will be shown in the functions list display. To return to the full list, just remove the text from the Search field and click on Search By Name again. You'll refer back to this window often to find the parameters of a specific function while writing your scripts.

Although you can access any function using *gimp_procedure_run()*, most of the PDB is directly abstracted by the *GIMP::Fu* module, making it easy to access just about any feature or plug-in using the function name directly. The interface allows for using procedural calls

```
$mask = gimp_layer_mask($layer);
```

or by accessing the GIMP functions using an object-oriented syntax, such as

```
$mask = $layer->mask;
```

The first step in writing your Perl-Fu scripts is to include the appropriate perl modules. There are 16 modules available, two of which (GIMP and GIMP::Fu) you'll always use, and three others (GIMP::Data, GIMP::Pixel, and GIMP::UI) which you may want if you have more specific needs:

GIMP

This module handles the direct Gimp-Perl communication and must be included in all Perl-Fu scripts. Although you can probably write Perl-Fu scripts using just this module, chances are good you'll want the next one too.

GIMP::Fu

This module provides much of the abstraction and user interface access that your scripts will use. Most Perl-Fu scripts will include this module.

GIMP::Data

Scripts can read and store data directly in the GIMP using this module. This is useful for keeping script data persistent across invocations. Note that this module may be superseded by features of Gimp::Fu.

GIMP::Pixel

If you need pixel level access to images, you'll need to include this module.

GIMP::UI

This module provides scripts to use user interface features normally found in libgimpui (the GIMP User Interface Library) such as Layer and Image menus and buttons for accessing brushes.

All the other modules are normally not needed in user scripts since GIMP::Fu most likely supersedes them.

The basic format for a Perl-Fu script looks like this:

```
#!/usr/bin/perl

use Gimp qs (:auto);
use Gimp::Fu;

register ...;

sub PF_my_script {
  ...
}

exit main;
```

The first line is simply the path to where the Perl executable lives on your system. This line is commonly used by all scripting languages on Unix systems. Since the GIMP simply executes scripts like any other Unix script, you will need to add this line just as you would with any other Perl script.

The next two lines include the GIMP Perl modules most likely to be used by all Perl-Fu scripts. If you'd like to be able to trace the output from the script (using the Perl Control Center) you can add the following line:

```
Gimp::set_trace(TRACE_ALL);
```

The next line is a call to register the script in the PDB. The format of this call is as follows:

```
register(
    "Script Name",
    "Short, one line description".
    "Longer, multi-line help message",
    "Author name",
    "Copyright information",
    "Date of release (or other relevant date information)",
    "Menu/Path/To/Script",
    "Types of Images script works on",
    [
    Input Parameter List...
    ],
    [
    Return Parameter List...
    ],
    \&function_name
);
```

Each of the parameters to the register function is fairly self-explanatory, but a few need to be expanded upon. The first is the Menu/Path/To/Script. This line is used to tell the GIMP where you want the script to be located in the GIMP's menu hierarchy. The first part of this text (all the parameters enclosed in double quotes are text strings) can be either <Image> or <Toolbox>. If your script works on a single image, then you'll want to use the former. If it works independent of any specific image, then you can use the latter. What comes after these is the menu path to your script. If any part of that path doesn't exist, it's created. So

```
<Toolbox>/Muse/Radical
```

would create a new menu next to the *Xtns* menu on the Toolbox, which will do strange things to the way your toolbox looks, but that's sort of up to you. Alternatively,

```
<Image>/Filters/Blur/NewBlur
```

will politely drop your new script in the existing *Filters->Blur* menu, accessible from any Image Window. Note that the last entry in the path is the text that is displayed for users to invoke your script. This differs from the name you gave it as the first parameter to the register function, which is used as the name in the PDB for your script.

The next parameter after the menu path describes which types of images your script will work on. The GIMP can handle RGB, indexed, and grayscale images, plus versions of RGB and indexed with alpha channels. More than one type can be specified by commas separating the text, and the asterisk can be used to wildcard certain types. Table 17-1 summarizes these options.

Table 17-1 Types of Images Supported by GIMP

Option	Meaning
RGB, RGBA, RGB*	RGB Images, RGB with alpha images, or either, respectively.
INDEXED, INDEXEDA	indexed images, indexed with alpha images, respectively.
GRAY	grayscale only images.
*	Any type of image.

Note that these options only make sense for scripts that work on specific images, so this parameter is ignored if the menu path starts with <Toolbox>.

The Input Parameter List

Scripts can accept input from users or have them passed in by other scripts that call them via the PDB interface. The input parameter list in the register function defines what parameters to accept and their types. Each line in the parameter list has the following format:

```
[ type, "name", "description" [, defaults , optional args] ]
```

The *type*, *name*, and *description* are mandatory for each parameter. The *defaults*, while not mandatory, will allow you to provide reasonable defaults for the parameters should users or callers not provide any values. The *optional arguments* are necessary for some types of parameters, such as sliders or spinners. Note: The brackets around the defaults and optional args aren't necessary as shown, although some defaults or optional args may be Perl lists which do require their own brackets.

There are quite a few types you can specify for script parameters, ranging from variations on integers and strings to brush and pattern names. The complete list is too long for this text, but we can show an example set of input parameters that would cover the range of types.

```
[ [PF_INT32,    "Count",    "Number of iterations",2     ],
  [PF_FLOAT,    "Time",     "A seed value",       0.555  ],
  [PF_STRING,   "Name",     "String to display",  "Muse" ],
  [PF_COLOR,    "Border",   "Red,green and blue",[255,0,0]],
  [PF_IMAGE,    "Image",    "An image id"                ],
  [PF_DRAWABLE,             "Drawable","A drawable id"   ],
  [PF_CHANNEL, "RGBA",      "A channel id"               ],
  [PF_LAYER,    "Layer",    "A layer id"                 ],
  [PF_TOGGLE,   "Yes or No","Work on a copy?"    1       ],
  [PF_SLIDER,   "Blur",     "Amount to blur",     45,     [0,100,1] ],
  [PF_SPINER,   "Angle",    "Rotation Angle",     30,     [0,180,1] ],
  [PF_FONT,     "Font",     "Font for name text"         ],
  [PF_BRUSH,    "Brush",    "Brush to use for painting"  ]          ],
```

The return parameters list is just like the input parameter list, but specifies the values returned from the script. If no values are returned, then you can leave this list empty.

The Functional Subroutine

The last parameter in the register function is a reference to a Perl subroutine. This subroutine is actually where you start your real work. In it, you'll make your calls to PDB functions in order to create and manipulate layers, masks, selections, and just about anything else the GIMP offers. In the sample script later in this chapter I called the subroutine *PF_my_script*, but you should use something more descriptive (in the previous register function example I simply called it *function_name*). Be sure to use a name that isn't already in use in the PDB or the results will be unexpected! You can use the *Xtns->DB Browser* to search for the name in the database.

Input parameters are passed to your subroutine via the @_ Perl array. From that point on you have control of what gets done with the arguments. The first two elements of this array are always the image id and the drawable id no matter what else you require as input parameters. It's important to remember that fact if your script expects to work on the image from which the script was invoked. To use these arguments, you can do something like

```
my($img,$layer,$xlfd,$string) = @_;
```

as the first line of your subroutine. In this example, we assume four parameters have been passed in, the last two of which were ones we explicitly asked for in our register function.

Return values from your script should be passed in directly in the return() call of your subroutine, such as:

```
return($width, $height);
```

The last thing in your script will always be:

```
exit main;
```

This hands control of your script back to the GIMP.

◆ Sample Program

Now it's time to look at an example script. GIMP Perl scripts can be written using either an object-oriented syntax or a procedural interface, or both. It turns out the choice of which to use has less to do with which works better than maintainability. For this example, mixing methods seemed to make the code easier to read.

To get started, let's take a look at a short script called DodgeGFX. This script implements steps that brighten up the dark regions of an image. For example, if you've ever photographed a friend in a shadow with a background lit brightly with sunshine you know that the shadowed region can be underexposed (hiding details). This script will use a trick to bring out those details in the shadows without affecting the lighter regions of the image.

It's a pretty simple process, one that lends itself well to a scripted solution. The steps are:

1. Duplicate the image into a new layer.

2. Desaturate the new layer.

3. Add a layer mask to it.

4. Copy the desaturated new layer into the mask.

5. Blur the mask.

6. Invert the mask, if necessary.

7. Adjust the levels of the mask.

8. Adjust the brightness and contrast of the mask.

9. Change the new layers mode to Screen.

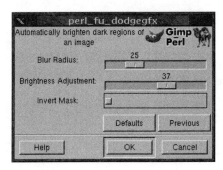

FIGURE 17-1 DodgeGFX GIMP Perl script interface

The code for this script follows. After that we'll look at the important aspects of the script in more detail.

```perl
0#!/usr/bin/perl
#
# DodgeGFX - Automatically brightens an images dark regions.

# Make use of the perl interface to the Gimp internals.
use Gimp qw(:auto);

# Make use of the perl interface to the Gimp UI.
use Gimp::Fu;

# The main routine, where processing for this script really starts.
sub DodgeGFX_Run {

    # Grab the input parameters.
    my($img, $drawable, $blur_radius, $brightness, $invert) = @_;

    # Start an undo group so this whole thing can be undone with a single
            # undo operation.
            eval { $img->undo_push_group_start };
```

```perl
    # Duplicate the specified layer.
    $newlayer = $drawable->gimp_layer_copy(1);
    $img->add_layer($newlayer, 0);

    # Desaturate it.
    $newlayer->desaturate();

    # Add a layer mask.
    $newmask = $newlayer->create_mask(0);
    $img->add_layer_mask($newlayer, $newmask);

    # Copy the desaturated layer into the mask.
    $newlayer->edit_copy();
    $newmask->edit_paste(1);
    $float = $newmask->edit_paste(1);
    gimp_floating_sel_anchor($float);

    # blur the mask.
    $newmask->plug_in_gauss_iir($blur_radius, 1, 1);

    # if requested, invert the mask.
    if ( $invert == 1 )
      {
          gimp_invert($newmask);
      }

    # Update the brightness of the layer.
    $newlayer->brightness_contrast($brightness, 0);

    # Set the Layer's mode to screen.
    $newlayer->set_mode(SCREEN_MODE);

    # End the undo group.
    eval { $img->undo_push_group_end };

    # Update the windows and return.
    gimp_displays_flush();
    return();
}


# Register this script with the Gimp's PDB.
register (
   "dodgegfx",                                        # plug-in name
   "Automatically brighten dark regions of an image", # short description
   "blah blah blah",                                  # long description
   "Michael J. Hammel <mjhammel\@graphics-muse.org>", # Author
   "Private License - Copyright 1999 Michael J. Hammel",# Copyright info
   "First release - August 1999",                     # release info
   "<Image>/Filters/GFXMuse/DodgeGFX",                # where to install
   "RGB*, INDEXED*",                                  # where to install
```

```
    [
        [ PF_SLIDER,
            "Blur Radius",
            "Larger blurs smooth the enhancement",
            25, [0, 100, 1]
        ],
        [ PF_SLIDER,
            "Brightness Adjustment",
            "For low contrast images, increase the bright-
            ness",
            0, [-127, 127, 1]
        ],
        [ PF_TOGGLE, "Invert Mask", "", 0 ]
    ],
    \&DodgeGFX_Run                          # main routine
);

# Hand control back to the Gimp.
exit main();
```

Let's break this script down, starting at the top. This script will use two of the GIMP Perl modules, *GIMP* and *GIMP::Fu*. The first provides access to the GIMP PDB. This is what lets you access the GIMP's plug-in API. It's what you need to access the blur, selection, paint, and other functions of the GIMP. We import this module using the line

```
use Gimp;
```

The second module, GIMP::Fu, is a convenience tool that provides a simplified and consistent user interface for GIMP Perl scripts. GIMP::Fu is the module that provides the register function, which in turn is what you use to describe the buttons, sliders, and input fields you'll have in the interactive version of your script. Keep in mind that your scripts can run both interactively (with a window) or noninteractively, or called from another script or plug-in. The line which imports GIMP:Fu looks like this:

```
use Gimp::Fu;
```

If you're interested in designing your own user interfaces, you can skip using GIMP::Fu and just use the GIMP module along with the Perl-Gtk interface directly. We'll talk about how to do this, and why you might want to do so, a little later in this chapter.

Moving on, you'll see the definition of a subroutine called *DodgeGFX_Run*. This subroutine could be called anything, but it is where your scripts do most of their real work. Later, when we get to the register function, we'll be referencing this routine.

The Register Function

Before we look at the internals of the DodgeGFX_Run routine, we should take a look at that *register* function. Although it might not look like it, register is a function and it's part of the GIMP::Fu package. The first argument to this function is the name of the script as it will be used in the PDB. But there's a catch: The name must be all lowercase. If it's not, it won't work. You'll get an error message on the console (or from wherever you started the GIMP).

The rest of the arguments are commented but a couple deserve more detail. First, the long description is the text that is displayed with the Help button (the Help button is automatically provided by GIMP::Fu). You can put this into a variable and then reference it from within the register function, just to make the code a little more readable.

The next argument of interest is the menu location. This is where you tell GIMP::Fu to install your script in the menu hierarchy. In this case, I've asked for my script to be installed in the Image Window's menus, under the Filters submenu. I'm also asking that a new subcategory be created under the Filters menu called GFXMuse, and that this script will be under that menu.

The second thing to notice is that I've asked the GIMP to create a new submenu under filters. Creating new menus is done automatically by the GIMP as long as the base location is recognized. There are two base locations, either <image> for the Image Window menus or <toolbox> for the toolbox menus. You can't add these filters to the other commonly used menus, such as those in the Layers and Channels dialog. If you try using <layers> instead of the other base locations, the GIMP would simply ignore your plug-in.

Input Arguments

Two arguments below the menu location is a Perl list construct that defines both the input arguments passed to your subroutine and the look of the user interface. The arguments are a little hard to grasp at first, but they make sense once you get the hang of it.

Talking in Perl speak now, each element of the input argument list is a list itself. These element lists are made up of four mandatory and one optional element. The first element is the type of display feature to use for interactive use of the script—buttons, text input, color selectors, etc. In this example, in the first element list, I use a PF_SLIDER. This means the user interface will have a horizontal slider that can be used to set a value. PF_SLIDER is one of many possible options here: PF_INT, PF_TOGGLE, PF_COLOR, and PF_GRADIENT are others.

The next field is the name of the parameter. Although most of the scripts I've seen make this look like a Perl variable name, it doesn't appear to be. In my example I used a name with spaces in it (which is not allowed as a Perl variable name—at least not as far as I know). This name is the text placed in the user interface to the left of the display feature we just defined. A caveat: Using spaces in the name makes the display look better, but may cause warnings to be printed on the console during startup for the GIMP. As far as I can tell, you can ignore the warnings.

After the name is the text used in the tooltip for this display item. This should be descriptive text, but not too long. If you need to make a thorough explanation, use the long description field of the register function.

One thing you can't do using just GIMP::Fu is generate a menu of layers or images. This is because you don't know what those layers or images are prior to calling the register function. If you need to do this, you'll need to make use of the GIMP::UI package. The only problem here is that the GIMP Perl documentation doesn't explain how I stick a new option menu created with GIMP::UI into the user interface.

The last field on an input parameter list element is optional and contains display feature-specific values. For the slider, I provided a list of three values: the default value, the low value, and the high value. If you have done any GTK programming this should be fairly familiar to you.

After the input arguments you can place a set of output arguments. However, this script doesn't return any values so that list of arguments is left out.

Finally, the reference to the subroutine we defined earlier is added. This is the actual name of the routine. Unlike the first argument to register, this one is case-inspecific.

Back into the Subroutine

Now let's get back into the subroutine. Arguments into your script are positional, that is, you don't have to give specific names to the arguments, you just have to be sure you list your variables in the same order as the GIMP will pass them to you.

All scripts located under the <image> base path get the image and layer id passed in by default. These scripts tend to work on specific images or layers, so this makes sense. The image id is the first argument and the layer id is the second argument. Your input arguments come after those. Scripts that get installed under the <toolbox> base path do not get passed the image or layer ids. In my example, you'll see that I have the image and layer id variables ($img and $drawable, respectively) listed first, followed by my three input variables ($blur_radius, $brightness, and $invert). Notice that my variables are listed in the same order as they've been defined in the register functions list of input arguments. It's easy to get these mixed up and cause some strange errors, so double-check them before pulling your hair out. Oh, if you're not familiar with Perl, this line:

```
my($img, $drawable, $blur_radius, $brightness, $invert)
= @_;
```

is used to assign the input arguments to their variables. If you've done shell scripting, @_ is sort of like $*—it contains the entire set of input values.

The first functional call to the GIMP's internal routines is the line to start an undo group.

```
$img->undo_push_group_start;
```

Undo grouping allows you to perform multiple operations from within your script but allows the user to undo them all with a single Ctrl-Z keypress. It's a simple thing to do, and your users will really appreciate it, so get in the habit of making this call at the start of all your scripts.

At the end of the script you'll see the companion call which ends the undo grouping:

```
$img->undo_push_group_end;
```

Everything between these two calls gets grouped for a single undo operation.

The next call to the GIMP internals comes right after the undo group start call. Here, I duplicate the current layer. A couple of things to note here. First, I've called the layer variable "drawable." You'll hear the term drawable used quite a bit with the GIMP. It is a generic term referring to just about any object which can be directly drawn in; layers and masks are the most common.

In any case, the variable drawable is used as an object and the layer copy routine is accessed as a method from this object:

```
$newlayer = $drawable->gimp_layer_copy(1);
```

The single argument, "1," tells the method to add an alpha channel to the layer if it doesn't already have one. If you look in the PDB, the *gimp-layer-copy* function actually has two arguments. The first is the layer id and the second is the alpha channel setting. Here, we don't have to give the layer id because the method is called in context to the layer identified by the drawable variable. For those of you who, like me, are not familiar with object-oriented programming, this can be a little tricky. You'll have to look at the PDB entry for the function you want to call and then determine what input arguments are applicable.

Alternatively, you can use the procedural interface:

```
gimp_layer_copy($drawable, 1);
```

Most of the example script uses the object-oriented interface, but a few places use the procedural calls. The main reason for mixing the two methods is to make the code more readable. Well-written, easily maintained code needs to read like a story. If you can't follow the story, you aren't going to be too happy being forced to read the whole thing.

An interesting call comes when we blur the image:

```
$newmask->plug_in_gauss_iir($blur_radius, 1, 1);
```

What makes this different from other calls is that this is not a core GIMP feature; it's a call to another plug-in. Notice the prefix, *plug_in*. Although this particular plug-in, the Gaussian Blur IIR, is likely to be available to all users (since it's part of the basic GIMP distribution), not all plug-ins will be available for every user. As a script writer, you may want to verify that the plug-ins you need are available before allowing the script to run. A call to *gimp_procedural_db_query()* should probably be made to verify those plug-ins are available and, if not, allow the script to exit gracefully. Reporting errors visually isn't possible using GIMP::Fu, so you'll probably end up writing error messages to an error file.

Further along, you'll find this line:

```
$newlayer->set_mode(SCREEN_MODE);
```

Here I've made use of an enumerated value—SCREEN_MODE. This can be done in a number of places, such as with setting brush and layer modes. Other options include SCREEN_MODE, COLOR_MODE, ADDITION_MODE, and so forth.

Fitting it all Together

So how does all this work? The register function calls *gimp_install_procedure*(), passing in the appropriate arguments so your script will be seen by the GIMP and other plug-ins and scripts. Then control is returned to the GIMP via the *exit main*() call. When a user accesses your script, the GIMP looks up the procedure name in the PDB and makes a call to the subroutine you provided in your register function. At this point your script can call other subroutines as needed. Control is returned to the GIMP when you call your last *return*() statement.

Using GIMP Perl without the GIMP::Fu interface

The only problem with using GIMP::Fu is that it's not all that interactive. It does provide a simplified user interface that most script writers will find sufficient, but if you need a complex interface you may want to skip GIMP::Fu.

GIMP::Fu is a convenience function that does nearly all of the user interface coding for you. To get around it, you would have to use the Gtk package. Note that the naming here stinks—"Gtk" with lowercase "tk" is the Perl binding to GTK+ (all uppercase), the user interface toolkit for creating windowing applications under X. Anyway, you would first give your script access to the Gtk and GIMP packages:

```
use Gtk;
use Gimp;
```

Then you would have to write your application following the same basic layout as a plug-in based on the C API. This would include proper naming of data structures and routines. You could look at GIMP/UI.pm for a little example of how this might work. It's not a job for the faint of heart, however.

GIMP:Fu will automatically save runtime parameters between runs. If you don't use GIMP:Fu, you might want to make use of the GIMP::Data module to save this information manually.

The question, of course, is whether or not using GIMP Perl is really appropriate for plug-ins which require more complex interfaces. That is mostly a developer's choice. There are no clear guidelines for determining which is better, although Gtk (the Perl binding for GTK) is still a little buggy and incomplete. If this causes you problems, you might be better off just using the C interface for your plug-in.

RECAP

In this chapter we examined, in depth, the basic parts to a GIMP Perl script. This includes the register function, the procedural and objected-oriented syntax for accessing the GIMP functions, and the modules necessary to provide that access and a user interface.

18 Site Design 4: Image Galleries

IN THIS CHAPTER

- Goals for This Site Design Project
- Page Layout Considerations
- The Tiled Background
- The Logo
- The First Thumbnail
- Automating the Process
- Generating HTML
- Recap

We've covered everything you need to use the GIMP to generate images for the Web, from using stock logo plug-ins to color management with Curves and Levels to effects processing with the GIMP filters to animation design and scripting with Perl. All that's left is to tie it all together to generate a Web site of your own!

In this chapter we want to build a Web page gallery of thumbnail images linked to their full-sized versions. To accomplish this, we'll divide the project into two pieces: establishing a process for generating a single thumbnail and then automating the process to produce a whole series of images and output the actual HTML.

◆ Goals for This Site Design Project

As always, we want a fast-loading page, this time with 12 thumb-nails. The thumbnails will be placed in a four-row table with three cells in each row. Each thumbnail should be scaled down to be 128 pixels wide but with the aspect ratio (width to height) maintained. As an added flare, we'll convert each thumbnail into an old photograph over a drop shadow. The thumbnails also all need to be in JPEG format, reduced in quality to save file size.

Aside from the table of thumbnails, we'll want a banner of some kind (a simple logo) across the top. We'll also want links to next and previous pages (though we won't consider what those pages might be). Finally, we want a tiled background that pro-vides the appearance of some kind of light-colored texture.

Although we could stretch the project to handle any number of images to be placed on multiple pages, we'll assume only 12 images here and leave the larger project to the properly motivat-ed reader.

◆ Page Layout Considerations

In addition to a table of thumbnails, the gallery page needs only a few other minor features: links to the next gallery page (we assume we'll have one), the banner across the top, and the tiled background. The layout for this kind of gallery is very straight-forward: centered logo at the top, some space between the logo and the thumbnail table, and the centered thumbnail table. The tiled background provides no page layout issues for us; it simply sits in the background tiled across the entire page.

◆ The Tiled Background

Making a tiled background is simple when you start with a tiled pattern:

1. Open a new Canvas window. Make it 256x256 pixels with a white background.

2. Double-click the Bucket Fill tool to open its Tool Options dialog.

3. Select Pattern Fill.

4. Click on the Pattern Quick Tool to open the Pattern Selection dialog.

5. Select the Paper (100x100) pattern.

6. Click inside the Canvas window. The paper pattern will fill the background.

FIGURE 18-1 The paper tile pattern

Since this pattern is already tiled, and as long as we don't apply any filters that change that aspect, we've already handled the hard part. Next we apply some filters. Don't worry, these shouldn't break the tiled aspect of the pattern.

7. Open *Filters->Distorts->Scratches*.

8. Set Angle X to 30, Angle Y to 70, Gamma to 0.30, Smoothness to 4, and Length to 50. Apply the filter.

9. Open *Filters->Map->Bump Map*.

10. Set Azimuth to 155, Elevation to 37, Depth to 4; select the Sinusoidal mapping and the "Compensate for Darkening" option. Apply the filter.

FIGURE 18-2 Scratches applied to the pattern make it appear more random

FIGURE 18-3 The bump map simulates depth, giving the pattern a plaster or cement appearance

All that's left now is to apply a Levels modification.

11. Open the *Image->Colors->Levels* dialog.

12. Set the input levels to 0, 2.25, and 225. This should require that you only change the middle value.

13. Apply the changes by clicking on OK.

The changes made with the Levels dialog lightened the color of the texture. We want a background that has a little character, but not one that distracts the visitor from the real content on the site. This tile should do the trick.

FIGURE 18-4 Our background pattern is complete

To verify the tile aspect of the image has not been lost after running these filters, select *Image->Transforms->Offset* and click on the *Offset by (x/2),(y/2)* bar. Then click on the OK button. The image should change noticeably but there should be no seams running vertically or horizontally through the middle of the image. If there are, then the tiling has been compromised.

To fix the tiling, follow these steps.

1. Select the Clone Tool from the Toolbox.

2. Click on the Brush Quick Tool to open the Brush Selection dialog.

3. Select a soft-edged brush, such as the Circle Fuzzy (19) brush. Don't pick a really large brush—we want to make fairly small changes here.

4. Hold the Shift key down and left-mouse click somewhere in the upper right quadrant of the image. That's the source location. Release the shift key.

5. Now left-mouse click and drag over the visible seams.

The seams should start to go away. You're pasting the source region over the seams with the Clone Tool. If the cloning leaves visible marks around the brush you can try reducing the brushes opacity a little too.

Save the image to a file named tile-bg.jpg. We'll integrate it into the Web page later when we work on our HTML. Now we're ready for our logo.

◆ The Logo

We want a seamless logo overlaid on the background, one that appears to meld into it. This is fairly easy to do using the background we just created and the Carved logo from the Script-FU logo collection.

1. Open the Script-Fu->Logos->Carved dialog from the Toolbox's Xtns menu.

2. Set the text for the logo.

3. Set the font size appropriately. We used a size of 50 pixels, which may be a little large for some displays.

4. Set the background image to the name of the file you saved the tiled background to (if you did as we suggested, that would be tile-bg.jpg). You may need to use a fully qualified path for this.

5. Click on the OK button.

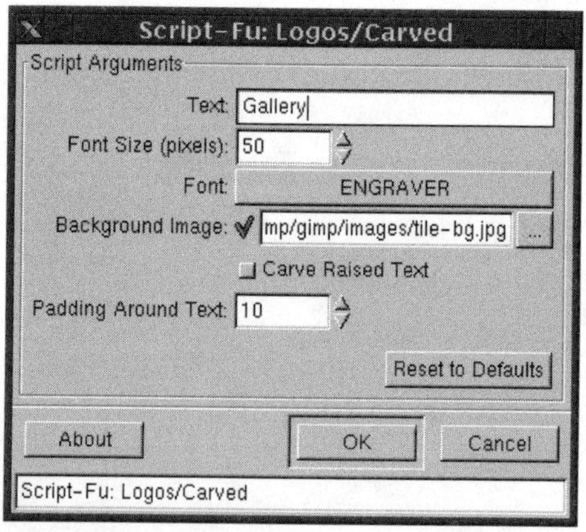

FIGURE 18-5 The Carved logo dialog set for our example

The logo is generated using the Engraver font, which is available in the FreeFonts collection available from many Linux Web sites. If you don't have this font you can try another font, though the results may not be quite as dramatic.

The key to this logo is that we use the same background tile as the one we'll use for the background of our gallery page. Because of the random nature of the pattern (which is part of the reason it tiles so well), the logo images fit in over the background seamlessly. You can't see the edges of the logo!

In our example we actually made three logo images, one each for "Web," "Professionals," and "Gallery," and then centered them vertically on the page. We did this to make the text fit using a 50 pixel font. A smaller font may have permitted us to string all of that text on one line (and in a single logo image), but to make the effect more visible in this example we used a bigger font.

FIGURE 18-6 The gallery page with the background and logo images

◆ The First Thumbnail

We've assumed that we'll have 12 images for our gallery that are large and need to be processed in some way to generate the thumbnails. We'd like a nice thumbnail gallery that appears somewhat uniform (though that may not always be the case). The thumbnails should be 128 pixels wide, but maintain their aspect ratio. The Old Photo and Drop Shadow filters will be applied to all of them as well. The resulting image will need to be saved in the JPEG format using as much quality reduction as is reasonable. The steps for processing therefore are:

1. Resize.

2. Apply Old Photo filter (Script-Fu->Decor->Old Photo).

3. Apply Drop Shadow (Script-Fu->Shadow->Drop Shadow).

4. Flatten the image.

5. Save as a JPEG image.

Let's process the first image manually. By doing so we can specify more clearly the steps we'll need to automate later, including the actual parameters to filters and other GIMP features. We also use this as a dry run to make sure the results are what we really want.

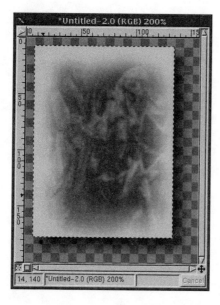

FIGURE 18-7 The first thumbnail

This looks pretty good, but when we try to flatten the layers we lose the transparent areas along the edges. Those areas come from the Drop Shadow filter resizing the image to fit in the shadow. Without resizing, we wouldn't see the shadow. So we have to allow the resizing. So what do we do about the transparent regions?

There are two options here, but only one of them actually solves our dilemma. The first option is to save the file as a GIF instead of as a JPEG. This would mean converting the image to indexed and then merging the visible layers (instead of flattening). The problem with this option is that the shadow, which has soft edges when the image is in RGB format, turns into a hard-edged black region—one that doesn't look all that much like a shadow—when the conversion to indexed is performed. We could use an indexed palette of 256 colors, but that's not optimal for use on the Web.

The alternative is to remove the transparency by placing the background tile in this image as the background layer (i.e., the lowest layer). This solution will work because (a) the tile will fit seamlessly into the existing page background (as we've proven with the logos) and (b) because no scaling of the tile needs to be performed. The latter issue is important. If we scale the original image down to 128 pixels first, then the tile (at 256 pixels wide) will be wider than the thumbnail. We can cut and paste the tile into a thumbnail, move it to the bottom layer, and then merge the visible layers using the Clip to Image option. With the tile image as the background we can save it as a JPEG and preserve the drop shadow appearance!

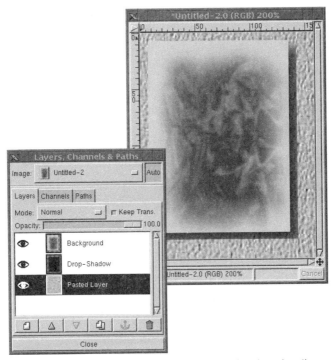

FIGURE 18-8 Background Tile pasted into the thumbnail

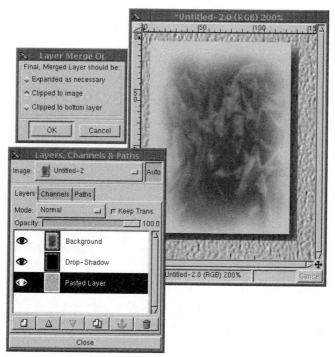

FIGURE 18-9 The layers are merged, clipped to the thumb-nail image size

A little experimentation shows that reducing the image quality in the Save As JPEG dialog to 30% (0.30) gives us an image that is under 4000 bytes but maintains good quality. We'll use that same level for all our images. The quality you use will depend on the images you use, though use of the Old Photo filter (which reduces the color range of the image) will probably permit you to get close to a 30% quality level.

Note that when we applied the Drop Shadow filter the image was automatically resized. In our example it changed to 158 pixels in width. Since all our thumbnails will end up this size, we'll just leave it, though if you really wanted 128 pixels or less you'd have to scale the original image down even further before applying the drop shadow.

FIGURE 18-10 The completed thumbnail (zoomed to double-normal scale in the GIMP) with a sample Web page

◆ Automating the Process

Now we need to automate the steps for processing a single image. Ideally, we'd feed a set of images to a GIMP Perl script and let it process them all, but the only difference between processing one image and a set of images is how you open and close files in Perl. That's a Perl issue and not a GIMP one, so we'll leave the larger project for your own experimentation.

The first thing we want to do is define the user interface. We need to specify the following items:

1. The width in pixels we want the image to be.

2. The image to use as the background layer.

3. The filename to use for the saved image.

4. The directory to save the image to.

The register function for our script will therefore look something like this:

```
$long_description="
This Perl-Fu script processes an image into a thumbnail
with a drop shadow placed over the specified background.
The background can be a tile or color. The image is run
through the Old Photo filter first before the drop shadow
is applied.";

$short_description="Process an image into a thumbnail for a
gallery";

$author="Michael J. Hammel <mjhammel\@graphics-muse.org>";
$copyright="Private License - Copyright 2000 Michael J.
Hammel";

register (
    "gallerygfx",           # plug-in name
    $short_description,#  short description
    $long_description,     # long description
    $author,                # Author
    $copyright,             # Copyright info
    "First release - September 2000",  # release info
    "<Image>/Filters/GFXMuse/GalleryGFX",# where to install
    "RGB*",                 # images to work on
    [
        [ PF_SPINNER,
            "thumbnail_width",
            "Specify the width, in pixels, that you want the
thumbnail to be.",
            128, [20, 200]
        ],
        [ PF_IMAGE,
            "background_image",
            "What image should be used as the background?"
        ],
        [ PF_STRING,
            "output_file_name",
            "What name should be used for the thumbnail
image file?",
            "tn.jpg"
        ],
        [ PF_STRING,
            "output_directory",
            "Where should the file be saved?",
            "/tmp"
```

```
        ]
    ],
    \&GalleryGFX_Run        # main routine
);
```

The PF_IMAGE field will present a menu of currently open images. Users will select which image to use as the background tile from this menu. In essence, they would open the background tile, open each image one at a time, and run this script, selecting that background each time. Note that the thumbnail width, output file name, and output directory will be remembered each time you run this script (or any GIMP Perl script).

The next thing to do is define the layout of the code. The order of processing was determined to be like so:

1. Resize the image.

2. Apply the Old Photo filter (Script-Fu->Decor->Old Photo).

3. Apply the Drop Shadow filter(Script-Fu->Shadow->Drop Shadow).

4. Copy the background image into this image as the bottom layer.

5. Flatten the image.

6. Save it as a 30% quality JPEG image.

The first thing to do is grab the input parameters:

```
# Grab the input parameters.
my($img, $drawable,
$thumbnail_width,
$background_image,
$output_file_name,
$output_dir) = @_;
```

Then we calculate the thumbnail dimensions based on the requested width.

```
# We'll know the width, but we have to compute the height
# to maintain the aspect ratio.
my $image_width = $img->gimp_image_width();
my $image_height = $img->gimp_image_height();
my $height =
int(($thumbnail_width/$image_width)*$image_height);
my $width = int($thumbnail_width);
```

Now we can scale the image down to its thumbnail size.

```
# Scale the image to specified size.
gimp_image_scale($img,$width,$height);
```

...which we follow by passing it through the Old Photo script.

```
# Apply an "old photo" look to it.
script_fu_old_photo($drawable, 0, 1, 1, 1, 0);
```

Since the Old Photo script generates new layers and then flattens the image again, we can't be certain that the drawable id (which identifies the layer in the image) is currently active. So we let GIMP tell us before we move on:

```
$drawable = gimp_image_get_active_layer($img);
```

Now we can apply the Drop Shadow filter:

```
# Apply the Drop Shadow filter to it.
script_fu_drop_shadow($drawable,
"8", "8", "15", [0,0,0], "100.0", 1);
```

Drop Shadow leaves multiple layers in the image, so let's clean up. Note that we can't flatten the image if there are transparent regions in it—those regions would get converted to the background color. We'll use Merge Visible layers instead:

```
gimp_image_merge_visible_layers($img, 0);
```

Once again, make sure we have the correct id for the layer that's left:

```
$drawable = gimp_image_get_active_layer($img);
```

The two filters have been applied. The next step is to copy in the tile image, move it to the bottom layer, then flatten the image. We do this by getting the active layer of the tile background image, selecting all of that layer, doing an *Edit->Copy* followed by *Edit->Paste* into the thumbnail image, and converting the floating layer this creates into a new layer that we move to the bottom of the thumbnail image. Note the extra call to *gimp_selection_none()*—this turns off the selection we just made. No sense leaving around bits and pieces of our actions, right?

```
my $new_drawable =
gimp_image_get_active_layer($background_image);
gimp_selection_all($background_image);
```

```
gimp_edit_copy($new_drawable);
gimp_selection_none($background_image);
$new_drawable = gimp_edit_paste($drawable, 0);
gimp_floating_sel_to_layer($new_drawable);
gimp_image_lower_layer_to_bottom($new_drawable);
```

Now we can flatten the image because the newly pasted tile background is the bottom layer and has no transparent regions.

```
gimp_image_flatten($img);
```

Now make sure all the Canvas windows have been updated:

```
gimp_displays_flush();
```

Finally, save the image to the specified file.

```
my $filename = join("/", $output_dir, $output_file_name);
$drawable = gimp_image_get_active_layer($img);
file_jpeg_save($drawable, $filename, $filename, 0.30, 0,
1, 0, "", 0, 1, 0, 0);
```

The full listing will look like this. Note that there are some extra lines inserted to provide visual progress updates to the user. We leave it as an exercise for the reader to look up in the PDB and see what these calls mean.

```
# Make use of the Perl interface to the Gimp internals.
use Gimp qw(:auto);

# Make use of the Perl interface to the Gimp UI.
use Gimp::Fu;

# Gimp:set_trace(TRACE_ALL);

# The main routine, where processing for this script
# really starts.
sub GalleryGFX_Run {

    # Grab the input parameters.
    my($img, $drawable,
        $thumbnail_width,
        $background_image,
        $output_file_name,
        $output_dir) = @_;

    # We'll know the width, but we have to compute the
height
```

```
# to maintain
# the aspect ratio.
my $image_width = $img->gimp_image_width();
my $image_height = $img->gimp_image_height();
my $height =
 int(($thumbnail_width/$image_width)*$image_height);
my $width = int($thumbnail_width);

# Display a progress indicator.
gimp_progress_init("GalleryGFX is working...", -1);

# Scale the image to specified size.
gimp_image_scale($img,$width,$height);

# Apply an "old photo" look to it.  The sleep() is a
delay
# to allow the script to finish before we try to run
# any other plug-ins on it.
script_fu_old_photo($drawable, 0, 1, 1, 1, 0);

sleep(1);
gimp_progress_update(0.25);
sleep(1);
gimp_progress_update(0.50);

$drawable = gimp_image_get_active_layer($img);

# Apply the Drop Shadow filter to it.
script_fu_drop_shadow($drawable,
    "8", "8", "15", [0,0,0], "100.0", 1);

sleep(1);
gimp_progress_update(0.75);
sleep(1);
gimp_progress_update(0.90);
gimp_image_merge_visible_layers($img, 0);

$drawable = gimp_image_get_active_layer($img);

# Copy the background tile into the image and make it
# the background.
my $new_drawable =
     gimp_image_get_active_layer($background_image);
gimp_selection_all($background_image);
gimp_edit_copy($new_drawable);
gimp_selection_none($background_image);
$new_drawable = gimp_edit_paste($drawable, 0);
gimp_floating_sel_to_layer($new_drawable);
gimp_image_lower_layer_to_bottom($new_drawable);

# Flatten the image.
```

```perl
    gimp_image_flatten($img);

    # Update the windows and return.
    gimp_displays_flush();

    # Save the image to a file.
    my $filename = join("/", $output_dir,
$output_file_name);
    $drawable = gimp_image_get_active_layer($img);
    file_jpeg_save($drawable,
        $filename, $filename, 0.30, 0, 1, 0, "", 0, 1, 0, 0);

    # gimp_progress_update(0.99);
    return();
}


$long_description="
This Perl-Fu script processes an image into a thumbnail
with a drop shadow placed over the specified background.
The background can be a tile or color. The image is run
through the Old Photo filter first before the drop shadow
is applied.";

$short_description="Process an image into a thumbnail for a
gallery";

$author="Michael J. Hammel <mjhammel\@graphics-muse.org>";
$copyright="Private License - Copyright 2000 Michael J.
Hammel";

# Register this script with the Gimp's PDB.
register (
    $short_description,# short description
    $long_description,                 # long description
    $author,                           # Author
    $copyright,                        # Copyright info
    "First release - September 2000",  # release info
    "<Image>/Filters/GFXMuse/GalleryGFX",# where to install
    "RGB*",              # images to work on
    [
        [ PF_SPINNER,
            "thumbnail_width",
            "Specify the width, in pixels, that you want the
thumbnail to be.",
            128, [20, 200]
        ],
        [ PF_IMAGE,
            "background_image",
            "What image should be used as the background?"
        ],
        [ PF_STRING,
            "output_file_name",
```

```
                "What name should be used for the thumbnail
        image file?",
                "tn.jpg"
        ],
        [ PF_STRING,
                "output_directory",
                "Where should the file be saved?",
                "/tmp"
        ]
    ],
    \&GalleryGFX_Run    # main routine
);

# Hand control back to the GIMP.
exit main();
```

One other note: There are a number of calls to sleep() in this code. These calls are necessary to work around a problem with serializing calls to plug-ins from other plug-ins. This problem was unresolved at the time of this writing but may have been fixed by the time it reached your hands. If it has been fixed, then leaving the calls to sleep() in place won't hurt anything—other than to slow the script down just a tad.

◆ Generating HTML

All that's left is to run this script to generate our thumbnails and write up some HTML to handle it. It may sound like a lot of work, but it's not. In fact, it's mostly a bunch of cutting and pasting. Here's the code:

```
<HTML>
<HEAD>
</HEAD>

<BODY background="images/tile-bg.jpg">

<CENTER>
<IMG SRC="images/logo1.jpg"><br clear=both>
<IMG SRC="images/logo2.jpg"><br clear=both>
<IMG SRC="images/logo3.jpg">
</CENTER>

<table align=center>

<tr>
```

```
<td align=center valign=middle><IMG
SRC="images/tn1.jpg"></td>
<td align=center valign=middle><IMG
SRC="images/tn2.jpg"></td>
<td align=center valign=middle><IMG
SRC="images/tn3.jpg"></td>
</tr>

<tr>
<td align=center valign=middle><IMG
SRC="images/tn4.jpg"></td>
<td align=center valign=middle><IMG
SRC="images/tn5.jpg"></td>
<td align=center valign=middle><IMG
SRC="images/tn6.jpg"></td>
</tr>

<tr>
<td align=center valign=middle><IMG
SRC="images/tn7.jpg"></td>
<td align=center valign=middle><IMG
SRC="images/tn8.jpg"></td>
<td align=center valign=middle><IMG
SRC="images/tn9.jpg"></td>
</tr>

<tr>
<td align=center valign=middle><IMG
SRC="images/tn10.jpg"></td>
<td align=center valign=middle><IMG
SRC="images/tn11.jpg"></td>
<td align=center valign=middle><IMG
SRC="images/tn12.jpg"></td>
</tr>

</TABLE>
```

FIGURE 18-11 A full page of thumbnails with the background and logo

RECAP

And that's it! Congratulations! You've found your way through the levels, layers, and filters that make the GIMP the powerful Web tool you can't live without. Now it's time to stroll forward, confident in your new skills, to dazzle the world!

A Toolbox Reference

The Toolbox is the main window for the GIMP from which the most commonly used tools can be accessed. In the 1.2 release, the Toolbox can be resized to allow any rectangular layout (rows and columns) that suits the user's needs. The default configuration is shown in Figure A-1. This appendix is a quick reference guide to the tools in the toolbox, providing their keyboard shortcuts and descriptions of what each tool is used for. Screenshots of the tool and its Tool Options dialog are also provided. Remember that the Tool Options dialog is opened by double-clicking on a Tool icon in the Toolbox. Keyboard shortcuts represent the keys that can be pressed within a Canvas window or the Toolbox in order to activate that tool.

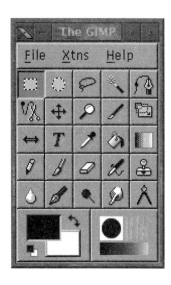

FIGURE A-1 The default Toolbox layout

The tools have been organized into the following categories for easier reference:

Selection Tools

- Rectangular
- Elliptical
- Freehand
- Fuzzy
- Bézier
- Intelligent Scissors

Transformation Tools

- Move
- Zoom
- Crop
- Transform
- Flip

Paint, Text, and Color Tools

- Text
- Color Picker
- Bucket Fill
- Blend Tool (Gradients)
- Pencil
- Paintbrush
- Eraser
- Airbrush
- Ink Tool

Artist Tools

- Clone
- Convolver
- Dodge and Burn
- Smudge
- Measure

Colors and Patterns

◆ Selection Tools

Tool: Rectangular Selection

Shortcut: **r**

FIGURE A-1A
Rectangular Selection
Icon

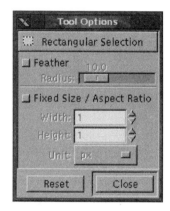

FIGURE A-1B Rectangular Selection
Tool Options

Selects a rectangular region of an image in the current layer using a moving dotted outline. The outline is referred to as *marching ants* due to their appearance, although this behavior can be disabled from the Preferences dialog.

TOOL OPTIONS

Feather: Allows for an antialiased edge of Radius width pixels to be centered over the edge of the selection.
Fixed Size / Aspect Ratio: Allows the user to create selections of the specified aspect ratio (width to height) in the specified units (pixels, points, inches, etc.) using a single click and drag. The selection is anchored on the click point and opened in the direction of the drag. The default ratio is 1 pixel.

Tool: Elliptical Selection

Shortcut: **e**

FIGURE A-2A Elliptical
Selection Icon

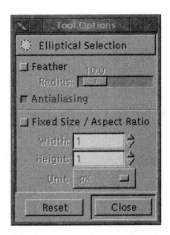

FIGURE A-2B Elliptical Selection Tool
Options

Selects an elliptical (oval or circular) region of an image in the current layer using the marching ants outline.

TOOL OPTIONS

Feather: Same as Rectangular selection.
Fixed Size / Aspect Ratio: Same as Rectangular selection.
Antialiasing: Allows smoother-edged elliptical selections without feathering.

Tool: Freehand Selection

Shortcut: **f**

FIGURE A-3A Freehand
Selection Icon

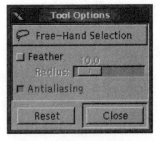

FIGURE A-3B Freehand Selection Tool
Options

Allows selection of any shaped region using a freehand drawing method. Click and drag around the region of interest. When done, release the mouse button and the start and end points will be joined by a straight line, closing the selection loop.

TOOL OPTIONS

Feather: Same as Rectangular selection.
Antialiasing: Allows smoother-edged elliptical selections without feathering.

Tool: Fuzzy Selection

Shortcut: **z**

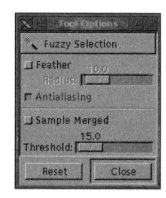

FIGURE A-4A Fuzzy Selection Icon

FIGURE A-4B Fuzzy Selection Tool Options

Selects a continuous region of pixels that are within a threshold range in value from the source pixel clicked on by the user.

TOOL OPTIONS

Feather: Same as Rectangular selection.
Antialiasing: Allows smoother-edged elliptical selections without feathering.
Sample Merged: By default, the Fuzzy Select tool will select pixels based on their values in the current layer. The Sample Merged option will select pixels by the visual appearance, that is, by their merged values for all layers.
Threshold: The maximum value above the seed pixel below which all pixels are selected.

Tool: Bézier Selection

Shortcut: **b**

FIGURE A-5A Bézier Selection Icon

FIGURE A-5B Bézier Selection Tool Options

Allows the selection of any region using Bézier curves. Curves are modifiable using control points and handles. Click around region to drop control points. Click again in the first control point to close the selection but not activate it. Click in any control point and drag outward to view handles. Click on handle end points and drag to adjust the curve. Hold the Control key down, click, and drag a control point to move its location. Once the curve is complete, click inside the outline of the path created to activate the selection.

TOOL OPTIONS

Feather: Same as Rectangular selection.
Antialiasing: Allows smoother-edged elliptical selections without feathering.

Tool: Intelligent Scissors Selection

Shortcut: **i**

FIGURE A-6A Intelligent Selection Icon

FIGURE A-6B Intelligent Selection Tool Options

Intelligent Scissors attempts to find edges in an image between two click points where the color variations follow distinct visual outlines. The user clicks along the visual line to drop control points and the Intelligent Scissors automatically provide a freeform line between the nearest two control points which, with luck, follows the visual outline. The outline must be closed by clicking on an existing control point. Once the outline is closed, the selection may be activated by clicking inside the outline.

TOOL OPTIONS

Feather: Same as Rectangular selection.
Antialiasing: Allows smoother-edged elliptical selections without feathering.

◆ Transformation Tools

Tool: Move

Shortcut: **m**

FIGURE A-7 Move Icon

Moves the current layer or selection.

NO TOOL OPTIONS.

Tool: Zoom (Magnify)

Shortcuts: **Shift-m, =, -**

FIGURE A-8A Zoom Icon

FIGURE A-8B Zoom Tool Options

Zooms in or out on the current image. Works only on the image as a whole and not on individual layers. *Shift-m* activates the zoom tool so that clicks in the Canvas window will perform the zoom. A zoom selection can also be made using the mouse in this mode. The = (equal sign) key permits a quick zoom in and the − (minus) key zooms out.

TOOL OPTIONS

Allow Window Resizing: When set, the Canvas window automatically resizes to fit the zoomed region.
Tool Toggle: Sets the direction of the magnification for clicked zooms.

Tool: Crop

Shortcut: **Shift-c**

FIGURE A-9A Crop Icon

FIGURE A-9B Crop Tool Options

Crops a region manually or by using the current selection.

TOOL OPTIONS

Current Layer Only: Crop applies to the current layer only. If not set, crop is applied to the entire image.
Allow Enlarging: If set, crop boundaries can extend beyond the current layer's boundaries.
Tool Toggle: If Allow Enlarging is not set, these toggles determine the behavior of crop regions outside the boundaries of the current layer. The Crop option will limit the action to the current boundaries. The Resize option will permit crop boundaries outside of the current layer boundaries.

Tool: Transform

Shortcut: **Shift-t**

FIGURE A-10A
Transform Icon

FIGURE A-10B Transform
Tool Options

Provides four types of transformations of the current layer or selection: rotation, scaling, shearing, and perspective. Each transformation will change the current layer or selections pixels, with selections being converted to floating selections when the action is performed.

To use a transform, select it from the Tool Options dialog. Then click inside the current layer or selection. If Show Grid is enabled in the Tool Options dialog, then a grid will be displayed, otherwise an outline with control points on the corners is displayed. Click and drag anywhere to perform the transformation. The line or control point closest to the click point will be modified.

Each transform type also has its own dialog for setting and/or showing exact parameters of the transformation.

TOOL OPTIONS

Transform: Allows selection of the type of transformation.
Tool Paradigm: Variations on quality of the transform.
Show Grid: When enabled, shows grid lines in layer to be transformed.
Smoothing: When enabled, performs smoothing along edges of the transformed region.
Show Path: Should always be set.
Clip Result: When enabled, causes the transformed region to retain the original layer or selection dimensions.

Tool: Flip
Shortcut: **Shift-f**

FIGURE A-11A Flip Icon

Figure A-11b Flip Tool Options

Flips the current layer or selection either horizontally or vertically.

TOOL OPTIONS

Tool Toggle: Selects the direction of the flip.

◆ Paint, Text, and Color Tools

Tool: Text
Shortcut: t

FIGURE A-12A Text Icon

FIGURE A-12B Text Tool Options

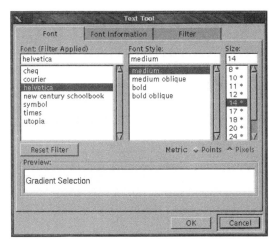

FIGURE A-12C Standard Text Tool dialog

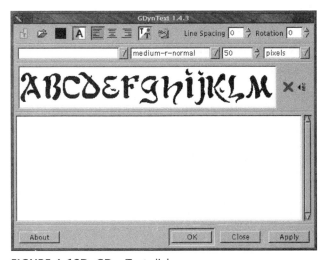

FIGURE A-12D GDynText dialog

Adds text to the current layer or to a new layer.

TOOL OPTIONS

Antialiasing: Allows smoother-edged elliptical selections without feathering.

Border: Sets the number of pixels to pad to the outside edges of the text. Some fonts need this to be set to something other than 0 in order to be rendered properly.

Use Dynamic Text: Uses the alternative Text Tool called GDynText.

Tool: Color Picker

Shortcut: **o**

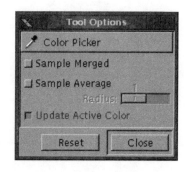

FIGURE A-13A Color Picker Icon

FIGURE A-13B Color Picker Tool Options

Selects and shows the color values for the pixel clicked on by the user. When active and the user clicks on a layer, a dialog window opens to show the chosen pixel's color in RGB and Hex values.

TOOL OPTIONS

Sample Merged: Same as Fuzzy Selection.
Sample Average: Chooses the color based on the average color value of all pixels in the current layer within the radius specified of the chosen pixel.
Update Active Color: When enabled, causes the foreground color to be set to the color of the chosen pixel.

Tool: Bucket Fill

Shortcut: Shift-b

FIGURE A-14A Bucket Fill Icon

FIGURE A-14B Bucket Fill Options

Fills the selected region or layer with a solid color or pattern. The fill will be composited with the existing pixels based on the Opacity and Mode selected in the Tool Options dialog.

TOOL OPTIONS

Opacity: The transparency used in the fill. A setting of 100 means to use a fully opaque fill, while a setting of 50 means the fill is 50% transparent.
Mode: The compositing mode to use.
Sample Merged: Same as Fuzzy Selection.
Threshold: The fill will operate on all pixels within the selected region or layer that is contiguous and within the threshold value of the pixel which the user clicks on to perform the operation.
Fill Type: Use either the foreground, background, or a pattern for the fill operation.

Tool: Blend Tool (Gradients)

Shortcut: **l**

FIGURE A-15A Blend Icon

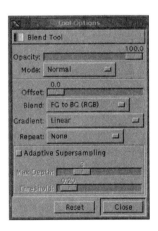

FIGURE A-15B Blend Tool Options

Fills the selected region or layer with a gradient pattern. The fill will be composited with the existing pixels based on the Opacity and Mode selected in the Tool Options dialog.

TOOL OPTIONS

Opacity: Same as Bucket Fill.
Mode: Same as Bucket Fill.
Offset: Changes the rate at which the gradient changes from dark to light.

Blend: Determines what to use for the starting and ending colors of the blend.

Gradient: Determines the direction and shape of the blend.

Repeat: Adds a repeating pattern if the length of the blend is shorter than the space it needs to fill. The length of the blend is determined by the distance the mouse is dragged across the Canvas window.

Adaptive Supersampling: When enabled, increases the quality of the blend along edges in repeated and shaped blends.

Tool: Pencil

Shortcut: **Shift-p**

FIGURE A-16A Pencil Icon

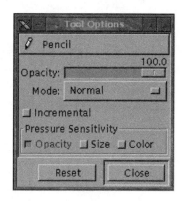

FIGURE A-16B Pencil Tool Options

Draws lines using hard-edged brushes only. The pencil tool will ignore the soft edges provided by some brushes in the Brush Selection dialog.

TOOL OPTIONS

Opacity: Same as Bucket Fill.

Mode: Same as Bucket Fill.

Incremental: Increases the amount of application over a given region with multiple passes of the same brush stroke. A single stroke consists of pressing and holding the left mouse button, dragging it around the Canvas window, then releasing the mouse button.

Pressure Sensitivity: Sets parameters for use with drawing tablets.

Tool: Paintbrush

FIGURE A-17A Paintbrush Icon

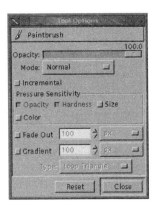

FIGURE A-17B Paintbrush Tool Options

Shortcut: **p**

Draws lines using hard- and soft-edged brushes. Unlike the pencil, the paintbrush will honor soft edges provided by some brushes in the Brush Selection dialog.

TOOL OPTIONS

Opacity: Same as Bucket Fill.
Mode: Same as Bucket Fill.
Incremental: Same as Pencil.
Pressure Sensitivity: Same as Pencil.
Fade Out: Sets the rate at which ink runs out on each brush stroke. If not enabled, ink continues to flow at an even rate throughout the entire brush stroke.
Gradient: If enabled, allows the Paintbrush to paint using the currently active gradient.

Tool: Eraser

Shortcut: **Shift-e**

FIGURE A-18A Eraser Icon

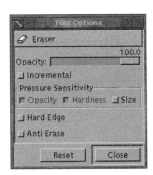

FIGURE A-18B Eraser Tool Options

Removes pixels from the current layer. If the current layer does not have an alpha channel, then erased pixels are changed to the current background color.

TOOL OPTIONS

Opacity: Same as Bucket Fill.
Incremental: Same as Pencil.
Pressure Sensitivity: Same as Pencil.
Hard Edge: When enabled, causes the Eraser to ignore soft edges in the active brush.

Tool: Airbrush

Shortcut: **a**

FIGURE A-19A Airbrush Icon

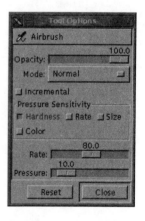

FIGURE A-19B Airbrush Tool Options

Paints using soft-edged brushes in a manner similar to blowing paint on a canvas from an airbrush gun.

TOOL OPTIONS

Opacity: Same as Bucket Fill.
Mode: Same as Bucket Fill.
Incremental: Same as Pencil.
Pressure Sensitivity: Same as Pencil.
Rate: Similar to the spacing option in the Brush Selection dialog, this option determines how often paint is blown (i.e., the pump rate) by the gun.

Pressure: Determines the rate at which paint is applied. Higher values mean more paint is being blown by the airbrush gun with each pump.

Tool: Ink Tool

Shortcut: **k**

FIGURE A-20A Ink Tool Icon

FIGURE A-20B Ink Tool Options

Designed specifically for use with drawing tablets, this tool operates much like the regular paintbrush but using a brush that can be manually shaped. The effect is to produce lines that simulate an old-fashioned ink pen, such as those often used in calligraphy.

TOOL OPTIONS

Opacity: Same as Bucket Fill.
Mode: Same as Bucket Fill.
Adjustment: Sets the size and angle of the pen manually. These options provide manual control of the pen for those using a standard mouse instead of a drawing tablet.
Shape: Used interactively to change the shape of the pen. Click on the small button and drag it. The Type toggles set bounds for the shape of the brush as well.
Sensitivity: Sets the parameters associated with use of a drawing tablet.

◆ Artist Tools

Tool: Clone

Shortcut: **c**

FIGURE A-21A Clone Icon

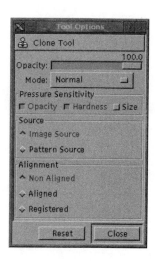

FIGURE A-21B Clone Tool Options

Copies a brushed-sized region to another part of the image. Hold down the Control key and click on the source location to copy from, move the mouse to the destination, then left-click the mouse and drag. The distance from the source and destination pixels is kept constant during the drag, which means the source changes as you drag. Release the mouse button, move to a new destination, and begin again to reset the cloning to be sourced from the original location.

TOOL OPTIONS

Opacity: Same as Bucket Fill.
Mode: Same as Bucket Fill.
Pressure Sensitivity: Same as Pencil.
Source: When set to Image, the source location is taken from the current layer. When set to Pattern, the source is taken from the currently active pattern.
Alignment: Sets the source to stay constant so repeated cloning operations either reproduce (aligned) or overlap (nonaligned).

Tool: Convolver

Shortcut: **v**

FIGURE A-22A Convolver Icon

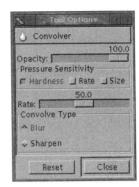

FIGURE A-22B Convolver Tool Options

Blur or sharpen a region interactively based on the currently selected brush shape. Applied in the same manner as the Paintbrush.

TOOL OPTIONS

Opacity: Same as Bucket Fill.
Pressure Sensitivity: Same as Pencil.
Rate: How fast to apply the operation. Higher values mean more blurring or sharpening with each brush stroke.
Convolver Type: Either blur or sharpen.

Tool: Dodge and Burn

Shortcut: **Shift-d**

FIGURE A-23A Dodge and Burn Icon

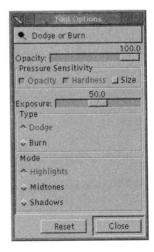

FIGURE A-23B Dodge and Burn Tool Options

Dodge (lighten) or burn (darken) a region of an image interactively using the currently selected brush. Applied in the same manner as the Paintbrush.

TOOL OPTIONS

Opacity: Same as Bucket Fill.
Pressure Sensitivity: Same as Pencil.
Exposure: How fast to apply the operation. Higher values mean the effect is applied more.
Type: Either Dodge or Burn.
Mode: Apply effect to one of the three levels of lightness.

Tool: Smudge

Shortcut: **Shift-s**

FIGURE A-24A Smudge Icon

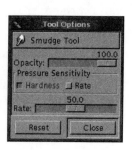

FIGURE A-24B Smudge Tool Options

Smears pixels interactively. Applied in the same manner as the Paintbrush.

TOOL OPTIONS

Opacity: Same as Bucket Fill.
Pressure Sensitivity: Same as Pencil.
Rate: How fast to apply the operation. Higher values mean the effect is applied more.

Tool: Measure

Shortcut: **None**

Interactive method of measuring the distance between pixels and the angle from horizontal. Left-mouse click anywhere in the window and drag to measure distances and angles.

TOOL OPTIONS

Use Info Window: When selected, a dialog window opens showing the measured values. The same values are also displayed in the information box at the bottom of the Canvas window.

FIGURE A-25A Measure Icon

FIGURE A-25B Measure Tool Options

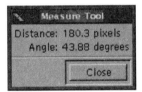

FIGURE A-25C Measure Info Window

◆ Colors and Patterns

Tool: Foreground/Background Selection

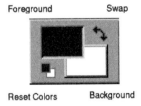

FIGURE A-26 Foreground and Background selection

These items in the Toolbox are used to set the foreground and background colors. By clicking on either the foreground or background boxes you can open the Color Selection dialog, which offers multiple methods of selecting a color. Clicking on the reset icon returns the foreground and background to their default colors. Clicking on the swap arrows will switch the foreground and background colors.

Tool: Patterns, Gradients, and Brush Quick Tools

Clicking on any of these buttons will open the associated dialog, allowing you to select a new active pattern, gradient, or brush.

Brush Selection   Pattern Selection

Gradient Selection

FIGURE A-27 Quick Tool icons in the Toolbox

B Color Management Tools Reference

The GIMP provides a wealth of color management tools for the Web professional. This appendix provides a quick reference to some of the most useful ones.

◆ Referenced Tools

- Curves
- Levels
- Hue, Saturation, Lightness
- Color Balance
- Threshold

Tool: Curves

Menu path: **Image->Colors->Curves**

The Curves dialog is used to adjust the overall brightness for all pixels of a layer or selection, or to adjust the brightness of specific channels. The dialog opens with a diagonal line to represent the existing brightness curve, with the lower left being the darkest pixels and the upper right being the brightest. By clicking and dragging in the graph area of the dialog you can adjust the curve. Each click will add new grab points which allow changes to specific ranges (between the grab points to either side of the point being adjusted).

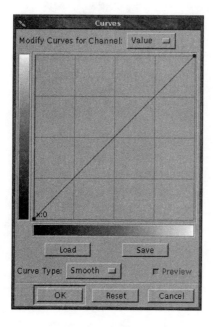

FIGURE B-1A Curves dialog

With the Curves dialog open, clicking the left mouse button in the Canvas window will cause a vertical line to be drawn on the graph at the point associated with the brightness of the selected pixel.

TOOL OPTIONS:

Curve Type: The curve is kept smooth by default. The Curve Type menu allows the user to change to freehand drawings which affect much smaller ranges of pixels.

Preview: Changes to the curve are reflected in the Canvas window immediately when this button is enabled.

Load/Save: Allows the loading and saving of curves to/from files.

Example:

A simple gradient is converted to a wave form gradient by adjusting the Value curve as shown.

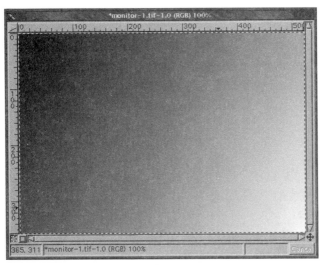

FIGURE B-1B Initial gradient

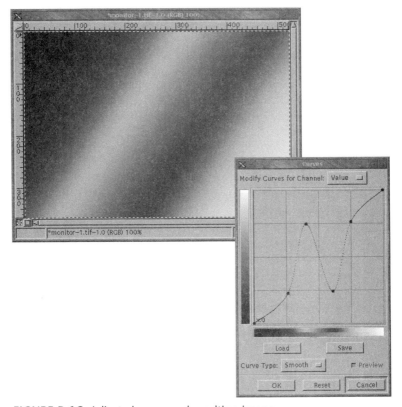

FIGURE B-1C Adjusted curve and resulting image

Tool: Levels

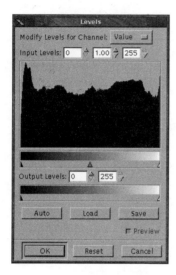

FIGURE B-2A Levels dialog

Menu path: **Image->Colors->Levels**

The Levels dialog is similar to the Curves dialog in that it deals with the relative brightness of the image. However, instead of allowing changes to a range of pixels at a given brightness, the Levels dialog allows changes to the overall distribution of brightness between specified values for the black and white points in an image. In essence, the Levels dialog makes the distribution of pixels fit a curve that runs between the value for the darkest pixel you want (which may or may not be fully black) and the lightest pixel you want (which may or may not be fully white).

Adjustments to a selection or layer's brightness using the Levels dialog is handled by changes to the black, white, and midpoints of the displayed histogram. These are also known as the overall input levels. Moving the black and midpoints to the right darkens the image, while moving the white and midpoints to the left brightens the image. Changes to the black and white points affect specific pixels by stretching the existing histogram, while changes to the midpoint changes the distribution of the levels in the histogram.

By default, the overall value of pixels is adjusted. Changes to individual channels can be done by changing the selected option in the channel menu at the top of the Levels dialog.

TOOL OPTIONS:

Input Levels: Allows manual setting of the input levels. The left field is for the black point, the middle field for the midpoint, and the right field for the white point.

Output levels: Allows changing the overall brightness of the image uniformly across all pixels.

Auto: When selected, the histogram is stretched to force the currently darkest pixel to become fully black and the currently brightest pixel to become fully white. This also has the effect of stretching the distribution of the brightness levels to fit within the new range.

Preview: Changes to the curve are reflected in the Canvas window immediately when this button is enabled.

Load/Save: Allows the loading and saving of curves to/from files.

Example:

The levels of the previous example are adjusted to enhance the wave form.

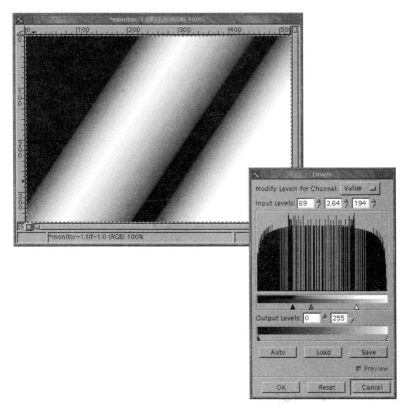

FIGURE B-2B Adjusted levels and resulting image

Tool: Hue, Saturation, Lightness

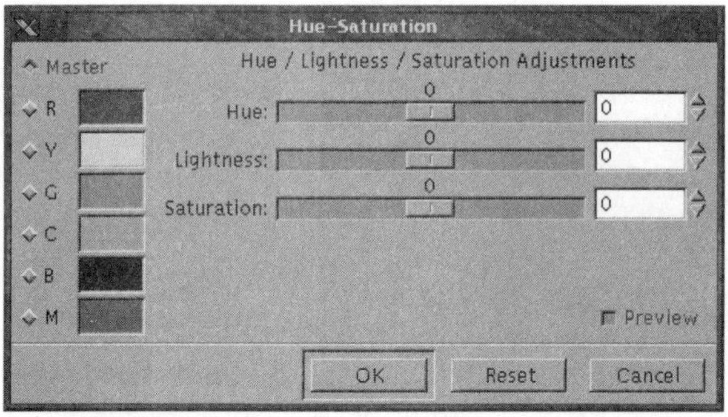

FIGURE B-3A Hue, Saturation, Lightness dialog

Menu Path: **Image->Color->Hue-Saturation**

Hue, Saturation, and Lightness are characteristics of color beyond the more common red, green, and blue components. Each of these characteristics can be adjusted individually across the entire image as well as applied to the red, green, blue, cyan, magenta, and yellow channels of pixels in the current layer or selection.

TOOL OPTIONS:

Hue, Saturation, Lightness: Sliders that adjust each of these color components.
Master Toggle: Set by default, this toggle causes any changes to be applied across all color channels of the current layer or selection.
Color Toggles: Each toggle is mutually exclusive, allowing operation on specific color channels.
Preview: Set by default, this toggle allows changes to be viewed immediately.

Example:

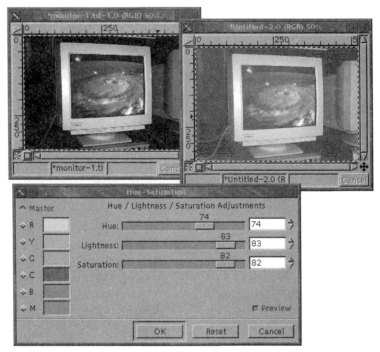

FIGURE B-3B Hue, Saturation, and Lightness-adjusted image

Tool: Color Balance

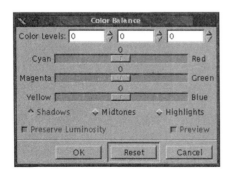

FIGURE B-4A Color Balance dialog

Menu Path: ***Image->Color->Color Balance***

Color Balance allows you to change the color in an image in a manner similar to the Curves tool. The main difference between Color Balance and Curves is that Color Balance can isolate the changes to certain brightness levels (known as Shadows, Midtones, and Highlights), while Curves allows a finer grain control, even down to individual pixel value changes.

Color Balance functions by allowing you to mix colors between pure red, green, and blue and their complimentary colors (cyan, magenta, and yellow, respectively). Complimentary colors can be mixed to produce white light.

Since this tool operates primarily on color and very little on brightness, it is difficult to show a reasonable example in a grayscale image.

TOOL OPTIONS:

Color Levels: Text input values that range from –100 to +100, with each box left to right corresponding to the colors sliders below them.

Cyan/Red Slider: Mixes colors between the complimentary colors of Cyan and Red.

Magenta/Green Slider: Mixes colors between the complimentary colors of Magenta and Green.

Yellow/Blue Slider: Mixes colors between the complimentary colors of Yellow and Blue.

Shade Toggles (Shadows, Midtones, Highlights): Selects which lightness level within the current layer or selection to operate on.

Preserve Luminosity: When set, forces hue (color) changes to not affect brightness levels. This means bright images stay bright even if their colors change.

Preview: Allows changes to be reflected immediately in the Canvas window.

Tool: Threshold

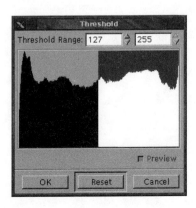

FIGURE B-5A Threshold dialog

Menu Path: *Image->Color->Threshold*

Like the histogram shown in the Levels dialog, the Threshold tool shows an image in black and white and allows the user to select a contiguous region within the histogram. The selected region is shown in black and white in the Canvas window. Because the effect is to convert a layer or selection to black and white, the Threshold tool is a quick way to generate a layer mask from a duplicate of an original layer. Be sure to duplicate the original, however, since Threshold will modify that current layer.

TOOL OPTIONS:

Threshold Range: The selected range. The text input fields can be used to manually select the range or the mouse can be used to interactively select the range within the histogram. Note that only a single contiguous range is permitted.

Preview: Allows changes to be reflected immediately in the Canvas window.

Example:

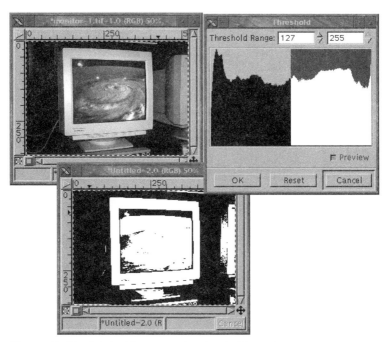

Figure B-5b Original image and a threshold version

C Effects Filter Reference

Effects filters provide a means to modify existing images in predefined ways, generating both recognizable and bizarre results. While not all effects filters are useful in a day-to-day Web design environment, many will find their way into your work over time as both stand-alone tools as well as Web image pipeline processing tools.

◆ Referenced Tools

Blurs

- Blur
- Gaussian Blur IIR
- Gaussian Blur RLE
- Motion Blur
- Selective Gaussian Blur

Distorts

- IWarp
- Polar Coordinates
- Ripple
- Waves
- Wind

Lighting Effects

- FlareFX
- GFlare
- SuperNova

Mapped Effects

- Bump Map
- Displace
- Map Object

Filter: Blur

Menu path: ***Image->Filters->Blur->Blur***

FIGURE C-1A Blur dialog

The simplest of all blur filters, Blur simply mixes pixels with their neighbors using their combined average values. The randomization options determine if a pixel will or will not be blurred. A random number is generated for each pixel and if the value chosen is within randomization percentage, then the pixel is blurred. This filter offers very soft blurs which are not very dramatic in their visual effect.

TOOL OPTIONS:

Random Seed, Time: Sets the seed values for choosing random numbers. If Time is chosen, the seed value is set to the time value used in the current blur and displayed in the Random Seed field the next time blur is used. This allows using the exact same settings for successive uses of the Blur filter.

Randomization Percentage: Sets the percentage of pixels that are to be actually blurred. 100% means all pixels get blurred.

Repeat: Number of times to apply process over all pixels in the selected region.

Filter: Gaussian Blur IIR

Menu path: *Image->Filters->Blur->Gaussian Blur IIR*

FIGURE C-2A Gaussian Blur IIR

This first of the two Gaussian Blur filters is best suited for scanned images such as photos or line drawings. Both Gaussian Blur filters require a radius of greater than one, and the blur amount is based on the standard deviation of the normal distribution of pixel values within the specified radius of the pixel being blurred.

TOOL OPTIONS:

Horizontal, Vertical: Determines the dimensions of the radius of pixels to examine in calculating the blur.
Units Menu: Determines the units of dimensions (pixels, points, inches, etc.) for the blur radius.

Example:

FIGURE C-2B Gaussian blurred image with its original

Filter: Gaussian Blur RLE

Menu path: ***Image->Filters->Blur->Gaussian Blur RLE***

FIGURE C-3A Gaussian Blur RLE dialog

Exactly the same as the Gaussian Blur IIR filter except the algorithm used is more suited to images generated by computer, such as 3D raytraced images.

TOOL OPTIONS:

Identical to Gaussian Blur IIR

Filter: Motion Blur

Menu path: ***Image->Filters->Blur->Motion Blur***

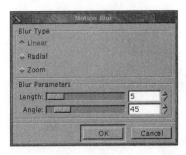

FIGURE C-4A Motion Blur dialog

Simulates motion in multiple directions.

TOOL OPTIONS:

Blur Type: Linear generates left to right motion blurs; radial produces a blur with the appearance of radial lines; and zoom generates motion away from the viewer.
Length: Applies to the apparent length of a linear blur and depth of a zoom blur. Does not affect radial blurs.
Angle: Applies to the direction of the linear blur. Does not affect either other type of motion blur.

Example:

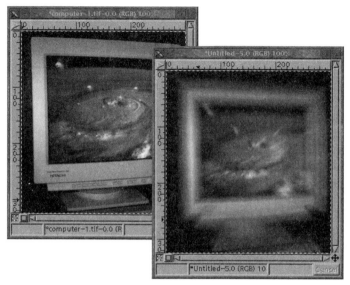

Figure C-4b Motion blurred example

Filter: Selective Gaussian Blur

Menu path: ***Image->Filters->Blur->Selective Gaussian Blur***

FIGURE C-5A Selective Gaussian Blur's Perl-Fu interface

A variation on the Gaussian Blur filters, the Selective Gaussian Blur filter can, with the right value for Max Delta, smooth an image without losing any image details. The effect is to make a photographic image look painted or drawn. The resulting image will look much cleaner. However, the trade-off is that this filter can take exceptionally long to process even relatively small images.

TOOL OPTIONS:

Blur Radius: The radius, in pixels, from the source pixel to use in computing the blurred value.

Max Delta: The maximum difference between the source pixel and its neighbor, below which the neighbor is used in the blur computation.

Example:

FIGURE C-5B Original image and its painted version

Filter: IWarp

Menu path: ***Image->Filters->Distorts->IWarp***

One of the most interesting effects filters available in the standard GIMP distribution, IWarp allows you to distort images interactively from within a selection or entire layer.

Click inside the Preview window and drag to modify the image. The type of modification is determined by the Deform mode. The amount of distortion is determined by the Deform Radius and Deform Amount sliders. The animate options will automatically generate a series of layers that range from the original image to one with the distortions specified, interpolating the sequence to move transitions smoothly from beginning to end.

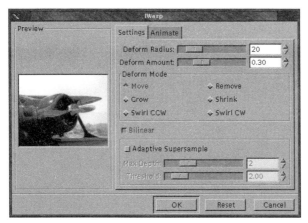

FIGURE C-6A IWarp dialog

TOOL OPTIONS:

Deform Radius: Number of pixels from source; click in preview to modify.

Deform Amount: Higher values make larger changes with less mouse movements.

Deform Mode: Move drags pixels around, Grow expands the pixels, Remove restores pixels to their original settings (a sort of interactive undo), Shrink pulls pixels in towards the mouse position as it's dragged around the images, and the Swirl options twist the pixels around the mouse in either clockwise or counterclockwise directions.

Bilinear: Produces, in some circumstances, a slightly smoother distortion.

Adaptive SuperSampling: When enabled, higher values produce high-quality distortions at the expense of longer computation times. Not often used for Web production due to the small size of images.

Animate: When enabled, causes IWarp to generate a series of layers that simulate a warping from the original image to the final, distorted image.

Number of Frames: Specifies the number of frames to generate between original and final distorted image.

Reverse: Generates from final back to original.

Ping-Pong: Generates frames from original to final and back again.

Example:

FIGURE C-6B IWarped image

Filter: Polar Coordinates

Menu path: ***Image->Filters->Distorts->Polar Coords***

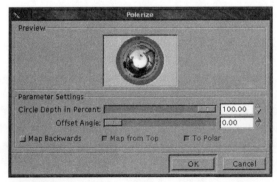

FIGURE C-7A Polar Coordinates dialog

Maps the selection or layer pixels from their current rectangular coordinates to polar coordinates. The effect can be adjusted to set which pixels are used for the outside and inside of the mapping, as well as to set the circular mapping back into rectangular coordinates.

Mapping from rectangular to polar coordinates causes the image to be wrapped into a visually circular image. The empty space left in the rectangular Canvas window will be set to the current background color.

TOOL OPTIONS:

Circle Depth in Percent: 100 percent causes a closed circular mapping, while lesser values leave gaps in the circularly mapped image.

Offset Angle: Moves the closed line of the mapping around the central point. This has the effect of rotating the gap produced around the center of the image.

Map Backwards: When checked, causes the mapping to start with the right side of the image instead of the left.

Map from Top: When checked, the top row of pixels is mapped to the center of the circular image and subsequent rows are mapped towards the outside. When unchecked, the bottom row is mapped to the center of the image.

To Polar: When checked, the mapping is to a circular image. When unchecked, the mapping unfolds the circular mapping back to a rectangular image.

Example:

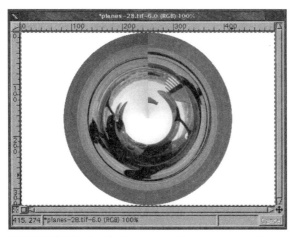

FIGURE C-7B Original image with mapped version

Filter: Ripple

Menu path: ***Image->Filters->Distorts->Ripple***

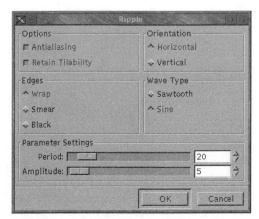

FIGURE C-8A Ripple dialog

Causes wave-type effects. Option for smearing edges may not work in all cases. While good for Web-based images, Ripple's limited periodicity makes it unsuitable for images destined for large prints. Ripples generate flow across the image from left to right or top to bottom.

TOOL OPTIONS:

Antialiasing: Smoothes the waves to prevent stairstepping, though with certain amplitudes and periods this may not help much.

Retain Tileability: Attempts to maintain the tileability of the original image.

Orientation: Direction for individual waves to propagate.

Wrap: Causes left edges to wrap to the right, and so forth.

Smear: Causes the edges to be maintained, smearing them outward to fill space left by pixels moved by waves.

Black: Causes edges left blank by waves to be filled with black.

Wave Type: Sine waves are smooth; sawtooth are straight edges (jagged).

Period: Larger values stretch the waves in the direction of their propagation.

Amplitude: Larger values make the distance between crest and trough wider for individual waves.

Example:

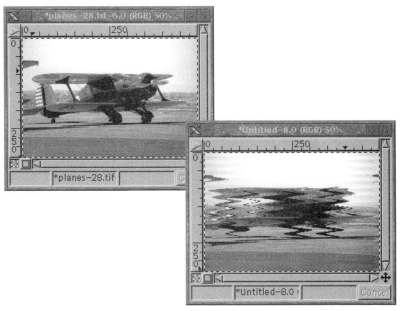

FIGURE C-8B Original and rippled version

Filter: Waves

Menu path: ***Image->Filters->Distorts->Waves***

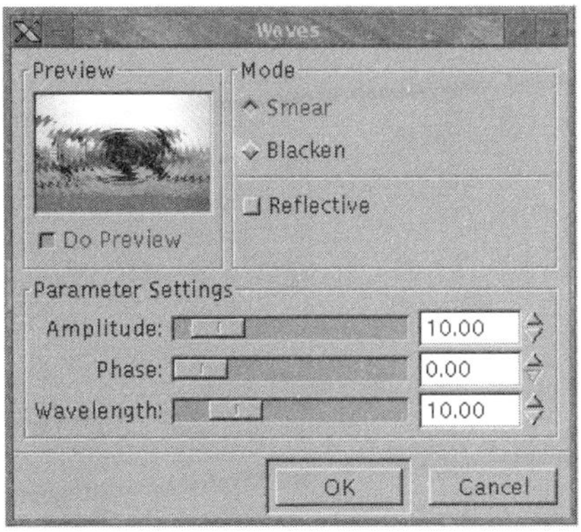

FIGURE C-9A Waves dialog

Similar to Ripple using the default settings, Waves can generate very unusual effects from ordinary images when its options are set to their upper ranges. The Waves filter forms waves, centered in the selection or layer, that radiate outward.

TOOL OPTIONS:

Mode: Smear causes edges to be maintained, while blacken causes edges that are pulled away by the wave calculations to be filled in with black.

Amplitude: Higher values create wider distances between crests and troughs in individual waves.

Phase: Changes the starting point for the direction from which the wave begins to flow.

Wavelength: Higher values increase the number of visible waves radiating out from the central point.

Example:

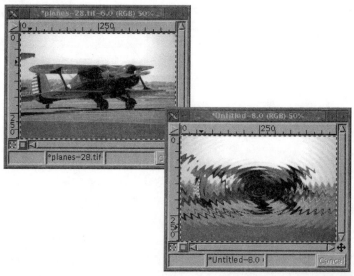

FIGURE C-9B Same original image used for Ripple is now passed through the Waves filter

Filter: Wind

Menu path: **Image->Filters->Distorts->Wind**

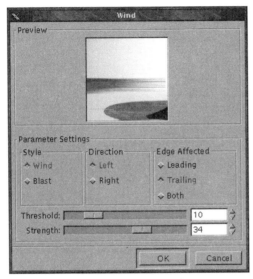

FIGURE C-10A Wind dialog

Smears an image in the specified direction and manner. Similar in style to the motion blur, but with less uniformity to the blurring.

TOOL OPTIONS:

Style: Wind produces an effect that looks similar to dunes being blown, with streaks blurred along visible edges in the image. Blast is a less smooth version of the same thing.

Direction: Determines from which direction the wind would be blowing.

Edge Affected: Where Wind determines a visible edge to exist in the image, this option determines which side of the edge is modified by the effect.

Threshold: Higher values cause less of the image to be affected.

Strength: Higher values cause longer streaks.

Example:

FIGURE C-10B Wind applied to original image.

Filter: FlareFX

Menu path: ***Image->Filters->Light Effects->FlareFX***

FIGURE C-11A FlareFX dialog

Produces simple lens flares. A lens flare is the ring of light, often with spikes radiating from its central point, generated by bright lights causing reflections in a cameras lens.

TOOL OPTIONS:

X, Y, and Preview Window: Allows specifying the exact location of the center of the main flare or, with the Preview Window, the interactive setting of the central point.

Example:

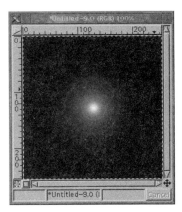

FIGURE C-11B Simple FlareFX on black background

Filter: GFlare

Menu path: ***Image->Filters->Light Effects->GFlare***

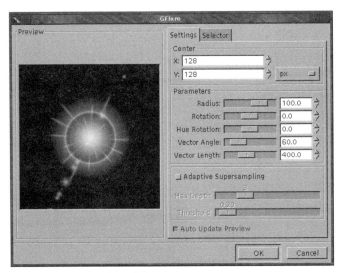

FIGURE C-12A GFlare dialog

Similar to FlareFX but with a large number of additional features. Shape, color, location, number of reflections, and spikes can all be specified. Flares can be saved and edited. A primary flare is positioned and orientated with secondary flares of varying sizes, distributions, and appearance.

TOOL OPTIONS:

Center: Positions the center of the primary flare.
Radius: Size of primary flare.
Rotation: Rotates the rays emanating from the center of the primary flare around its center.
Hue Rotation: Changes the color of the primary flare.
Vector Angle: Changes the rotation of the line of secondary flares around the center of the primary flare.
Vector Length: Changes the length of the line of secondary flares. Larger values stretch the secondary flares further out from the center of the primary flare.
Adaptive Supersampling: Produces smoother effects in some cases at the expense of longer computation times.
Selector: Allows selection of preexisting (i.e., saved) flares.
New/Copy/Delete/Edit: Allows the creation of new flares, copies existing flares, deletes existing flares, or edits existing flare designs.

GFLARE EDITOR OPTIONS:

Glow, Ray, and Second Flare Paint Options: Sets the opacity and blend modes for each aspect of the primary and secondary flares.
Glow Gradients: Sets the shape, angle, and size of the gradient applied as the glow of the primary flare.
Glow size, rotation, and Hue Rotation: Defines the size, rotation and color of the glow. Rotation may not be visible unless the angular gradient changes the shape of the glow.
Ray Gradients: Sets the shape, angle, and size of the gradient applied as the rays that emanate from the center of the primary flare.
Ray Size, Rotation, and Hue Rotation: Defines the size, rotation, and color of the rays emanating from the center of the primary flare.
Ray Spike Number: Sets the number of visible spikes for the primary flare.
Ray Spike Thickness: Sets the width of the spikes.

Second Flares Gradients: Similar to Glow Gradients but applies to secondary flares.
Second Flares Size, Rotation, and Hue Rotation: Same as for Glow options but applies to secondary flares.
Shape of Secondary Flares: Either circular or multisided polygons.
Random Seed: Sets the seed value for the random numbers used to determine the location of the secondary flares.

Example:

FIGURE C-12B Sample GFlare, one of the predefined settings (effect is not as obvious in black and white)

Filter: SuperNova

Menu path: **Image->Filters->Light Effects->SuperNova**

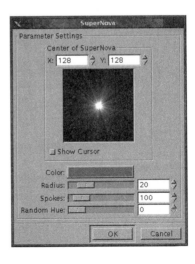

FIGURE C-13A SuperNova dialog

Generates an effect similar to FlareFX but with more defined spokes and no secondary flares.

TOOL OPTIONS:

Center of SuperNova, Preview: Allows setting the effects center manually or interactively.
Color: Sets the color of the effect.
Radius: The size of the effect in pixels.
Spokes: The number of spokes generated.
Random Hue: Higher values vary the color of the radiating spikes at a higher rate. A value of 0 causes all spikes to maintain the hue defined by the Color option.

Example:

FIGURE C-13B Sample SuperNova on a black background

Filter: Bump Map

Menu path: **Image->Filters->Map->Bump Map**

The Bump Map filter provides a simple method of adding depth to 2D images. It works by using a source image's pixel values, ranging from 0 (black) to 255 (white), to specify shadows on a destination image. While this effect works to varying degrees on just about any image, most Web developers will find this filter useful to generate simple 3D frames around images and page sections.

Bump Map can be used to add depth to an image by duplicating the original layer, blurring the duplicate, and using it as the source to bumpmap the original.

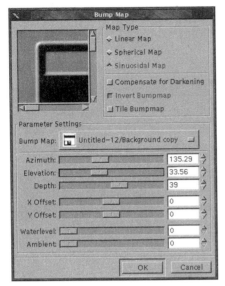

FIGURE C-14A Bump Map dialog

TOOL OPTIONS:

Map Type: Various computational methods for producing the bump map. Linear and Sinuosidal often produce very similar results. Spherical mapping tends to be less dramatic than the other two. Computations for all three usually take about the same time for all images.

Preview Window: Shows only a portion of the resulting image, defaulting to the upper left corner. The window can be moved using the sliders or by clicking inside the preview and dragging it around.

Compensate for Darkening: Increases the brightness of the resulting image so that it matches the brightness of the original image.

Invert Bump Map: Inverts the values of the source image to produce the bump-map effect.

Tile Bump Map: If the source image is smaller than the destination and this option is set, then the source image is tiled across the destination image. Otherwise, the source image is used once.

Bump Map: The source image used to apply shadows to the destination image.

Azimuth: Determines the direction from which the simulated lighting shines, as in the angle to the front, side, or back of the viewer.

Elevation: Also determines the direction of the light source, but here as in how high it is in the sky.

Depth: The simulated depth in the image. Higher values mean bigger shadows.

X, Y Offsets: Adjusts the position of the source image in relation to the destination image.

Water Level: Applies only to source images with Alpha channels. Higher levels of transparency mean lower application of bumpmapping. Increasing the water level increases the amount of Bump Map applied when higher levels of Alpha are present in the source image.

Ambient: Higher values add more light to the image. Since Bump Maps tend to darken an image and the Compensate option may not provide enough light to bring out details, ambient light can be used to brighten a bump-mapped image back near its original levels.

Example:

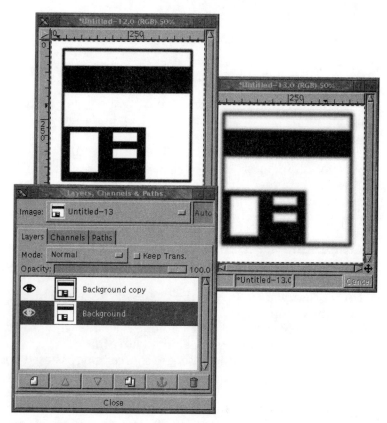

FIGURE C-14B Original and blurred version

FIGURE C-14C Bump-mapped image with blurred version used as the source on the original

Filter: Displace

Menu path: *Image->Filters->Map->Displace*

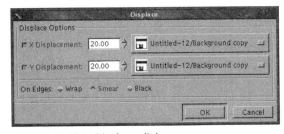

FIGURE C-15A Displace dialog

Moves pixels in the original image by the specified amounts multiplied by the intensity of the corresponding pixels in the displacement map image.

TOOL OPTIONS:

X, Y Displacement: Number of pixels to move.
Option Menus: Used to select the image or layer to use as the displacement multiplier.

On Edges: Determines what to do at the edges of the original image.

Example:

FIGURE C-15B Displaced version

Filter: Map Object

Menu path: **Image->Filters->Map->Map Object**

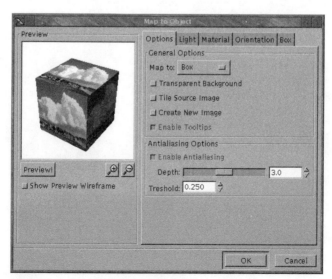

FIGURE C-16A Map Object dialog

Maps a source image onto one of a number of three-dimensional shapes, from a simple plane to boxes, cylinders, and spheres. The direction, color, and intensity of a source light can be set along with the reflectivity of the object on which the image is mapped.

Map to Object will map either an entire layer or the current selection to the object chosen in the Options page of the dialog. Because the detailed effects of lighting and material can be lost on images designed for the Web, Web designers will find this filter most suitable for simple mappings of images with little original detail.

TOOL OPTIONS:

Map To: Sets the 3D object the source image will be mapped to.

Transparent Background: When set, the image generated will have a transparent background; otherwise, the current background color is used.

Tile Source Image: When set, maps the source image to the object by tiling it to fit the object's dimensions. Note that the object's size is only configurable for cylinders.

Create New Image: When set, causes a new Canvas window to be opened with the rendered object.

Antialiasing: These options increase the quality of the rendering. Higher depth values tend to create high-quality renderings, but at the cost of higher compute times.

Light / Lightsource Type: Point lights apply lighting evenly, like a distant sun would do. Directional light applies a cone of light, like a spotlight would do.

Light / Lightsource Color: Specifies the color of the light applied to the object. Primarily affects the light reflection on the object.

Light / Position: Moves the light in space around the object. A position of 0, 0, 0 would be at the objects center. To move the light so it is on the same side of the object as the viewer (and thus display the lighting reflections), use a positive Z value. Y values move the light up and down; X values move it left and right.

Material / Intensity Levels: These values adjust the effect of the light coming from all directions, not just the actual light source. Ambient sets the general light of the entire scene. Higher values brighten and fade the scene. Lower diffuse values even out the reflected light over the entire object's surface, dimming its appearance. Higher values focus the intensity of overall reflection, increasing it more towards the light source's actual reflection.

Material / Reflectivity: Each option here adjusts the effect of the reflection of the light coming directly from the light source.

Diffuse works as it does under the Intensity Levels option, but specifically for the light source reflection. Specular values determine the purity of the light's reflection. The higher the value, the more pure the color at the center of the reflection. Highlight changes the size of the reflection.

Orientation / Position: Specifies the location of the center of the object.

Orientation / Rotation: Specifies the rotation of the object around its access.

Box / Map Images to Faces: Specifies what images to use for the six faces of a box.

Box / Scale: Stretches the object and image the amount specified.

Cylinder / Cap Faces: Specifies the images to use on the ends of the cylinder.

Cylinder / Size: Stretches the cylinder length and radius.

Example:

FIGURE C-16B Image mapped to a rotated box

Rendering Filters Reference

The GIMP's rendering filters are designed to generate images irrespective of existing image content. Web designers will find these filters most useful for generating backgrounds and eye-catching logos.

◆ Referenced Tools

- QBist
- Flame
- Plasma
- Solid Noise
- FSCompose
- GIMPressionist
- Sphere Designer

Tool: QBist

Menu path: ***Filters->Render->Pattern->QBist***

FIGURE D-1A QBist dialog

QBist renders a pattern in the current layer, overwriting the current contents of that layer. The pattern is selectable from a set of nine options. Selecting any pattern in the QBist dialog makes it the current pattern, places it in the center tile of the dialog, and updates all the other tiles with new patterns. Once the current pattern is acceptable, clicking on the OK button will render that pattern scaled to fit in the current layer.

Because QBist is destructive to the current layer's contents, you will usually want to add a new, transparent layer and make it the active layer prior to running QBist.

TOOL OPTIONS:

Pattern Tiles: Middle tile is current pattern. Clicking on any tile makes that the current selection and updates all other tiles with variations of that pattern.

Load: Load a saved pattern from a file.

Save: Save the current pattern to a file.

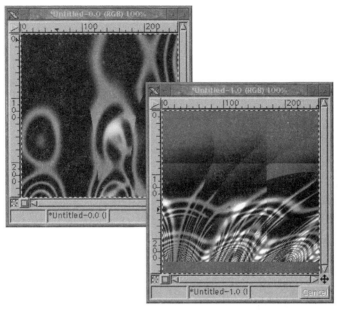

FIGURE D-1B   QBist pattern example

Tool: Flame

Menu path: *Filters->Render->Nature->Flame*

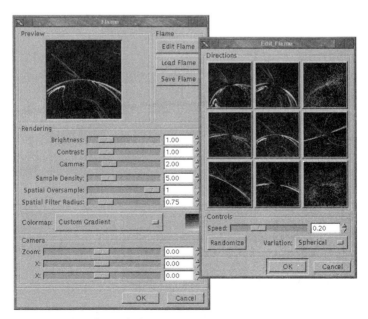

FIGURE D-2A   Flame dialog

One of the most interesting filters available in the GIMP, Flame produces wisps and tendrils of color that, in some forms, resemble the fingers of an open flame.

Flame's interface is a little more daunting than most GIMP filters, but it's not all that complex after you've used it a little. The Edit option allows you to choose the style of design to render. This subdialog works much like QBist's dialog, where selecting a tile makes it the active pattern and updates all the other patterns in the dialog. Besides the basic difference in pattern appearance, Flame also provides much more control over the shape, size, brightness, and scale of the image than does QBist. Like QBist, you can also save and load existing Flame patterns to and from a file. Additionally, Flame provides a means of applying color schemes to the patterns by using existing or user-defined gradients.

Flame renders its contents over the current layer's pixels. Only the pattern is rendered, however. The black background shown in the Preview window is not rendered. This means that Flame can be used to overlay a pattern on an existing image.

TOOL OPTIONS:

Preview Window: Displays the pattern that is to be rendered in the current layer.
Edit Flame: Opens the Edit window to allow selection of the pattern and its parameters.
Load Flame / Save Flame: Loads and saves patterns to and from a file.
Rendering / Brightness: Increases the brightness of all pixels in the pattern.
Rendering / Contrast: Increases the range of brightness between the brightest and darkest pixels in the pattern.
Rendering / Gamma: Changes the gamma level for the pattern, essentially brightening or darkening the image.
Rendering / Sample Density, Spatial Oversample, Spatial Filter Radius: These options have very little visual impact.
Colormap: Allows selection of the gradient or solid color to use in the pattern.
Camera: Sets the position of the rendering within the Canvas window. Changes to these options will update the Preview window automatically. Zoom enlarges or shrinks the pattern, while X and Y move it around the window.
Edit / Speed: Changes the complexity of the pattern. Higher values add more variation between tiles.
Edit / Variation: Changes the way the pattern is generated.

Edit / Randomize: Updates all the tiles with new patterns based on the speed and variation settings.

FIGURE D-2B Sample rendering of Flame pattern

Tool: Plasma

Menu path: ***Filters->Render->Clouds->Plasma***

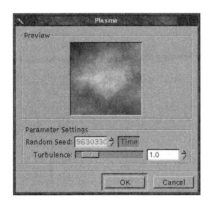

FIGURE D-3A Plasma dialog

One of the simplest rendering filters, Plasma is used to generate a colored, random pattern that resembles a cloud of smoke. When desaturated and processed with the Curves and Levels filters, Plasma can produce effects ranging from simple smoke to elements of fire and explosions.

TOOL OPTIONS:

Random Seed: Allows the user to set a specific value for the random seed. This permits exact reproductions of any given Plasma pattern.
Time: Set by default, this button is used to specify the current time as the seed value for the pattern to be generated.
Turbulence: Higher values here create more turbulent patterns. The default setting of 1 can also be lowered. A value of 0 generates a multicolored gradient pattern with nearly discernible edges between colors.

FIGURE D-3B Simple Plasma and Curves adjusted version

Tool: Solid Noise

Menu path: ***Filters->Render->Clouds->Solid Noise***

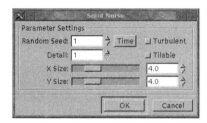

FIGURE D-4A Solid Noise dialog

With a user interface much like Plasma, Solid Noise produces a moderately different rendering. The image still resembles smoke, but without color and in more condensed wisps.

Solid Noise can be used to generate cigarette and cigar smoke or, more commonly, forms of cottonlike clouds.

TOOL OPTIONS:

Random Seed: Used to generate the random nature of the noise, this field can be set to specific values to reproduce prior results.
Time: When set causes Solid Noise to use the current system time as the random seed.
Detail: Higher values provide a wider spread to the noise. The maximum value is 15, which produces a rendering similar to that produced by Plasma.
Turbulent: Higher values produce more condensed or clumped sections in the noise.
Tileable: When set forces the edges of the rendering to be tileable.
X/Y Size: Stretches the rendering the specified amount in either the X or Y direction.

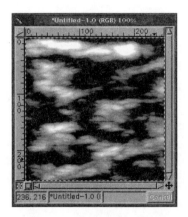

FIGURE D-4B Sample cloud pattern generated with the Solid Noise filter

Tool: IFSCompose

Menu path: ***Filters->Render->Nature->IFSCompose***

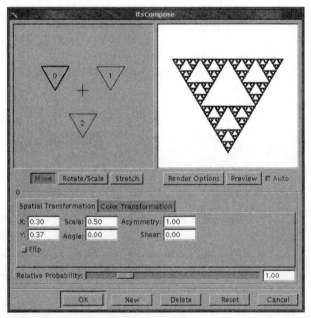

FIGURE D-5A IFSCompose dialog

One of the most sophisticated filters in the standard GIMP distribution, IFSCompose is a tool for generating fractal patterns found most often in nature. This includes, but is not limited to, trees, limbs, leaves, flowers, and other plant life.

IFSCompose is powerful but requires practice to truly master. The interface, while not complex, is not completely intuitive. The numbered objects in the upper-left box are known as *transformations* and define weighted centers to the fractal design displayed in the upper-right (preview) box. By moving, rotating, scaling, adding, and deleting these objects you can drastically change the shape of the fractal form.

Initially, IFSCompose displays three transformations which form a Serpinski triangle in the preview window. New transformations (added using the New button at the bottom of the dialog) are added at the current center (represented by the crosshairs) of the box in the upper left.

Pressing and holding the right mouse button in this window will open a menu that allows a few hidden options such as recentering the transformations, undoing the last change, and selecting all transformations at once. Holding the Shift key while left-mouse clicking in a transformation will add that object to the selected transformations. In this way, you can edit multiple transformations at a time.

Position and shape for individual transformations can be set manually using the options in the Spatial Transformation page in the middle of the dialog. The Color Transformation provides means for changing their colors.

TOOL OPTIONS:

Move: When set, clicking and dragging in the transformation window will move the selected transformations.

Rotate / Scale: When set, clicking and dragging will either rotate or scale the transformation depending on the direction of drag and location of initial click.

Stretch: When set, clicking and dragging in the transformation window stretches the transformations but maintains their area.

Render Options: Opens a small dialog for setting the way IFSCompose works internally. Can be set to use smaller blocks of memory for its calculations, which is useful for large numbers of transformations.

Preview / Auto: Options for previewing changes automatically or manually.

Spatial Transformation: Provides the means to manually position, orientate, and scale individual transformations.

Color Transformation: Provides color change options for individual transformation. Simple sets the initial color, which can then be broken down into component mappings for red, green, blue, and black using the Full options.

Relative Probability: Higher values increase the weight of the selected transformations. Higher weights shift the rendering towards the position, size, and orientation of that transformation. *Left-mouse Click in Transformation Edit Window:* Opens a menu with undo/redo and selection options.

FIGURE D-5B Rendered IFSCompose image

Tool: GIMPressionist

Menu path: *Filters->Artistic->GIMPressionist*

Possibly the most creative of the standard filters, and the one most likely to be a favorite among real artists, GIMPressionist offers enormous flexibility along with a fairly intuitive interface.

GIMPressionist takes an existing image and applies a set of modifications based on brush and paper types along with brush stroke direction, orientation, and frequency. The number of options available is large, but their groupings are fairly intuitive and most have Tips available that explain their use.

TOOL OPTIONS:

Paper: Selects the texture upon which the new painting will be applied.

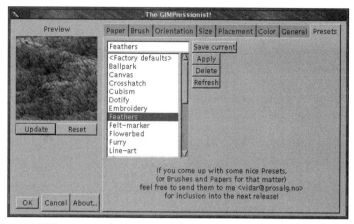

FIGURE D-6A GIMPressionist dialog

Brush: Selects the brush type, its aspect ratio (height to width size), brightness (gamma), and amount of embossing it will have. The Select menu allows the use of an existing layer as a brush.

Orientation: Specifies the number of directions to stroke (given a starting angle) and the angle span from one stroke to the next. The Orientation toggles (Value, Radius, etc.) specify which patterns to follow for the brushstrokes. These force the strokes to follow certain patterns. The Manual toggle will use the values set in the Orientation Map Editor, which is opened by clicking on the Edit button.

Size: Specifies the size of the stroke. Higher numbers of sizes increase the variation in lengths of strokes. The min and max values specify the minimum and maximum lengths in pixels for strokes. The Size toggles, like the Orientation toggles, vary the stroke lengths by existing patterns in the current image. The Size Map Editor can be used to manually specify the number and length of strokes to use.

Placement: Varies the position of strokes throughout the image. Higher density values force strokes to clump together.

Color: Like Placement, these options use existing image contents to determine the color of strokes.

General: These options affect various attributes of the individual brushstrokes, backgrounds, and shadows.

Presets: These options allow using predefined configurations and saves the current configuration as a new, named preset.

Orientation Map Editor: Adds, modifies, and edit vectors that define the orientation of brush strokes. Each option, including the Vector window, offers tips on their use.

Size Map Editor: Adds, modifies, and edits vectors that define the size of brushstrokes. Each option, including the Vector window, offers tips on their use.

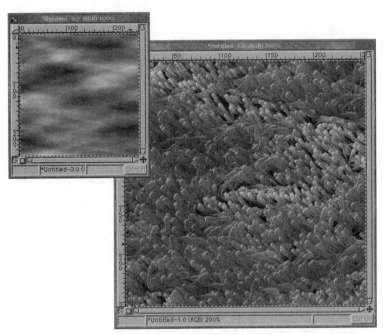

FIGURE D-6B Original image and its GIMPressionist processed version

Tool: Sphere Designer

Menu path: *Filters->Render->Sphere Designer*

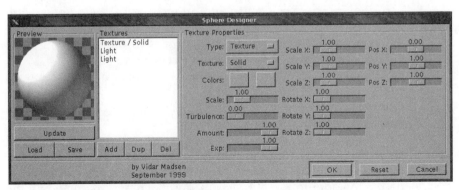

FIGURE D-7A Sphere Designer dialog

Designed by the same developer, Vidar Madsen, who brought GIMPressionist to the GIMP, Sphere Designer provides a means of designing planetscapes. The rendered image will overwrite existing layer data, so be certain to create a new layer prior to using Sphere Designer.

TOOL OPTIONS:

Textures: The list of layered textures and lights. The first entry is the lowest to the surface and the bottom entry is the farthest out.
Add / Dup / Del: Adds a new layer to the bottom of the list, duplicates the currently selected layer (added to the bottom of the list), or deletes the currently selected layer.
Load / Save: Loads and saves configurations.
Update: Changes the type automatically to update the preview window. All other changes require the Update button to be pressed to view modifications to the configuration.
Reset: Located at the bottom right of the dialog, this button resets Sphere Designer to its default configuration.
Type: Texture layers define a pattern on the surface. Bump Map layers add simulated depth. At least one light layer is required to see the texture and Bump Map layers.
Texture Menu: Applied to both textures and Bump Maps, these options define basic patterns to be modified using other options in the dialog.
Colors: Sets gradient style coloring for all layers.
Scale: Larger values stretch the textures and Bump Maps across the surface of the sphere but have no effect on lights.
Turbulence: Larger values cause larger amounts of random turbulence in textures and Bump Maps.
Amount: Smaller values darken a texture but have no effect on Bump Maps or lights.
Exp.: Smaller values enhance a textured layer's effect on the overall appearance of the sphere.
Scale X/Y/Z: Scales a texture or bump map in the X, Y, or Z directions.
Rotate X/Y/Z: Rotates a texture or bump map in the X, Y, or Z directions.
Position X/Y/Z: Moves a texture or bump map in the X, Y, or Z directions.

FIGURE D-7B A planetscape designed with Sphere Designer

E GIMP Keyboard Shortcuts

While tools like the GIMP are better used interactively employing the mouse or drawing tablet, there are many features that can be accessed directly from the keyboard using keyboard shortcuts. In fact, any feature with a menu entry can be accessed through the keyboard even if there is no default keyboard shortcut for it. That's because all the GIMP menus are user-configurable. To change the shortcut you move the mouse over the menu entry (don't click on it) and type the new shortcut keys. If you want to use Shift, ALT, or CTRL keys, be sure to press these first and hold them down while you press the letter key that completes the shortcut sequence. For example, to set the Print option to ALT-Shift-P you would open the File menu from a Canvas menu, move the mouse over the Print option, hold down ALT and Shift together, then press the P key.

The shortcuts listed here are the defaults for GIMP 1.2. Use this reference to verify the keystrokes you want to use that aren't already in use. Note that using an existing shortcut a second time will remove it from its current location.

The following abbreviations are used in the following tables:

Ctrl   The Control key
ALT   The ALT key

Note that all letter keys are listed in uppercase for clarity; only where *Shift* is listed is the key actually the uppercase version.

All Toolbox options work only with the mouse over the Toolbox. Canvas menu shortcuts apply to the currently active window. Layer menu options apply only when the mouse is in the Layers and Channels window and a layer has been clicked on.

Not all menu entries have default keyboard shortcuts.

Toolbox Options

File New	Ctrl-N
File Open	Ctrl-O
Quit	Ctrl-Q
Help	F1
Contextual Help	Shift F1
Layers, Channels, and Paths Dialog	Ctrl-L
Tool Options	Shift-Ctrl-T
Brushes Dialog	Shift-Ctrl-B
Patterns Dialog	Shift-Ctrl-P
Gradients Dialog	Ctrl-G
Palettes Dialog	Ctrl-P
Open a Previous Image	Ctrl-x, where x is 1 to 9 or the maximum Recent Documents value set in the Preferences dialog.

Canvas Menu File Options

New	Ctrl-N
Open	Ctrl-O
Save	Ctrl-S
Close (Closes current Canvas window)	Ctrl-W
Quit (Complete exit from the GIMP)	Ctrl-Q

Canvas Menu Edit Options

Undo	Ctrl-Z
Redo	Ctrl-R
Cut	Ctrl-X
Copy	Ctrl-C
Paste	Ctrl-V
Clear	Ctrl-K
Fill with Foreground Color	Ctrl-,
Fill with Background Color	Ctrl-.
Cut Named Buffer	Shift-Ctrl-X
Copy Named Buffer	Shift-Ctrl-C
Paste Named Buffer	Shift-Ctrl-V

Canvas Menu Select Options

Invert	Ctrl-I
All	Ctrl-A
None	Shift-Ctrl-A
Float	Shift-Ctrl-L
Feather	Shift-Ctrl-F
Sharpen	Shift-Ctrl-H

Canvas Menu View Options

Zoom In	=
Zoom Out	–
Info Window	Shift-Ctrl-I
Navigation Window	Shift-Ctrl-N
Toggle Selection	Ctrl-T
Toggle Rulers	Shift-Ctrl-R
Toggle Statusbar	Shift-Ctrl-S
Toggle Guides	Shift-Ctrl-T
Shrink Wrap	Ctrl-E

Canvas Menu Image Options

RGB Mode	ALT-R
Grayscale Mode	ALT-G
Indexed Mode	ALT-I
Offset Transform	Shift-Ctrl-O
Duplicate	Ctrl-D

Canvas Menu Layer Options

Anchor Layer	Ctrl-H
Merge Visible Layers	Ctrl-M
Previous Layer	Prior (Page Up key, usually)
Next Layer	Next (Page Down key, usually)
Raise Layer	Shift-Prior
Lower Layer	Shift-Next
Layer to Top	Ctrl-Prior
Layer to Bottom	Ctrl-Next

Canvas Menu Tool Options

Reset Default Colors	D	Move	M
Swap Colors	X	Magnify	Shift-M
Text Tool	T	Crop / Resize	Shift-C
Color Picker	O	Transform	Shift-T
Rectangular Select	R	Flip	Shift-F
Elliptical Select	E	Bucket Fill	Shift-B
Free Select	F	Blend	L
Fuzzy Select	Z	Pencil	Shift-P
Bézier Select	B	Paintbrush	P
Intelligent Scissors	I	Eraser	Shift-E
Airbrush	A	Clone	C
Convolve	V	Ink	K
Dodge / Burn	Shift-D	Smudge	Shift-S

Canvas Menu Filters Options

Repeat Last (reruns last filter without dialog)	ALT-F
Reshow Last (reopens last filter dialog)	Shift-ALT-F

Note: None of the actual filters come with default keyboard shortcuts installed.

Index

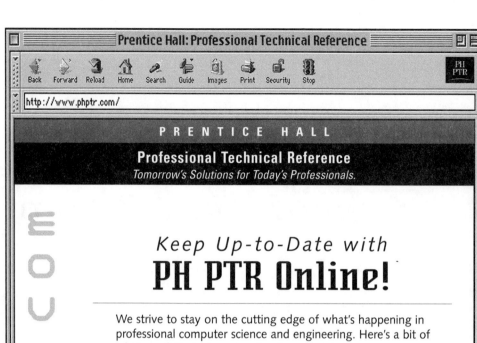

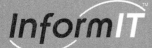
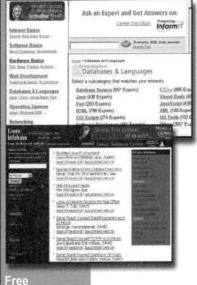

RELY ON
Essential Guides for ALL the Web Skills You Need!

Everything a working professional needs to get up and running on today's hot Web tools and technologies.

**ESSENTIAL DESIGN
FOR WEB PROFESSIONALS**
BY CHARLES J. LYONS

© 2001, Paper, 236 pp., 0-13-032161-3

**ESSENTIAL PHP
FOR WEB PROFESSIONALS**
BY CHRISTOPHER COSENTINO

© 2001, Paper, 168 pp., 0-13-088903-2

**ESSENTIAL ASP
FOR WEB PROFESSIONALS**
BY ELIJAH LOVEJOY

© 2001, Paper, 276 pp., 0-13-030499-9

**ESSENTIAL FLASH 5
FOR WEB PROFESSIONALS**
BY LYNN KYLE

© 2001, Paper, 261 pp., 0-13-091390-1

**ESSENTIAL GIMP
FOR WEB PROFESSIONALS**
BY MICHAEL J. HAMMEL

© 2001, Paper, 252 pp., 0-13-019114-0

**ESSENTIAL COLDFUSION 4.5
FOR WEB PROFESSIONALS**
BY MICAH BROWN & MICHAEL FREDRICK

© 2001, Paper, 212 pp., 0-13-040646-5

Also Available:

**ESSENTIAL JAVASCRIPT
FOR WEB PROFESSIONALS**
BY BARRETT, LIVINGSTON, & BROWN

© 2000, Paper, 208 pp., 0-13-013056-7

**ESSENTIAL PERL 5
FOR WEB PROFESSIONALS**
BY BROWN, BELLEW, & LIVINGSTON

© 2000, Paper, 208 pp., 0-13-012653-5

**ESSENTIAL CSS & DHTML
FOR WEB PROFESSIONALS**
BY LIVINGSTON & BROWN

© 2000, Paper, 208 pp., 0-13-012760-4

**ESSENTIAL PHOTOSHOP 5
FOR WEB PROFESSIONALS**
BY EIGEN, LIVINGSTON, & BROWN

© 2000, Paper, 304 pp., 0-13-012833-3

WWW.PHPTR.COM/ESSENTIAL